Ess
Arti

@nd online

Complete Issues
articles · opinions · statistics · contacts

Get nstant online access to this book by logging on to:
www.completeissues.co.uk

User name:_____

Password: _____

See page 2 for details of **Complete Issues** ⟶

The book

The articles you will find in this volume have been chosen because they are relevant, interesting and well written. They include:

- **thought-provoking discussion pieces**
- **opposing viewpoints**
- **personal accounts**
- **informed insights**

We looked at thousands of articles from a wide variety of newspapers, magazines and online journals. You'll find material from little known sources as well as from well respected national media – all selected with the needs of UK users firmly in mind.

The Essential Articles book is an attractive item on any library shelf. Its bright, magazine-style format entices readers to browse and enjoy while learning about current issues and dilemmas, making even difficult issues approachable.

Online

We are constantly expanding our online service. We have now integrated our major publications in the Complete Issues Website – a complete source of opinions, facts, figures and further research. Go to: **www.completeissues.co.uk**

This brings together our three main publications – Essential Articles, Fact File and Key Organisations – and allows users to search and browse all books together, past and present editions, and to view and download those they've purchased.

As well as being able to access all the articles in both PDF and editable formats, there are additional references and links. Your purchase of the book entitles you to use this on one computer, however, buying a site licence makes the service and the material available to **all** students and staff at **all** times, even from home.

We have included a checklist poster of major topics or key words in the current Essential Articles and Fact File for you to display. You can record your log-in details on this and on the front page of this book to make access to the online service quick and easy.

If you do not yet have the other publications in the Complete Issues Package you can upgrade here: **www.completeissues.co.uk**

Unique features

UP-TO-DATE: A new edition is published every year.

RELEVANT: To the UK and its education system and to advanced learners of English.

ORGANISED: Articles are grouped by theme, cross referenced, indexed and linked on the page to closely related pieces and statistics. Our online searches will find even more!

STIMULATING: Each article has an accompanying group of questions to raise awareness of the issues.

ATTRACTIVE: Full colour and eye-catching with appealingly designed pages and great photos.

EASY TO USE: You don't have to worry about copyright issues as we've cleared these. Because you have both the book and online access you can use Essential Articles in different ways with different groups and in different locations. You can simultaneously use it in the library, in the classroom and at home.

FLEXIBLE: You can make paper copies, use a whiteboard or a computer. Different groups or individuals can be using different parts of the book at the same time. Editable text makes it even more adaptable.

BOOSTS LIBRARY USE: The posters provided free with each volume list the topics in Essential Articles and its sister publication Fact File and make it very easy to find the issues you are looking for. You can put one of your free posters in the library/LRC and one elsewhere – in the staff room, in a corridor, in a subject area. If you would like more copies of the poster just let us know.

SAFE: Although we have included controversial, hard-hitting articles and tackled difficult subjects, you can be confident that students are not going to encounter inappropriate material that an internet search might generate.

ADDITIONAL BENEFITS: Subscribers to Essential Articles and Fact File are entitled to 10% discount on all our other products. They also receive occasional free posters to help promote library use and reading in general.

Contents

> He began to believe that there were calories in almost everything that would make him gain weight ... shampoo, soap, pencils ... Page 34

Contents

> 66 I'll sidestep being identified with the racists and will not fly the flag 99
> Page 47

> 66 In England alone 650,000 homes are classed as overcrowded 99
> Page 50

> 66 **How is it that birds living on a tiny island in the middle of the South Pacific are dying because of our wasteful lifestyle?** 99
> Page 68

Contents

> 66 I've never supported direct action because I've always felt that setting fire to cars... only adds to the general misery of any given situation 99
> Page 92

> 66 Cornish goods are being taken on tours of Britain to end up being sold in branches of Tesco right next door to where they were made 99
> Page 101

Contents

> 66 What's needed is... officers to look out for and challenge men on dark streets 99
> Page 140

Alcohol

Safety **Friends**
Drunkenness
Government Law
Cheap Booze
Family Responsibility
Alcoholism
Health

I like a drink, but collectively we have a problem

Luisa Dillner

Britain is on an almighty bender and only by raising drink prices can we lower consumption

I like a drink as much as the next person but the latest public health statistics are enough to make you choke on your chardonnay. Alcohol is to blame for two admissions to hospital every minute, according to data from the North West Public Health Observatory. The Observatory's publication of local alcohol profiles in England shows there were 954,469 admissions to hospital related to alcohol in 2009, an increase of nearly 10% from 2007/8.

Statistics

Separate statistics reveal that deaths from alcoholic cirrhosis for men in Scotland have more than doubled since the late 1980s; in England and Wales they rose by around 70%. For women, rates have gone up by a half.

Drink problem

Professor Mark Bellis, the director of the Observatory, is keen to emphasise the ubiquitous nature of the problem. "It is time," he said, "to recognise that we are not a population of responsible drinkers with just a handful of irresponsible individuals ruining it for others." So is

SOME ISSUES:

Do you think that generally people drink too much? What is an acceptable amount to drink?

Do you think increasing the cost of alcohol will help solve the problem?

See also:
A face that should haunt a generation,
p118, *Essential Articles 13*

Home brew,
p10, *Fact File 2010*

www.acdaction.org.uk

it time to acknowledge that we might have a collective drink problem? Almost every week sees another sector of society vilified in the media for its reckless consumption. Such unlikely drinking buddies as young women (ladettes), chavvy men, middle-class mothers, the over-65s and the managerial and professional classes have all been targeted by the media as problem drinkers.

History repeating itself

Indeed, alcohol has been a moral stick with which to beat various sections of society for many centuries. The 12th-century historian William of Malmesbury blamed the defeat of the English at the battle of Hastings on their binge drinking the night before. In contrast, the Normans, apparently, stayed in and prayed. As a nation, we are still embarrassed by our alcohol habits, seeing our drinking as

less refined than that of other Europeans, who seem able to eat a meal and drink alcohol at the same time.

Do we really want help?

It is perverse of us, then, to shriek "nanny state" at any government intervention to reduce our alcohol intake. Or to react with irritation to a public health doctor reciting the medical consequences of harmful drinking. Alcohol is arguably a fabulous drug in moderation. It helps us unwind and it lubricates social interaction. Tony Blair used it every evening to relax. Yet, for all our warm feelings towards the grape and grain, we can also be found railing against the drunken teenagers vomiting over kerbs in our town centres on a Saturday night.

Alcohol is up there with sex and drugs as a social evil, for which any government is

damned if it initiates policies to control its consumption and damned if it doesn't.

What can be done?

But what can a government do? It can reach for obvious solutions. Putting labels on bottles of alcohol promoting sensible drinking is visible, but there's no evidence it works. Education is an even weaker suggestion. Children at school are already warned about the dangers of alcohol, drugs and unprotected sex, but believe that they are invincible.

To have a hope of managing the costs of alcohol to society, we need to grapple with the truth that our drinking habits have changed. Since the 1950s, our alcohol intake has doubled. We have desocialised drinking and taken it into the privacy and unregulated arena of our homes. It's much cheaper to drink at home, so we no longer dress up and

go to the pub but fill up our supermarket trolleys, kick off our shoes and uncork a bottle or two of wine.

We drank 760ml of alcohol at home per person per week in 2006 compared with 527ml in 1992. Outside the home, it was 733ml in 2001/2 and 443ml in 2008. So the amount we drink in pubs versus home has flipped. The strength of wine has increased from 9% in the 1970s to an average of 12.5% today, allegedly due to public demand. In bars, glasses have almost doubled in size.

Perhaps without realising it, one in three men and one in five women now drinks above the recommended level of four units a day for men (a pint of beer is 2 units and a glass of wine is 2 units) and three for women. The professional and managerial classes now drink more than anyone else and while rates of drinking among the young are slightly falling, they are rising among women and older people. Alcohol is over 60% more affordable now than it was 20 years ago.

Price change

So, given that it's as cheap as chips to get drunk, one has, regretfully, to consider whether putting the price up may reduce our consumption. There is a relatively close link between the price of alcohol and the amount a population consumes. The figures from the British Beer & Pub Association suggest the recession may be reducing the amount people drink already. In Scotland, the SNP have mooted the idea of charging a minimum 45p per unit of alcohol, an idea that has support from many medical organisations but none at all from other political parties.

Would it work?

Opponents have argued this amounts to a disproportionate tax on the poor who, it's assumed, scream for the 10 cans for £5 offers in supermarkets, but research from Aberdeen University shows that people from all income groups buy similar amounts of cheap alcohol. Dr John Foster, from the

University of Greenwich says that such a tax would only really hit people who drink strong beers (and cider drinkers).

Wine has about 10 units per bottle and its price would not rise dramatically, neither would that of normal-strength beer. To those who still say it is tough on poorer people, he argues that everyone has to pay the price for alcohol, be it through extra policing or the demands on the health service.

I find myself agreeing with him and I am not alone. Ben Page of Ipsos Mori says the public is divided over whether the Scottish Parliament should raise the minimum price of alcohol. A few years ago, there would have been an outcry over a price hike on our drug of choice. Sadly, the resocialising of our intake of alcohol by taking it back into locals is likely to be much harder.

The Observer, 5 September 2010
© *Guardian News & Media Ltd 2010*

Leave me alone with my glass of cheap beer

Steve Downes

I don't like being told what to do.

Ask my mum and dad, or any of my old schoolteachers.

In common with many other strong-willed (stubborn) people, I find that the one way to make me do the wrong thing is to tell me that it's the wrong thing.

Which is why I strongly object to any attempts by the government to educate people about the dangers of alcohol – or to influence behaviour by setting a minimum price per unit.

The latest reports claim that tens of thousands of lives could be saved in the next 20 years if a minimum price of 50p per unit is introduced.

Aside from the fact that these predictions can only be speculative, would increased alcohol prices really put people off? I doubt that they would. Petrol prices have risen at a rate of knots in recent years. But people are still filling up their tanks and driving their cars in their numbers.

By increasing the cost of alcoholic drinks, I think the government would have little or no impact on consumption rates, but could inadvertently encourage black-market booze operations to be established. Another concern that I have is that if alcohol becomes more expensive to buy, people

Would increased alcohol prices really put people off? I doubt that they would. Petrol prices have risen ... But people are still filling up their tanks

SOME ISSUES:

Do you think an increase in the price of alcohol will put people off drinking?

Does the government have a duty to do this? Or is it just interfering?

See also:
Alcohol & drugs section,
p7-16, *Fact File 2011*

are less likely to drink regularly in moderation and more likely to save their precious pennies for a fortnightly binge, which is much more dangerous.

There is also the little-publicised fact that alcohol consumption in Britain has been falling every year since 2002. That's because people are intelligent enough to work out the risks and moderate their behaviour – without being forced to do so by people who we elected to run the country, not inspect the contents of our shopping trolleys.

I put on a seatbelt when travelling in a car because I know that it is the right thing to do – not because meddling bureaucrats tell me to

Everybody knows how dangerous life can be. They make their own choices about how to respond to that, and have to live with the consequences.

I put on a seatbelt when travelling in a car because I know that it is the right thing to do – not because meddling bureaucrats tell me to. I lock my car when I leave it unattended because I don't want someone to nick my stereo – not because the police have come up with a punchy catchphrase. A cheaply-made public information advert with a blindingly obvious message and the pretend-grave voice of an actor will not change my ways. I refrain from drinking bucketloads of strong beer or spirits because I know that it is not good for me, makes me feel like death for up to 48 hours afterwards and encourages me to do things that are out of character – like smile, be sociable and dance. In life, we learn from our mistakes.

A few pence on a bottle of cider isn't going to put people off alcohol – any more than a lecture from mum, dad, a medic or a teacher will do the trick. The most effective way is to find out the effects for yourself. Cider nearly killed me once. And ever since, I cannot so much as smell the stuff without feeling nauseous. And vodka made me aggressive. As I am both a coward and totally inept at fighting, I soon gave that the cold shoulder. Ultimately, though, I think people object to being lectured about how they live.

While there are plenty of people who drink to the point of self-destruction, the vast majority of people simply like a glass of reasonably-priced red wine or a whisky to wind down in the evening. With the cost of living rocketing, wages stagnating and the economic outlook misty with a chance of murk, is this the time to force people to pay more for one of life's small pleasures?

Eastern Daily Press, 22 February 2011

Master Harold is about me as a little boy, and my father, who was an alcoholic. There's a thread running down the Fugard line of alcoholism. Thankfully I haven't passed it on to my child, a wonderful daughter who's stone-cold sober. But I had the tendency from my father, just as he had had it from his father.

There was no way of avoiding my father's drinking. He was a jazz musician with a band called the Orchestral Jazzonians in Port Elizabeth, South Africa. He had lost a leg

number. Got a voice, who spoke simply: "How can we help?" I said: I think I'm in trouble with my drinking. The voice asked if I wanted to attend a meeting. I said yes. I was given the address of an episcopal church in Gramercy Park, whose monthly meeting was happening that very evening. I went along and sat quietly, at the back of the group, and I listened to people. One man came up and said: "Welcome – I see you're a stranger, a new face." I said yes. He said: "Do you want to talk about anything?" I said no.

as a writer. Not that I needed to be drunk, but I needed the stimulus and the imaginative freedom that it gave me. Night-time is when I brainstorm; last thing, when the family's asleep and I'm alone, I think about the next day's writing and plan a strategy for my assault on the blank page. And for that I needed whisky.

That was the terror I lived with – that I would not be able to write again. That little devil was on my shoulder all through the next few years. Every time I wrote something, it was whispering in my ear: "You should have a couple of drinks – it will make everything so much better." I don't know

*That little devil was **whispering in my ear:** "You should **have a couple of drinks** – it will make everything so much better."*

in his childhood in an accident and was very often in hospital – it's what eventually killed him, when gangrene developed in the stump. I always had to smuggle in small bottles of brandy – that was his drink of choice – and sit at the bedside with these two little bottles in my side pockets while we waited for a moment when the eagle-eyed nurses weren't focused on us. Then I would slip them over and he would drink it under the sheets.

He was a great storyteller, and to reward me for the little favours I did for him he would re-tell potted versions of the wonderful adventure novels he had read as a boy, such as Conan Doyle's Sherlock Holmes stories or White Fang and Call of the Wild and The 39 Steps. I loved him. But it was a very conflicted love.

I took the napkin with me to the phone box at the back of the restaurant, called the

I have survived a lot of things in the course of my 78 years, and I know I have an instinct for survival. When the meeting was over, that instinct took me back to my hotel room and not to my bar. I don't think I slept that night. I knew I had an even more painful job ahead of me the next morning. When I met my producer, before the meeting to fire the young actor, he noticed that my hand was shaking and asked why. I told him I was going to try and stop drinking. He said: "Listen, take my advice – don't stop drinking today."

But I didn't drink anything that day. I never went back to Gramercy Park – the truth is, I don't like groups too much. I'm a loner. So I white-knuckled it. I had all the horrors that go with withdrawal, but I just sweated it out by myself.

The bigger problem was that I believed that, in a certain way, alcohol was necessary for me

whether that's true or not, and it's too late to worry about that now. But the next play I wrote, Road to Mecca, has proved over time to be one of my most successful. Now a pot of herbal tea is just as good for me as the two double whiskies I used to have before going to bed.

It is almost 30 years since that breakfast. I don't quite know how I did it, because I'm not somebody with a lot of self-control or willpower, but I haven't had a drink since. I call it my tea-bag birthday: 18 January 1982. On that day, every year, I get a box of herbal teas from the friend who scribbled the address on that paper napkin in the bar. I've never really shared the date with anyone else. But my friend remembers, and by God so do I.

The Observer, 31 October 2010
© Guardian News & Media Ltd 2010

Animals

Attack
Breeding
Animal testing
Experiments Zoos
Natural habitat Help
Captivity Rare species
Assistance animals
Disability

I'm proud I worked in an animal testing lab

I thought:
"You might not agree
but I'm doing
the right thing."

It was a surprise to me that I ended up working in an animal testing facility. I've been a vegetarian most of my life and I wanted to be a teacher when I was younger. Animal testing wasn't something I saw in my future.

I've always cared deeply about animals. My parents stopped eating meat because they disliked the way animals were farmed and slaughtered, and I felt the same way. Then I met my partner at university and when we graduated, he started working as a toxicologist, testing drugs that might potentially go on to be used for humans.

I was interested in his field of work; the more he told me, the more I understood and believed in it. My partner qualified for a Home Office licence, so he learned to handle animals in the right way and cause the least amount of trauma possible.

When a job came up, I applied. They checked me out thoroughly to make sure I had no affiliations with antivivisectionist groups. I started in a technical role away from the animal facility, preparing doses and equipment for clinical tests on humans.

After a few months, I asked to see where the animals were kept. In the back of my mind I saw the grainy black and white pictures of cats and monkeys in agony that appear on antivivisectionist stands. I was curious but reluctant, particularly to see the dogs. It was so hard to think of them in that environment. But they were bright-eyed and pleased to see us. They were kept in a different building from the rats, rabbits and mice, so the barking didn't disturb them. The animals were behind strengthened glass, not unlike you see in a pet shop. Everything was clean and they all seemed content.

You couldn't walk the dogs outside because it would interfere with the research, but there were play areas with toys. The husbandry staff talked

SOME ISSUES:

Is it right to test on animals?

What if that testing helped find a life-saving cure?

Would you work in that profession?

What sort of protest do you think is acceptable?

See also:
**Animal rights... and wrongs &
Animal research,**
p18-20, *Fact File 2011*

www.frame.org.uk
www.humaneresearch.org.uk
www.understandinganimalresearch.org.uk

My partner and I had cover stories. Most people did, for self-protection

to the animals and petted them. Seeing them reinforced my opinion that I was doing the right thing for the right reasons.

After a few years, I moved to my partner's department, assisting research scientists with paperwork. It was like any other company, once the doors were shut and you'd passed security. People socialised, just like any other workplace.

I was fairly comfortable telling close friends where I worked, although initially I told only people I thought would be sympathetic. As time went on, I became indignant about having to be defensive and got more relaxed about who I told. People sometimes pulled faces but often they just wanted to clarify what was involved. Many people think cosmetics are still tested on animals, so they'd assume we squirted perfume into rabbits' eyes.

I had to be more careful with people I didn't know well. My partner and I had cover stories. Most people did, for self-protection. You wouldn't call it a secret identity, but we gave people ideas that weren't exactly accurate. We kept it general and vague. I'd say I was an administrator. I was quite adept at sidestepping the conversation to avoid getting too deep into telling lies. I didn't get any thrill out of being secretive.

Our employer was happy to do as much as possible to protect us. An arrangement with the DVLA let us register our cars at another address so the plates couldn't be used to trace where we lived. Protesters often followed or photographed cars. A group of people rolled up every week to protest – security sometimes knew when to expect them and circulated advance warnings. They'd stand outside the gates shouting "Murderer!" and lie down to prevent people's cars coming out.

I stopped worrying about them – they were more of an inconvenience. It was sometimes scary wondering what they'd do, but they didn't throw bricks at our cars, they usually just shouted abuse. In some ways, they won simply by making us paranoid. I'd be much more fearful outside work, but I got used to it.

I was proud of my contribution, helping to test out potentially life-saving drugs

Having a bunch of people so set against you can make you become more determined. I thought: "You might not agree, but I'm doing the right thing." I was proud of my contribution, helping to test out potentially life-saving drugs.

Leaving was never about the work or the company – I moved away for family reasons. I work in administration now. It's a relief not having to hesitate or look around before saying what I do, but I was proud to work there and I'm always looking for that same sense of satisfaction.

The Guardian, 4 December 2010
© Guardian News & Media Ltd 2010

The latest assistance animal: a 'seeing-eye horse'

Blog:

We've had guide dogs, guide ponies, hearing dogs and even helping hand monkeys, but could disabled people riding 'seeing-eye horses' along the high street be the next big thing when it comes to employing assistance animals?

If Tabitha Darling of Fort Worth in Texas gets her way, they might be. Tabitha is legally blind, but also has a bone condition that can make walking painful. So instead of a guide dog or a wheelchair, she rides Trixie, a guide horse. The only problem is that she's riding her everywhere, including round the local supermarket.

The Americans with Disabilities Act says that stores cannot refuse entry to a service animal, but Tabitha's horsing around (sorry) in the aisles, weaving between the pickles and the sliced white loaves, is causing controversy in the local community - including amongst other disabled people. One Fort Worth resident who is also blind and physically disabled, but uses a more conventional combination of a seeing-eye dog and a wheelchair, says that Tabitha "doesn't need to be riding around like Lady Godiva in a store".

Well, I've checked the photos on the article, and from what I can see she's not naked like the infamous Godiva, but we'll leave that criticism to one side and focus on the horsey business. I guess their 'business' is part of the problem too, since horses aren't noted for nipping off to the nearest public toilet when they need to relieve themselves, if you catch my drift.

So what do you think? Is it a case of anything goes when it comes to assistance animals, and we should have the right to use any creature we want in any location we might find ourselves in, or should there be some level of practicality about it?

Written by Vaughan, Ouch! The BBC Disability Blog, 27 March 2009

SOME ISSUES:

Why might people object to this?

In what ways do you think animals may be able to help?

Are some animals more suitable than others?

Would you mind a horse in your local supermarket?

Ouch! **It's a disability thing**

dartmoor zoo's battle for survival

It's four years since *Benjamin Mee* bought Dartmoor zoo. But while Hollywood is turning his story into a film, his little zoo is struggling against extinction – just like the endangered species he cares for

SOME ISSUES:

What would it be like to run a zoo?

What is the main purpose of a zoo?

Are zoos worth the money they cost?

Is it fair to introduce a jaguar back into its natural habitat if the wild population is decreasing?

Compare this article to **The safest place for an animal is its natural habitat – not a zoo,** p26

www.biaza.org.uk

In 2006, while writing a book on humour in animals. I unexpectedly found myself becoming a zoo director. We were looking for a large house for my mother to live in with some of her children and grandchildren, and the details for Dartmoor zoo came up. We laughed, then we visited, and then realised that if we didn't buy it, most of its gorgeous animals would be destroyed. Six months later, I had a brand new line of excuses for submitting my copy late: "I'm afraid a wolf escaped and it took most of the day to get it

back, and now I'm a bit tied up with the council . . ."

I figured running a zoo would be harder than I thought. And I was right. Big bills (not just the ones belonging to our two macaw parrots) are a fact of zoo life. When one of our visitors thought it a good idea to throw a lifebelt into the tiger moat, naturally the cats bit it, and one broke a tooth. The cost: £4,200 – that's two thirds of a month's mortgage payment, or three keepers' wages, slightly less than our monthly electricity

Who knows, maybe one day we will build Eden Project-style biospheres on the moon, stocked with tigers, safe from poaching (you heard it here first).

bill, or slightly more than our insurance premium.

With all this money flowing out, I had to travel to France last week to sell the home in which my children grew up – complicated, inevitably, by some arcane French probate laws relating to the death of my wife Katherine in 2007. In two months' time I may be able to put our old house on the market, to feed to the ailing zoo – if it is still here to save.

Ironically, one of the man-made environmental catastrophes that is killing off animals – global warming – also appears to be killing off fragile zoos such as ours, which are almost entirely dependent on summer income. Since we took over in 2006, we have had three of the wettest summers on record. I am writing this in August, shivering in a fleece, looking out at yet another rain cloud. There are 30 visitors on our sodden site, instead of the expected 500.

There is, however, one tiny silver cloud among the black ones. Hollywood is taking an interest in our humble little zoo. You see, as a journalist (with credits including a DIY column for this newspaper), I naturally wrote a book about my experiences, imaginatively entitled *We Bought a Zoo.* Astonishingly, this was bought up by 20th Century Fox and is now being made into a film, directed by Cameron Crowe and starring Matt Damon. As me.

I haven't quite got my head around this, as zoo life has a way of keeping you in touch with the basics. I got that call from Hollywood with one hand down the storm drain. Last week, the electricity went off in the restaurant during peak service; Titus, our new Asian otter, chewed through his pond liner; and I was offered a bison, but had to turn it down. At this rate, the film about saving Dartmoor zoo first time round may be released too late to keep it going this time.

As it happens, today is National Zoo Awareness Day – but even that is not a day that celebrates zoos, or (as I see it) their enormous contribution towards safeguarding biodiversity. Rather, it is organised by the Captive Animals Protection Society, which wants to see zoos phased out completely and efforts concentrated on saving animals in the wild. Actually, I can see their point; I don't particularly like looking at animals behind wire either. But, as a zoo director, I understand that it is absolutely essential that we keep them there.

Every year, around 24 million people pay to visit members of the charity Biaza (British and Irish Association of Zoos and Aquaria). Together these institutions turn over £215m annually, of which £10.3m is currently donated towards 636 field global projects, saving everything from tree snails in French Polynesia and small carnivores in Vietnam to harvest mice in the UK. The Zoo Licensing Act also

What is clear, unfortunately, is that humankind is going to drive many more endangered species to extinction in the next 100 years

A zoo is a delicate ecosystem, a costly business that must entertain so it can also educate, while protecting as many endangered species as possible.

ensures some of the highest standards of husbandry anywhere in the world.

A zoo is a delicate ecosystem, a costly business that must entertain so it can also educate, while protecting as many endangered species as possible. Captive breeding programs in zoos co-operating worldwide have so far led to the successful reintroduction of about 800 species, but the situation is often complex.

Is it fair, for instance, to introduce a jaguar into the dwindling, broken-up patches of South American rainforest where the wild population is declining fast? Is it fair, too, or the people who live and farm there, and sometimes have to kill or be killed by jaguars? These messy questions take time to answer. Meanwhile, zoos do the potentially dangerous work of safeguarding viable breeding populations of jaguars, while economics, corruption, human nature and belated legislation thrash it out.

What is clear unfortunately, is that humankind is going to drive many more endangered species to extinction in the next 100 years. Extinctions now run at up to 10,000 times

the planet's historic baseline rate – an upward curve that exactly matches the increased energy requirements for the human population, which has trebled in the last 50 years and now grows by 10,000 every hour.

Who knows, maybe one day we will build Eden Project-style biospheres on the moon, stocked with tigers, safe from poaching (you heard it here first). But until that far-off day, I feel certain that zoos and wildlife parks – yes,

fences and all – will remain the best bet for keeping our most endangered creatures going. I just hope we can do the same for our zoo.

The Guardian, 31 August 2010
© Guardian News & Media Ltd 2010

RESPONSE:

The safest place for an animal is its natural habitat – not a zoo

It is false to claim that captive breeding protects endangered species
Garry Sheen

SOME ISSUES:

Are zoos really necessary?

Is it better for an animal to stay in the wild, even if it is in danger?

Do zoos give us the wrong impression – and stop us protecting habitats?

Compare this article to **Dartmoor Zoo's Battle for Survival,** p23. Whose point of view do you agree with most?

For a related conservation issue see **A British Noah's Ark,** p71.

See also:

Stuff the Tiger – long live extinction, p10, *Essential Articles 11* & **'Psycho' polar bear is 'addicted to humans',** p12, *Essential Articles 11*

Under threat, p17, *Fact File 2010*

www.captiveanimals.org

Talking of campaigns by our charity to phase out the keeping of animals in captivity, Dartmoor zoo owner Ben Mee says: "Actually, I can see their point; I don't particularly like looking at animals behind wire either" (Battle for survival, 31 August). He then adds the usual caveat: "But, as a zoo director, I understand that it is absolutely essential that we keep them there."

Are zoos really essential? Ben talks about them "protecting as many endangered species as possible". Yet of the 51 mammal and bird species at his zoo only seven are classed as threatened by the International Union for Conservation of Nature.

Zoos claim to be safer places for animals than their natural habitats. Mee questions whether it is "fair" to reintroduce a jaguar, because of not only the dwindling rainforest but also the impact "on the people who live and farm there". This view is highly dangerous for conservation, and many field scientists consider captive breeding to give a false impression that species are safe and that natural habitats don't need protecting. I can only hope Mee was joking when he suggested building "biospheres on the moon, stocked with tigers, safe from poaching".

Despite its claims, Dartmoor zoo itself has been responsible for killing animals – deer, as a result of "overpopulation", and a wolf who was ostracised by the pack, for example. More sinister is the line pushed by international zoo bodies that hybrid animals should be killed – such as three tiger cubs at a German zoo recently – because they use resources that could be spent on pure-bred animals. The Mee family bought the zoo without any prior experience, so not surprisingly Ben found it "harder than I thought" – so hard that its operating company has gone into liquidation despite a TV deal and a planned Hollywood

Of the 51 mammal and bird species at his zoo only seven are classed as threatened by the International Union for Conservation of Nature

Despite its claims, Dartmoor zoo itself has been responsible for killing animals

film. Let's hope they haven't started a trend for wealthy people with no experience to buy ailing zoos – Anna Ryder Richardson followed in their footsteps by getting a TV series based on her buying a zoo in Wales.

Mee talks about the alleged good work of members of the zoo-trade body, the British and Irish Association of Zoos and Aquaria (Biaza). Twice in the past year, we in the Captive Animals' Protection Society have exposed the practices of member zoos. One had a tiger-breeding programme with the owner of the country's most controversial animal circus.

The other was locking lions inside for up to 18 hours a day. Biaza revoked membership of the zoo connected to a circus but not the one keeping lions confined in a building that, according to government inspectors, had "no visible environmental enrichment" and "clear signs of substantial fighting". So how can Mee say we have "some of the highest standards of husbandry anywhere in the world"?

We need to urgently recognise that conservation means the protection and restoration of natural habitats, not keeping animals in cages. If we phase out zoos, and end captive breeding, resources can be used to protect habitats for the benefit of all fauna and flora.

Garry Sheen is development director of the Captive Animals' Protection Society

The Guardian, 21 September 2010
© *Guardian News & Media Ltd 2010*

Body image

Advertising
Family Bullying
Image Health
Sales Anorexia
Airbrushing
Cosmetic surgery
Obesity

Buy now –
pay the real price later!

Most people would do anything they can to avoid surgery. So why are so many people opting for both professional and backstreet cosmetic procedures in the name of physical perfection? Most people would expect any medical procedure to be carried out by a well-trained professional in clean, safe conditions using approved and tested treatments, right? So why do so many people suspend those expectations when the procedure is cosmetic? And why don't the resulting tragedies warn people of the risks they are taking in the pursuit of physical improvement?

TV, newspapers and magazines present both sexes with an ideal of attractiveness that for most of us is unattainable by nature alone. We are increasingly told we must resist ageing and remain young, with slimmer bodies but more enhanced curves. Is this why cosmetic surgery has increased? Are we giving in to the pressure?

Changing attitudes

Cosmetic surgery used to be the guilty secret of film stars, whose livelihood depended on their looks but whose fans would be shocked to discover that the superstar they idolised was not as 'naturally' good-looking as they thought. In contrast, there are celebrities today, such as Katie Price, who have built their entire careers on their surgically enhanced bodies. Celebrities now happily boast about their nips and tucks. Nobody raises an eyebrow at botox injections any more.

Such frankness has taken cosmetic procedures out of the closet and into the mainstream. It is no longer just fading film stars who seek physical

SOME ISSUES:

Do you think plastic surgery is a big deal?

Should it be so easy for people to be able to get plastic surgery?

What drawbacks do you think such easy access might have?

See also:

Little Miss Perfect,
p83, *Essential Articles 9*

It is no longer just fading film stars who seek physical perfection

perfection through surgical procedures, but people of all ages, genders and income groups who see this ideal, and want it for themselves. The more widespread it becomes, the more clinics open up and the more procedures are offered to satisfy that consumer demand – whether the consumer can afford it or not.

The website of a Cheshire cosmetic clinic neatly sums up why an increasing number of people are seeking cosmetic surgery. It is: "... an acceptable and sophisticated method of rejuvenating certain parts of the body that have begun to change with the ageing process ...looking our best makes us feel better." Apparently it provides you with "important psychological benefits... the feeling of well being, happiness". When you can achieve all that in a way that is said to be simple and acceptable – well, why not?

... gift vouchers, interest-free loans and – truthfully – loyalty cards!

The British Association of Aesthetic Plastic Surgeons, a professional body dedicated to improving training and standards, conducts an annual audit amongst its members. The 2011 figures show that despite the recession, BAAPS members carried out more procedures in 2010 than in 2009. The biggest increase was in the most visible areas of the body – facelifts, breasts and nose jobs. In contrast, areas that could be hidden or disguised by clothes or hairstyles – such as tummy tucks or ear correction – were down in popularity. Although women are more likely to use cosmetic surgery, the biggest percentage increase was among men – 'man boob' operations rose by 28%.

Almost certainly the figures from BAAPS are just the tip of the iceberg. It seems the higher the demand, the more easily accessible clinics make the whole cosmetic surgery process. And the more services they offer. As well as more major surgery, minor interventions, including 'lunchtime procedures', botox injections, injectable fillers and non-surgical facelifts are becoming more popular. Try Googling 'filler treatment' in your area to see just how easily accessible it is.

Attitudes towards what still is a surgical procedure have become so relaxed, that recently BAAPS protested when a large 'Health and Beauty' exhibition featuring organic foods, yoga accessories and makeup also offered visitors wrinkle-relaxing/lip-plumping injections and other medical treatments on the spot.

"It is outrageous but sadly unsurprising that serious medical treatments are being sold alongside cupcakes and vitamin supplements," said BAAPS president Fazal Fateh. The idea that consumers who reject chemicals on their vegetables would

consider synthetics injected into their own skins in a non-sterile environment at a bustling exhibition suggests that we are now seeing this as a lifestyle choice, rather than a medical risk.

Cost – the final frontier

As well as introducing new procedures, clinics are coming up with new ways to pay. Some major providers offer payment options more in line with supermarkets than medical centres – gift vouchers, interest-free loans and – truthfully – loyalty cards. SurgiCare, for example, says it "will help you have the procedure you want, at the time you want it" by offering interest free loans and 'Buy now and pay next year'. It encourages referrals "Every time you refer a friend, we will give you a £200 voucher or £100 cheque, when they proceed with their initial cosmetic surgery procedure or a £60 voucher or £30 cheque, when they proceed with their initial non-surgical, cosmetic treatment". As well as repeat visits, "Each time you have a non-surgical cosmetic treatment with us, we'll stamp your Loyalty Card; after your first three visits, you'll receive your first £60". It even has gift vouchers in £25 and £100 denominations – though you'd have to be pretty confident of your reception before you gave these as the "perfect birthday or Christmas present for that special someone".

Even websites like the popular Groupon – the major internet discounting service – will happily send you discounted offers, along with cheap meals for two and money off extreme sports.

The businesses involved, and BAAPS too, can agree that cosmetic surgery can be life changing, but that is the very reason why the surgeons feel that tempting promotions and offers should not be allowed. There is a fear that by making surgery more readily available, people – especially the young – are encouraged to have procedures they don't really need and which they think will solve other problems. By taking away any need to wait or save up the money, the providers are also removing the opportunity to reconsider the idea and the risks.

What are the risks?

As cosmetic surgery becomes more mainstream, we are forgetting that even procedures that seem quick and easy, carry risks. Behind the gloss and glamour are more than a few horror stories. In February 2011, for example, a 20-year-old British woman died in Philadelphia where she had travelled to have an injection of silicone to give her a fuller, rounder bottom – possibly to boost her career as a hip-hop dancer. The injection took place in a hotel near the airport not in a surgery. It seems likely that the silicone leaked into her bloodstream, the unqualified people who gave the injection are being sought by police.

But the risks don't just come with back street procedures. Denise Hendry, wife of Scottish footballer Colin Hendry, went for a 'routine' liposuction operation at a private hospital in 2002. The operation was botched leaving her with a bowel perforated in several places. She never recovered her health and after a seven-year battle with illness she died in July 2009.

At the time of writing, a businesswoman, Penny Johnson, has been awarded £6,190,884.92 in damages for a disastrous plastic surgery operation. In August 2003 she intended to have minor plastic surgery to her nose and dark circles under her eyes. However, the surgeon, Dr Fourie, proposed far more radical treatment, including replacement of her existing breast implants and a major facelift, with further surgery to her forehead and eyes.

She was left with nerve damage to the right side of her face giving her a permanent facial twitch. Her left breast is now deformed and gives her constant pain. These problems are likely to be with her for the rest of her life and have impacted on her work and her family life. She told a judge at the High Court in London: "My face is constantly contracting. I don't sleep and I have a permanent buzzing around my eye which can be so intense that I can't think about anything. I don't want to do anything any more. My husband has a separate life with my son which I'm not included in. I can't be a wife any more."

So while all agree that cosmetic surgery can be life changing, for the unfortunate ones, it is life changing for all the wrong reason. Yet still the mass media swamps us with images of surgically enhanced celebrities to admire and envy. On one page of a magazine there will be images of cosmetically enhanced stars, looking younger, slimmer yet curvier than ever, on the next page there will be a special offer telling us that we too can achieve physical perfection. But behind the white teeth and fake smile lies a risk and the cost of cosmetic surgery can be far higher than any 'buy now pay later' offer.

Sources: BAAPS & Various

10 vital pieces of advice about cosmetic surgery

Based on the BAAPS consumer safety guidelines

1. **Make your own decisions:** You are the real expert on your appearance and what worries you may have. You might need someone to help you decide what you should do, what can be done and what the risks are but this should be unbiased advice. Do not let anyone talk you into doing anything extra that was not a concern to you.

2. **Be informed:** Make sure you know about the limitations and risks of any procedure. No surgery is 100% risk free.

3. **Be comfortable:** Make sure you feel comfortable with the organisation, surgeon and clinic you have chosen.

4. **Know your surgeon:** Many people offering services are not even surgeons. Their impressive-sounding qualifications may mean nothing. Look for organisations connected with the Royal College of Surgeons or which have strong associations with NHS consultants. BAAPS can help you find someone in your area.

5. **Get the timing right:** If possible, you should avoid surgery around the time of major life events such as moving house, changing job, losing a loved one, the break-up of a relationship or the arrival of children.

6. **Beware of 'free' consultations** and avoid booking fees or non-refundable deposits. Nothing is really free. You shouldn't be locked into going ahead by any financial penalties.

7. **Think about location:** Do not travel a long distance or overseas for any surgery unless you are comfortable with the arrangements to follow up and manage any complications.

8. **Talk to your GP:** Many doctors are very happy to advise patients

9. **You can always change your mind:** You have this option to cancel right up until the time you go to sleep for surgery. The point of the surgery is to make you feel better about yourself - you need to be sure about it. There should be no penalty for cancellations.

10. **Take your time:** This is a serious commitment.

AIRBRUSHING IS OUT –

Debenhams Unveils Beauty Untouched

WARM SKINTONES

REMOVE HAIR →

SMOOTH FACE, REMOVE BLEMISH ON LIP, SMOOTH SKIN UNDER EYES.

← REMOVE HAIR

SKIM SHOULDER

ENHANCE SHADOW so CLEA APPEARS FULL

CLEAN UP UNDERARM

SKIM

SKIM WAIST

SKIM WAIST

SKIM ARM

SKIM LEG

SKIM LEG

First High Street retailer to use un-airbrushed images

Debenhams broke ranks with the rest of the high street by using un-airbrushed photography in a trial window to launch new swimwear lines for the summer.

It believes that over use of some digital photography techniques to create unrealistic body shapes and flawless skin may instead can make women feel more insecure about their natural looks and size.

Debenhams will be canvassing customer feedback on the raw images in a move which highlights the retailer's long standing commitment to encouraging positive body-image through minimal digital retouching.

Says Mark Woods, Director of Creative & Visual, "As a responsible retailer we want to help customers make the most of their beauty without bombarding them with unattainable body images.

"Our campaign is all about making women feel good about themselves – not eroding their self belief and esteem by using false comparisons.

"Not only does it make sense from a moral point of view, it ticks the economic boxes as well. Millions of pounds a year are spent by organisations retouching perfectly good images.

"As a rule we only airbrush minor things like pigmentation or stray hair and rely on

SOME ISSUES:

Do you think that it is right for companies to airbrush models in advertisements?

Are companies just improving the image or are they deceiving the customer?

Do images like this have a lot of influence on real people?

Do you think the model looks better before or after?

the natural beauty of models to make our product look great.

"We are proud to bring the issue of re-touching into the mainstream when the likes of Britney Spears and Madonna are using un-airbrushed but over-lit images as a shock tactic."

Caryn Franklin, fashion commentator and broadcaster, says, "Retailers do have the power to take a stance on digital manipulation. Fashion and beauty imagery that is honest, is absolutely crucial for all women to see. I'm delighted that Debenhams has taken the lead here and customer feedback will no doubt validate this important step."

Signage in the window will read: 'We've not messed with natural beauty; this image is un-airbrushed. What do you think?'

It will also show customers an example of just how much the image could have been altered; including all of the following:

- **Arms slimmed**
- **Legs made thinner**
- **Waist pulled in significantly**
- **Stray hairs tidied**
- **Skin tone changed and smoothed**
- **Creases in garments removed**
- **Under-eyes smoothed and lightened**
- **Cleavage enhanced**
- **Underarms tidied**

Jo Swinson, Lib Dem MP and co-founder Campaign for Body Confidence MP said, "It's great news that Debenhams will be using images of real women who have not been digitally manipulated to advertise their new swimwear range.

"More and more people are realising that airbrushing and other trickery are not necessary

Before

in order for women to look beautiful. I am sure that what this will demonstrate is that swimwear modelled by real women who have not been retouched can sell just as well as products advertised with extensive airbrushing, which has become the norm.

"Women can feel good about themselves knowing that beauty is not about achieving the unachievable."

Other advertisers regularly use digital techniques to slim waists, lengthen legs, perfect teeth, and even change eye colour and skin tone.

This is not the first time Debenhams has shown its commitment to promoting positive body image – in January the store ran a trial with size 16 mannequins in windows. The trial gathered customer feedback on a more representative size having a presence on the high street.

Also in February, Debenhams released images using disabled model Shannon Murray to launch the retailer's new Principles by Ben de Lisi range.

Women can feel good about themselves knowing that beauty is not about achieving the unachievable

AFTER

The window, which celebrates natural beauty, was unveiled at the Debenhams' Oxford Street store with staff members asking shoppers what they thought before the initiative was rolled out across the country.

Mark Woods says "We've been showing natural beauty for years and will continue to present women in a natural and positive way."

Source: Debenhams
September 2010

Boys don't cry

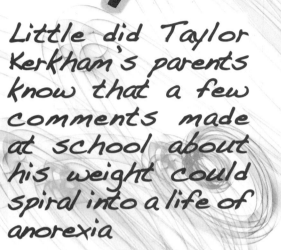

Little did Taylor Kerkham's parents know that a few comments made at school about his weight could spiral into a life of anorexia

Most 12-year-old lads spend their time obsessing over computer games, bikes or skate parks or frantically trying to find the most entertaining and, often, parent-worrying way of using up all of that energy they seem to have. But not Taylor Kerkham.

In fact he had so little energy and got so ill that he ended up spending five months in the Royal Manchester Children's Hospital – Taylor was worrying his parents for all the wrong reasons.

Why was Taylor so different to other boys? Because what started with a "few comments" made by his peers at school about him being a "bit chubby" caused Taylor to become anorexic.

Sometimes surviving on as little as half a tomato a day, Taylor's weight halved from eight stone (51kg) to just four stone (25kg) in only a few months.

Taylor recovering in hospital. At his lowest point he weighed just four stone
Image courtesy of MEN syndication

Taylor, from Stockport, said: "I was not fat but I was a bit chubby. Other children made comments and I wanted to be healthier, I wanted to lose weight. It started with watching TV, seeing programmes about healthy eating and then I started to look up calories in recipe books and on the computer."

What began as a healthy concern about his weight, soon spiraled out of control. His parents, Simon Kerkham and Cheryl Stevens, began to notice that something was wrong when his weight and body shape began to change drastically. His father, Simon, said: "He was not himself. He had always loved his food. He had terrible mood swings, it was frightening."

Yet Taylor had been so affected by the comments made about his appearance that he was determined to lose weight. "I could not relate to it at all. His strength of mind to pursue this was amazing, he was so determined" said Simon.

His mother Cheryl , said: "Every mealtime was a battleground. He would watch me cooking and then examine everything I was putting into the pan. He would shout if I added oil. He even pretended to drop his plate so that he wouldn't have to eat something he didn't like. He would give his food to the dog, he would hide it behind the sofa – we had to stay with him watching him all the time."

When his illness had the firmest grip, Taylor even began to believe that there were calories in almost everything that would make him gain weight, "When I wasn't eating enough my brain wasn't working as well, I thought there were calories in everything – not

SOME ISSUES:

Why do you think that people's comments had such a strong effect on Taylor?

Why do you think there is more help and support for girls than boys?

Do you think people generally think of anorexia as a female problem?

www.b-eat.co.uk

Taylor and his mother Cheryl. Image courtesy of MEN syndication

Despite the fact that one in ten anorexia sufferers are male they found that almost everything relating to anorexia was for and about girls

air – but everything solid or liquid, shampoo, soap, pencils and rubbers and stuff." He even began to hallucinate and began to believe that he was getting calories from smelling other people's food.

In desperation his parents took down mirrors and removed the batteries from their weighing scales. They constantly had to battle with him to get him to eat anything. One of the lowest points came when he had refused to eat for a day and a half. Things reached melting point when one day they forced him to eat a biscuit and it caused him to become so hysterical he threatened to commit suicide.

His mother, Ms Stevens said: "He'd even stopped drinking; he wasn't speaking properly, he started throwing everything around the house All I could do was phone the hospital." During his treatment he spent four weeks at Stepping Hill Hospital where he had to use a wheelchair but put on a few pounds thanks to

tube feeding. Staff had to monitor his heart rate every hour and someone stayed with him 24 hours a day to make sure he did not harm himself.

He then spent six months on a ward under the care of the Child and Adolescent Mental Health Services team at the Royal Manchester Children's Hospital.

In his counselling sessions Taylor talked about the illness taking over him and even gave it another name, the name of one of the people who had bullied him.

Now BMX-mad Taylor eats everything, though he still sticks to smaller portions. He is also enjoying being back at Stockport School and hopes to become a zoologist.

The anorexia not only reduced his weight but the lack of nutrition also affected his height. He is five feet tall but grew under half an inch in the seven months he was in hospital. Since he has been a healthy weight again he has grown nearly an inch in just two months.

Taylor said: "It is weird now, I can remember when I could only think about food and how I liked losing weight. It didn't matter what anyone else said, I just wanted to carry on. Talking about it now it seems like a long time ago, almost like it was another person."

He continues to have outpatient appointments, the family go for counselling together and they have support workers they can contact at any time.

Taylor and his family think it is important to raise awareness of eating disorders among boys as well as girls. When Taylor was diagnosed with anorexia, despite the fact that one in ten sufferers are male, the family found, when researching it on the internet, that almost everything relating to it was about and for girls. They hope that by raising the profile of Taylor and his illness, they can offer help to the many boys out there who also suffer from eating disorders.

Sources: Various

What should I do about my overweight niece?

Dear Agony Aunt,

My 12 year old niece is lovely, she is chatty and friendly and popular at school. The problem is she is very overweight. She says when she grows up she wants to work with food and become a chef. She loves baking and helping her mum in the kitchen, but I am very worried about her health.

I have suggested to my sister that she should encourage her to play outdoors more and exercise, and not to allow her so many treats. She says it is just puppy fat and that she is fine how she is.

They recently bought her a fridge for her bedroom which she stores chocolate and cans in.

I really believe this is the wrong way to raise a child. How can I speak to my sister and her husband about it?

Agony Aunt says... It's extremely difficult to criticise anybody's parenting methods, particularly if that person is a sibling. You do not want to offend them or cause an argument that might distance you from the family.

As she is interested in becoming a chef, maybe as her auntie, you could also cook with her, and encourage her to consider the health and nutritional aspects of food and cooking too. Maybe you could take her out to markets, where you get to walk around the stalls and consider the food together. This will be informative and double up as exercise too. If she has a computer fitness game, encourage her to use it, from a health and nutrition point of view.

If she is happy and content with herself, you really don't want to make her feel bad about her weight. Instead encourage her to consider the healthier parts of cooking and food.

About the fridge, maybe you could buy some fruit smoothies and nutritious snack bars for her to stock in there instead of cans and sweets.

Source: Adapted from original newspaper article

SOME ISSUES:

Whose responsibility is it to make sure the girl is a healthy weight?

Would you tell someone if you thought they should lose weight?

See also:
My brother is eating himself to death,
p113, *Essential Articles 13*

Britain & its citizens

Family Race
Nationality
Benefits Identity
Diversity Flags
Money
Poverty
Wealth
Housing

my britishness is more than skin-deep

It was claimed last week that by 2066, white Britons will be a minority, but should we really be worried by this?
Amardeep Sohi

Picture posed by model

I'm British, but Professor David Coleman has made me feel like a permanent immigrant. He's the Oxford University migration adviser who claimed last week that by 2066, white Britons will be a minority. He believes that this shift, based on skin colour will "represent an enormous change to national identity". But surely, national identity should be based on a system of values upheld by a population, not skin colour.

It wasn't until I ventured to India, the country of my parents' birth, that I realised how true this was.

Although my family originate from the Punjab, I was born and educated in London. Growing up, a real sense of being British was embedded within me, but I was always conscious of this "other" place from which my grandparents and parents had migrated in the 1960s, a reminder that resurfaces every time I have to tick the "Asian or British Asian" box on a form.

At 24, I finally made the journey to the Punjab. It was late by anybody's standards, but I was curious to visit the land my parents had left behind as children. A number of people were intrigued and keen to find out how I would react and I felt pressured to relate to the country that I

SOME ISSUES:

What is it that makes you British?

Does your skin colour affect your national identity?
What about your religious and cultural beliefs?

Is your family heritage more or less important than the country you are born in?

Would it matter if white Britons become the minority?

See also:
Who do you think you are?
p26, *Fact File 2011* &
Race relations,
p26, *Fact File 2010*
www.intermix.org.uk

was expected to look upon as the "motherland". I expected the experience to shed light on my family history, but it did so much more.

It confirmed what I had always known; first and foremost I was British. My ethnic background marginalised me in the UK, but my British upbringing did the same in India. When I ventured out, I was deemed the foreigner and even an attempt to blend in with traditional dress did little to dispel my British air and mannerisms. I was "the British girl" and the experience was dumbfounding.

But it wasn't just this reception that confirmed my sense of self. Although I was visiting a rural area, I naturally found myself comparing attitudes towards health, education, politics and even tax, all the things that bind a society.

The most striking difference was in healthcare. We Brits sometimes complain about the quality of care we receive in the NHS, but compared with a country where healthcare can only be

I came away with the realisation that our attitudes and contributions to society, whether they be financial, vocational or political, define who we are

obtained privately, isn't it a sign of our equality and sense of responsibility to one another? It soon became clear that I had a very British attitude to the elements which make up a society and this, I realised, is what defined me.

The trip was illuminating in so many ways and although I'm very proud of my heritage, I came away with the realisation that our attitudes and contributions to society, whether they be financial, vocational or political, define who we are. Skin colour and religious or cultural beliefs need not define national identity.

When Professor Coleman speaks of immigration in terms of colour, he is marginalising generations of Britons and disregarding decades' worth of contributions made to British society by immigrants and their offspring And he is playing into the hands of the far right. Immigration should remain on the agenda, but the arguments should be about numbers, not colour.

Focusing on the issue in terms of the effects on "white Britons" is short-sighted and reductive. National identity should be based on values we uphold collectively. Before there's a crisis of national identity, we would do well to remember that.

The Observer, 21 November 2010
© Guardian News & Media Ltd 2010

I long for diversity not to be a novelty

By Steve Downes

I've just returned from an eventful weekend with my wife in London. It included:

Getting lost twice, which was exacerbated by my genetic inability to ask for directions.

A "romantic" meal at the Liverpool Street Travelodge, with a typically miserable EastEnders episode playing at 120db on the flat screen telly in the corner.

A sleepless night – unfortunately for the wrong reasons: a man banging on a door down the corridor for two hours, and a girl being sick outside our room.

A wonderful performance of Blood Brothers at the Phoenix Theatre, marred slightly by Ryanair-style legroom and £6 for a warm glass of cheap white wine – in a plastic cup.

An epic journey home – via numerous tube stops, train from Stratford to Ipswich, bus from Ipswich to Stowmarket, train from Stowmarket to Norwich and car from Norwich to Cromer – because of underground and overground engineering works.

It was a great weekend, though, and one that was enhanced by the multi-lingual, multi-racial, cosmopolitan feel of the capital.

The sad thing is, I noticed. The different languages, shades of skin and cultural clothing caught my ear and eye. Such ethnic diversity is still a novelty for me. But should it be?

I certainly wish I was like children of pre-school age, who seem to see each other only as people, not colours or nationalities. It takes the unhelpful intervention of adults to disabuse them of that delightful innocence and infect their minds with prejudice.

SOME ISSUES:

Is there a mixture of cultures where you live?

Are race and culture the same thing?

How do you think racism should be tackled?

Do you think people should learn about the different cultures within Britain?

See also:

Who do you think you are?
p26, *Fact File 2011* &
Race Relations,
p26, *Fact File 2010*

The streets of Norwich. Photo courtesy of Nic McPhee

Although it is not a regular occurrence, I still hear plenty of examples of casual racism on the streets, in shops and in pubs.

London's more multi-cultural streets

A mixture of education about, and experience of, ethnic diversity would certainly give today's children the chance to escape the curse.

But I haven't been helped by being brought up in rural North Norfolk. I can still remember the names of three black/Asian children who went to the same schools as me. That's because they were the only three.

The situation has been improved in recent years by the arrival of people from Eastern Europe. They have brought a welcome dose of diversity to my home town. But the kaleidoscope of colours in the capital remains a distant dream, with white faces dominating the classrooms, even three decades on from my schooldays.

It's not that I want to falsely force the situation. I just long for my children to be so immersed in a multi-ethnic life that they do not pick up the bad habits of the generations that went before them.

Although it is not a regular occurrence, I still hear plenty of examples of casual racism on the streets, in shops and in pubs. I have even heard it much closer to home, which is demoralising indeed.

Some of it is genuinely sinister, but most of it is simply an ignorant offshoot of fear of the unknown.

It might be an insoluble problem for people who have the attitudes branded on their DNA through decades of conditioning.

But a mixture of education about, and experience of, ethnic diversity would certainly give today's children the chance to escape the curse.

I am currently flying through Harper Lee's wonderful, yet harrowing, novel To Kill a Mockingbird.

I think we are some way forward from the racial discrimination and bigotry that it describes in the Deep South of the USA in the 1930s. But we are also some way short of the ideal: a society so ethnically diverse that we don't even notice it.

Eastern Daily Press, 1 February 2011

My father, the racist

Chris Fox and his Indian partner are having a baby. Her family are thrilled and so are his – all except his father, who votes BNP and can't see past skin that isn't white

SOME ISSUES:

Would you have a relationship with someone your parents didn't approve of?

Does the writer have an over-optimistic view of his partner's family?

Are these opinions old-fashioned?

Is it right to go against your parents if you believe they are wrong?

Are mixed race relationships important?

See also:

Who do you think you are?
p26, *Fact File 2011*
Race relations,
p26, *Fact File 2010*
Sense of belonging,
p28, *Fact File 2010*

For more information go to:
www.intermix.org.uk

A baby's birth is surely the most joyous of all family events. With a new life and fresh innocence, the bonding of two families cooing over the new arrival seems inevitable. My partner is expecting our first child and her liberal Indian family have gone into overdrive to help us prepare for the baby and move to a new home. They are carrying boxes, buying appliances, giving us things for the baby and delivering unbelievable homemade Indian food.

We're grateful, not just for the amazing dishes, but for the support they have given us during the stress of house-buying and pregnancy.

In contrast, I'm getting the opposite of support from my father.

I've always know my dad was racist. I've disagreed with him all my life, not that he's noticed. No one else in the family shares his views, but he is oblivious to the opinions of others.

When it became clear that Mira and I were committed to being together, I tried to ease my father into the news, first telling him of my Indian friend, who was born in Kenya. He wasted no time in registering his objection. "Don't introduce her to me. I'm trying to send them all back," he harrumphed, about the sweetest girl I'd ever known.

Meanwhile, I was meeting, and being welcomed by, Mira's family. We went to her cousin's wedding in Gloucestershire and I was struck by the fondness between the elder uncles and aunts and the young nieces and nephews. Everyone mucked in to help, all the generations danced and celebrated together. It hit me that this is what a family is supposed to be like. They had a lot of love for each other and weren't shy about showing it. They also knew how to enjoy themselves. The laughter and dancing went on all night, and one or two of the old boys could be seen loitering by the door in the hope that the young ones were smoking more than tobacco. The ladies howled as a saucy aunt took the opportunity to cop a feel of my backside as I shook my generous booty.

On returning to London I visited my parents. After spending three happy days with Mira's family, it only took an hour with my dad for me to despair. I was subjected to a relentless torrent of bitterness about the government, immigration, television, the NHS,

Pictures posed by models

Tuesdays … it was all terribly, irredeemably foul. And it was all better in his day when you could leave your door open and be a hateful racist without anyone batting an eyelid.

Out of earshot of Mum, my dad told me I should "be careful" with Mira. It was a bit late for that, as we had just found out we were to have a baby, though it was too soon to make an announcement. His warning wasn't based on any knowledge of the person she is but on his assumptions about race and immigration. He suggested I would soon be putting up her relatives, and, even more absurdly, harbouring terrorists.

Depressed by his descent into risible paranoia, I took my leave, wondering how he had become such an ogre.

"He wasn't always like this," Mum said at the door. "I don't know what happened to him."

My dad was born into a large, poor, south London family in the 1920s. Seventeen at the outbreak of the second world war he became a stoker in the Royal Navy. By the time he was 21, he had sailed round the world, been sunk twice, seen good friends die and earned the eternal thanks of his country. By the time I was 21, the greatest suffering I had experienced was bleaching my hair.

"Don't introduce her to me. I'm trying to send them all back"

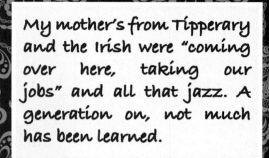

> My mother's from Tipperary and the Irish were "coming over here, taking our jobs" and all that jazz. A generation on, not much has been learned.

When he introduced my mother to his parents, my grandfather walked out. My mother's from Tipperary and the Irish were "coming over here, taking our jobs" and all that jazz. A generation on, not much has been learned.

Dad worked hard all his life and retired in his 50s. He had no idea what to do with himself without work to define him and, still haunted by his experiences in the war, he became an alcoholic. It took the threat of divorce from his devout Roman Catholic wife to drag him back from the brink.

Since then, his world has narrowed. He mourns a lost England, unable to recognise the multicultural country it has become as the one he fought for. "That's not patriotism," I tell him. "It's nostalgia."

In the last couple of years, he's spent all his time in a wheelchair and has only left the house to vote – for the BNP. The Daily Mail, television and the occasional like-minded visitor inform his perspective. So he has become a sour, entrenched, dogmatic bigot who only hears views that chime with his own racist – and even fascist – position.

With Mira pregnant, I knew I had to introduce her to my parents before announcing our news, lest I expose her to an even more difficult scenario. ("Hi Hitler. Let me introduce you to the mother of your Indian grandchild.") The reaction of friends and siblings to our happy surprise has been joyous and life affirming. I was a little nervous about telling my 23-year-old daughter, Dixie, that she was going to have a brother or sister but she was pragmatic and honest. She didn't know how she would feel about sharing her father for the first time, but she wanted to be involved. She is the reason I know

how uplifting raising a child is. She constantly fills me with pride, not because she's doing so well, but because she's a great addition to the world.

Her first reaction was, "Ha! Your life is over." Her second was, "What did Granddad say?"

Mum assured me Dad would behave when I brought Mira over to meet them. He would only have to be civil for five minutes before the three of us went out. "You're different to what I expected," he said, shaking her hand. "I heard you were from Kenya, so I thought you'd be a 6ft Zulu with a bone through your nose."

Really. That's what he said. And that's him on his best behaviour. If only Prince Philip had been there to laugh. He asked a few questions about her family background – very important to any self-respecting doctrinaire – and we parted. The introduction had gone well. Mum thought Mira was lovely and Dad hadn't expressed an opinion. I couldn't ask for more.

Mira had said it would be harder for me than for her, and she was right. She was untroubled before the visit and untroubled afterwards. She hasn't experienced much racism since coming to London at the age of nine and has a soft spot for old duffers. She's not easily offended and was quite happy to meet my dad and engage him, should he kick off. It might have been better than the faux civility.

Having breached introductions, it was time to drop the bombshell. I enlisted my brother and sister to join me, mostly so my dad could see how normal people react to good news.

Loyalty, respect and decency are central to his generation's values: loyalty to the country and your family. So could I expect him to be loyal, respectful and decent when I arrived to tell him that, after 23 years, I was to be a father again?

> He's spent all his time in a wheelchair and has only left the house to vote – for the BNP. The Daily Mail, television and the occasional like-minded visitor inform his perspective.

There's really only one way to put it. "Mira and I are going to have a baby!" Cue almost universal joy, screams and congratulations. Mum was thrilled and my brother and sister were delighted. "That's wonderful!" Mum said.

"Is it?" huffed my dad, who wheeled himself out of the room to calm down. The only person not to have congratulated me on the news was my father. He stewed all day, silently.

Meanwhile, Mira's family were cranking up to hysterical levels. Offers of help abounded and stamp-duty money was proffered for our new home. Food deliveries were increased, and I was getting progressively larger portions.

I was even more endeared to them by a tale from Mira's childhood. During the summer holidays, the extended family would cram into a car, including aunts, uncles and cousins. The kids would be in the boot and the adults squeezed into the seats as they headed excitedly for the airport. There they would sit in the departure lounge and watch the unfolding drama of people parting, while they had a picnic. For a treat they would go to arrivals.

I had to wait some weeks before my dad could broach the subject. He was "disgusted", he told me, that I was having a child "out of wedlock".

I laughed. "How could I marry an Indian girl with you?"

"I wouldn't come!" he barked, thinking it quite rational that I should marry because of his sudden bout of religious propriety, even if he wouldn't attend. But I knew it was his way of protesting without mentioning his real objection – her ethnicity was the problem.

There have been many mixed marriages in Mira's family, so race is not an issue for them. They, too, would like us to be married but accept that it is our choice.

Dad said he couldn't believe how "daft" I'd been, not even considering that I might be happy. He wanted nothing to do with it. He didn't want to know anything about the baby's progress. He maintained it was my Roman Catholic mother's feelings that concerned him, as according to him, she was secretly disgusted too.

That he hadn't even spoken to my clearly delighted mother about their imminent fifth grandchild seemed inhuman to me. I resented his lying about her to express his own opinions. I returned a similar level of vitriol, making clear that it was he, not me, who should be ashamed of his behaviour. We left it there.

I told him not to bother getting in touch if he wasn't going to apologise and, predictably, I haven't heard from him.

For the first time in my 49 years we're not talking. We've never had much in common, but talked most weeks, making each other laugh about football and family. I wasn't surprised, or that hurt, by his diatribe, but I was disappointed to see his lack of interest in my happiness and disrespect for my choices. He didn't ask about the woman who will be the mother of his grandchild, or how happy we are. His concern was how he felt about my situation: a triumph of ideology over parental concern.

Some have questioned the wisdom of a dispute with a father who is 88, in case "something happens". I can understand that, but it doesn't allow me to forgive the unforgivable. Having provided for it, he has dominated the family, laying down the law, mostly unchallenged. I'm not going to allow him to disrespect the woman I love, her family and our unborn child, and then go on to chat about the woes of Charlton Athletic.

It's a shame he won't know Mira. He would love her to bits if he could see past the colour of her skin. To me, it's shameful he has attempted to poison such a proud and blessed moment in his son's life. I can only hope the sight of a new baby will soften his silly head, but I'm not confident.

It took another generation to put it into perspective. As my daughter Dixie said: "Think of it this way, Dad – he'll be the last racist in the family."

Names have been changed

The Guardian, 29 January 2011
© Guardian News & Media Ltd 2011

> It took another generation to put it into perspective. As my daughter Dixie said: "Think of it this way, Dad – he'll be the last racist in the family."

WHY I WON'T FLY THE ENGLAND FLAG

Steve Downes

If someone asks me my nationality, I unhesitatingly reply "English".

I do not consider myself British, any more than many Scottish, Welsh and Northern Irish people do. When Andy Murray plays tennis, I'm not bothered if he does well. After all, he's Scottish, and he said (to my admiration, not anger) "anyone but England", when asked which team he would support in the last World Cup.

However, despite being proud to be an Englishman, I feel uncomfortable when it comes to one of the privileges of that identity – flying the George Cross. The red-and-white flag is supposed to be the ultimate symbol of pride and patriotism, as national flags are in so many countries.

On my recent extended visit to the United States, I was struck by how many people fly the Stars and Stripes in their gardens, on their houses and in their offices. I have witnessed the same phenomenon in India, Australia and France.

The same is not true in England. Here, we are somewhat timid when it comes to celebrating our national identity. I fear it is to do with the way our flag has been and continues to be hijacked by racists and ultra-nationalists who drape it over a multitude of sins and sickening views.

Last week, I decided to ignore my uncertainty and post a George Cross on my Facebook page. I simply wanted to show that I will be supporting England in the World Cup in South Africa next month – before, during and after their exit on penalties in the quarter finals. I soon regretted the move as I saw

SOME ISSUES:

What feelings do you have towards national flags?

What impression do you think flying this flag gives?

Is the flag part of your national identity?

Here, we are somewhat timid when it comes to celebrating our NATIONAL IDENTITY. I fear it is to do with the way our FLAG has been and continues to be hijacked by RACISTS and ULTRA-NATIONALISTS who drape it over a multitude of sins and sickening views.

a racist and anti-migrant undertone building up elsewhere on the social networking site.

The trigger for the tasteless was a rumour that the Metropolitan Police had banned England flags and England shirts from pubs in the capital during the World Cup.

The rumour – which turned out to be total rubbish – spread rapidly, with people posting it on their pages in high dudgeon. Pretty quickly, the apparently innocent sharing of the rumour turned to something more sinister. A flurry of comments followed, including "If we can't wear an England shirt, why should Sikhs wear turbans?" "If you want to ban England shirts, ban burkas." "If our flag offends you so much, why aren't you offended by our benefits?"

It is yet another example of our flag of national identity becoming a flag of convenience for the narrow-minded. Rightly or wrongly, I am now unlikely to fly an England flag during the World Cup. It's not that I won't be chewing my nails down to my elbows and crying when we get knocked out, it's just that I do not want people to identify me with the mindless minority.

I acknowledge that the current immigration system is far from perfect. I believe something needs to be done to make it fairer – both for those desperate people caught up in it and for this nation. But I find it sickening when I see dislike of a system mutate into hatred of the people who are caught up in it.

Quite simply, some people use the issue of immigration as a vehicle to transport their bullying, racist views.

They do the same when they hijack the George Cross and turn it into a symbol of hatred towards minority groups. What they seem to forget is that few people in England can lay claim to an unimpeachable "English" heritage. This is a nation built on centuries of immigration from scores of countries.

We are a mongrel nation, and our language is a magnificent merger of Celtic, Norse, Germanic, French, Saxon, Creole and numerous other tongues. The England that I live in is worth being proud of because of that cultural and linguistic cocktail.

Unfortunately, until I feel that there is a wider understanding of this in England, I'll sidestep being identified with the racists and will not fly the flag.

Eastern Daily Press, 25 May 2010

A STOP TOO FAR

A FATHER HAS BEEN THREATENED BY A COUNCIL WITH A "CHILD PROTECTION" ORDER FOR LETTING HIS SEVEN-YEAR-OLD DAUGHTER WALK 20 METRES FROM THEIR HOME TO THE BUS STOP ON HER OWN.

BY NICK BRITTEN

SOME ISSUES:

What age do you think is old enough for a child to walk to the bus stop on their own?

How far do you think is safe?

Who do you agree with – the parent or the council?

See also:
Just let parents get on with bringing up their children,
p86, *Essential Articles 13*

Mark McCullough, 32, received a letter from Lincolnshire County Council threatening to report the situation unless his daughter, Isabelle, was accompanied on her daily walk to catch the bus.

The short trip involves crossing a country road in the village of Glentham.

Either he or his partner Natasha Fegan, 33, are at home every day to see Isabelle off in the morning, and meet her when she returns home from school, but they allow her to make her own way from the house in Glentham, Lincs, to the bus stop on her own.

They have now been warned by Lincolnshire County Council that there must be a "change in arrangements", or they will face action.

Mr McCullough, who has four other children, was criticised at the same time for sending Isabelle to Normanby by Spital Primary School without a jumper.

He said: "This is more than upsetting. It has made me angry.

FOR A SEVEN-YEAR-OLD NOT TO BE ABLE TO WALK 20 METRES TO THE TOP OF THE COURTYARD AND CROSS A QUIET COUNTRY ROAD IS AN ABSOLUTE JOKE.

"IT SHOULD NOT BE FOR THE BUS DRIVER TO HAVE TO GET OUT AND SEE THE GIRL ACROSS THE ROAD."

"I am happy for Isabelle to walk from home to the end of the road and, if necessary, cross a country lane.

"I'm not going to wrap my children up in cotton wool.

"When I was a child I would go anywhere during the school holidays. I would be out at eight in the morning and not back until teatime.

"Admittedly I would not let the kids do that now because times are different. But for a seven-year-old not to be able to walk 20 metres to the top of the courtyard and cross a quiet country road is an absolute joke.

"I'm going to carry on as normal even if it means going to court."

Mr McCullough, a refuse collector, received the letter from the council on Friday.

It claimed the bus driver felt "obliged" to help Isabelle safely cross the road at the end of the day, and added: "Should there be no change in the arrangements for Isabelle's delivery to and collection from the bus stop, I will have no option but to consider reporting this as a child protection issue."

A council spokesman said the road was busy and that the bus driver, who reported the situation, felt it necessary of his own volition to get out of the bus and help the girl across.

He said: "We are simply trying to be responsible. She is only seven. We have had issues of children getting hurt or killed whilst crossing the road on their own.

"It should not be for the bus driver to have to get out and see the girl across the road."

Denise Carr, Lincs County Council's head of transport services, said "As a responsible authority we have expressed our concern that a seven-year-old is standing on a busy road alone each morning and then crossing the road unaccompanied.

"As the child was also left standing by the roadside on a cold morning without warm clothing we have raised our concern with the parents."

The Daily Telegraph,
14 September 2010
© Telegraph Media Group
Limited 2010

Let's take the HOUSING FIGHT to wealthy owners with empty spare rooms

The hidden truth about our housing crisis is that it is driven by under-occupation
George Monbiot

SOME ISSUES:

Is it fair that while some families live in overcrowded houses, other have rooms to spare?

Should people be allowed to own any house they want, if they can afford it?

Should owners of large houses be forced to take in lodgers?

Should single people move into smaller houses?

See also:

Great divide,
p80, *Fact File 2011*
Supply & demand,
p110, *Fact File 2011* &
Locked out,
p112, *Fact File 2011*

There are two housing crises in Britain. One of them is obvious and familiar: the walloping shortfall in supply. Households are forming at roughly twice the rate at which new homes are being built. In England alone, 650,000 homes are classed as overcrowded. Many other people are desperate to move into their own places, but find themselves stuck. Yet the new homes the government says we need – 5.8m by 2033 – threaten to mash our landscapes and overload the environment.

The other crisis is scarcely mentioned. I stumbled across it while researching last week's column, buried on page 33 of a government

In England alone, 650,000 homes are classed as overcrowded

document about another issue. It's growing even faster than the first crisis – at a rate that's hard to comprehend. Yet you'll seldom hear a squeak about it in the press, in parliament, in government departments or even in the voluntary sector. Given its political sensitivity, perhaps that's not surprising.

The issue is surplus housing – the remarkable growth of space that people don't need. Between 2003 and 2008 (the latest available figures), there was a 45% increase in the number of under-occupied homes in England. The definition of under-occupied varies, but it usually means that households have at least two bedrooms more than they require. This category now accounts for over half the homes in which single people live, and almost a quarter of those used by larger households. Nearly 8m homes – 37% of the total housing stock – are officially under-occupied.

The only occasions on which you'll hear politicians talk about this is when they're referring to public housing. Many local authorities are trying to encourage their tenants to move into smaller homes. But public and social housing account for only 11% of the problem. The government reports that the rise in under-occupation "is entirely due to a large increase within the owner-occupied sector". Nearly half of England's private homeowners are now knocking around in more space than they need.

Why is this happening? I've spent the past few days wading through official figures to try to find out. None of the most obvious explanations appear to fit.

Though the proportion of homes occupied by just one person rose sharply between 1961 and 2001, there has been no increase since then. The formation of single households can't account for the growth in under-occupancy between 2003 and 2008. The proportion of couples without children has also remained stable since 2001. Fertility rates have increased over this period – from 1.63 babies per woman in 2001 to 1.96 in 2009 – so a general absence of children doesn't explain it either. Nor can it be blamed on the elderly: except through devastating war, no population can age by 45% in six years. The divorce rate fell in 2008 to its lowest level since 1979. Marriage has declined, but cohabitation has risen. The overall rate of household formation rose only slightly during the period in which under-occupancy has boomed.

This appears to leave just one likely explanation: money. My guess, though I can find no research or figures either to support or disprove it, is that the richest third of the population has discovered that it can spread its wings. A report by the International Longevity Centre comes to the same conclusion: "Wealth ... is the key factor in whether or not we choose to occupy more housing space than is essential."

While most houses are privately owned, the total housing stock is a common resource. Either we ensure that it is used wisely and fairly, or we allow its distribution to become the starkest expression of inequality. The UK appears to have chosen the

Nearly 8m homes – 37% of the total housing stock – are officially under-occupied

second option. We have allowed the market, and the market alone, to decide who gets what – which means that families in desperate need of bigger homes are crammed together in squalid conditions, while those who have more space than they know what to do with face neither economic nor social pressure to downsize.

The only answer anyone is prepared to mention is more building: let the rich occupy as much space they wish, and solve the problem by dumping it on the environment, which means – of course – on everyone. I think there's a better way.

While reducing under-occupancy can't solve the crisis of provision by itself, and there will still be a need for new construction, a better distribution of the housing we've built already would help to relieve the pressure on both people and places. First, we need to see the problem. I suggest a new concept: housing footprints. Your housing footprint is the number of bedrooms divided by the number of people in the household. Like ecological footprints, it reminds us that the resource is finite, and that, if some people take more than they need, others are left with less than they need.

The next step is to reverse the UK's daft fiscal incentive to under-occupy your home. If you live by yourself, regardless of the size of your property, you get a 25% council tax discount. The rest of us, in other words, subsidise wealthy single people who want to keep their spare rooms empty. Those who use more than their fair share should pay for the privilege, with a big tax penalty for under-occupation. If it prompts them either to take in a lodger or to move into a smaller home in a lower tax band, so much the better.

> **Families in desperate need of bigger homes are crammed together in squalid conditions, while those who have more space than they know what to do with face neither economic nor social pressure to downsize**

I would also like to see an expansion of the Homeshare scheme, which could address several growing problems at once. Instead of paying rent, lodgers – who are vetted and checked by the charity that runs the project – help elderly homeowners with shopping, cleaning, cooking, gardening or driving. Typically they agree to spend 10 hours a week helping out, and to sleep in the house for at least six nights out of seven. This helps older people to stay in their own homes and lead an independent life, gives them companionship and security and relieves some of the pressure on social services and carers. It provides homes for people who wouldn't otherwise be able to afford them.

But we can't solve this problem unless we start to discuss it. It needs to be researched, debated, fought over. It needs to turn political. I can understand why neither the government nor the opposition dares to think about it: none of the major parties wants to pick a fight with wealthy householders. So it's up to us to give them no choice, by turning under-occupation into an issue they can't avoid. It cannot be left to the market, as the market works for the rich.

> **Those who use more than their fair share should pay for the privilege, with a big tax penalty for under-occupation. If it prompts them either to take in a lodger or to move into a smaller home in a lower tax band, so much the better**

• A fully referenced version of this article can be found on George Monbiot's website www.monbiot.com

The Guardian, 4 January 2011
© Guardian News & Media Ltd 2011

Drugs

Addiction
Recovery
Danger Harm
Health War
Pressure **Britain**
Therapy
Society

WHERE'S THE HARM?

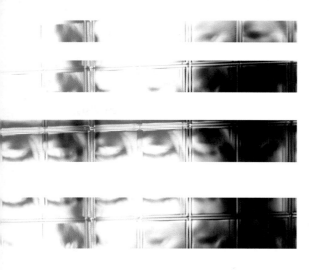

"Alcohol is more harmful than crack or heroin"

"Alcohol is more harmful than crack or heroin," reported The Daily Telegraph and many other newspapers in November 2010. The headlines were based on a study led by Professor David J Nutt, who used to be the head of the government's Advisory Council on the Misuse of Drugs until he was asked to resign for making similar claims. But do they give the correct picture?

Research puts alcohol harm ahead of heroin and crack. Yet alcohol is most harmful largely because it is most widely used.

Professor Nutt's study ranked 20 drugs according to the harms that he and other experts decided that they caused. Not surprisingly, heroin, crack cocaine and methamphetamine (meth or crystal meth) were found to be most harmful to individual users. They were also the illegal drugs most harmful to society and other people. However, because alcohol is legal and most widely available, it was found to be most harmful overall.

The research reminds us that alcohol misuse causes widespread social harm, but can the findings tell us about the potential dangers of drugs like crack and heroin which are not as widely used as alcohol?

HOW WERE THE DRUGS COMPARED?

The aim of this research was to assess and compare various harms from 20 recreational drugs in the UK so that the people who make decisions health, policing and social care could have useful guidance on the harms of drugs.

Groups of experts in drug policy-making rated the harms to both individuals and to communities. The substances included alcohol and tobacco as well as illegal drugs such as heroin, crack cocaine, cocaine, amphetamines and cannabis.

They scored the drugs according to 16 types of harm: nine harms related to the individual (such as health, death, relationships) and seven related to harms to others (such as crime and costs to the economy and

SOME ISSUES:

What do you think about the way the drugs were tested?

Does this change your opinion on drugs?

What role do TV and newspapers play in people's perception of drugs?

See also:
Alcohol section, p10-18

community). The group then assessed the relative importance of each harm to produce a 'score' for each drug, for harms to the individual, others and a combination of the two.

At a second meeting, experts from the Independent Scientific Committee on Drugs scored each drug on the 16 harm criteria and then discussed the importance of each of these criteria and the definitions that the previous group had produced. Each drug was given a score out of 100 (with 100 being the most harmful) on each of the 16 criteria. Each measure of harm was also assessed for its importance in the context of the UK.

THE SCORES
Crack cocaine (37), heroin (34) and methamphetamine (32) were considered the most harmful to individual users.

The three most harmful drugs to others were alcohol (46), heroin (21) and crack cocaine (17).

When the individual harm and the harm to others scores were combined, alcohol was the most harmful drug, scoring 72 out of 100. This was followed by heroin (55) and crack cocaine (54).

WHAT DOES IT TELL US?
The authors say that the way drugs are classified at the moment does not have much to do with the harm they cause. They also said that reducing harm from alcohol should be a target in a public health strategy.

The researchers were aware of some limitations to their approach:

• They only considered harms – some drugs do have benefits (for example, the commercial benefits to society of the tobacco and alcohol industries).

• Their results may not be relevant to countries with different cultures and legal systems.

• They did not include prescription drugs.

• They did not investigate the use of more than one drug or substance (for example, alcohol plus recreational drugs).

HOW HELPFUL?
For someone who wants to know about the harms of drug use, finding out which drugs are most harmful to individual users is important. Policy makers are more interested in the impact on society. Here there will always be differing opinions and controversy - and the part of the research that scored the harm for each drug could have been affected by personal opinion.

What the researchers tried to do was to put numbers on the wider impact of different drugs, but the fact remains that alcohol came top of the list largely because it is a legal, widely used drug.

THE CRITERIA:

Harms to the individual:
• **Death caused directly by drugs**
• **Death related drugs**
• **Damage caused directly by drugs**
• **Damage related to drugs**
• **Dependence**
• **Impairment of mental functioning caused directly by drugs**
• **Impairment of mental functioning related to drugs**
• **Loss of tangibles (income, housing, job etc)**
• **Loss of relationships**

Harms to others were:
• **Injury**
• **Crime**
• **Environmental damage**
• **Family problems**
• **International damage**
• **Economic cost**
• **Community**

Source: Adapted from NHS Behind The Headlines 'Study compares drug harms' www.nhs.uk/news/2010/11november/pages/study-compares-drug-narms.aspx

Breakthrough in Britain's war on drugs and crime

By Robert Verkaik

The long battle to break the link between drug addiction and criminal behaviour is being won, a ground-breaking study into the long-term success rates of treatment programmes suggests. Nearly a half of all addicts who participated in drug courses in 2005 have been found to be free from addiction and no longer committing crime four years after leaving treatment. For those with cannabis or cocaine habits the success rates are as high as 69 per cent and 64 per cent respectively.

The success rate among the 41,000 drug users involved in the National Treatment Agency for Substance Misuse and Home Office study is higher than previous government figures for reoffending rates for addicts on court rehabilitation orders.

The NTA tracked the post-treatment outcome of drug users over a four-year period. Almost half those discharged in one year subsequently demonstrated recovery from addiction. Of the remainder, about half directly returned to treatment. A further third were redirected back into treatment through the criminal justice system. Of those who left treatment but subsequently reoffended using drugs, 65 per cent went back into treatment.

Paul Hayes, chief executive of NTA, says: "Experts agree that heroin and crack cocaine users take several years to overcome addiction, and need repeated attempts before they do. This means annual statistical reports of numbers in drug treatment can present a distorted picture of a system that is subject to a steady ebb and flow of people coming and going over a longer time frame."

He added that the NTA could follow the treatment journey of individuals over successive years and demonstrate that positive change and recovery from addiction is possible.

SOME ISSUES:

How do you think we should help drug addicts?

Should we force addicts to seek help?

What should the government do about the problem?

See also:

The difference that rehabilitation can make was on show at a reunion organised by the charity Rapt

Success stories

Photo by Susannah Ireland

**"Hi, my name's Yana and I'm an addict,"
says a 37-year-old woman hunched over a
table on a podium in central London.**

"Hi Yana," shouts the audience of counsellors, prison
officers, probation workers, friends and fellow addicts.

Her obvious nervousness and vulnerability add to a heart-
warming moment of redemption and epiphany in a day
when scores of offenders reaffirm their new drug-free
lives.

Yet only five years ago Yana Stewart would have happily
smacked you in the face as soon as look at you.

In a life marred by misery and self-destruction it was
Yana's single piece of good fortune to find a place on
an intensive drug treatment programme run by the
Rehabilitation for Addicted Prisoners Trust (Rapt). The
charity's abstinence-based approach means that three
quarters of those who complete the course stay off drugs
and stay out of prison for life. Mike Trace, Rapt's chief
executive and Labour's former deputy drug tsar, says that
for a drugs rehabilitation programme to work it must be a
"life-changing" experience.

Yana went on to outline her life of addiction: "My mum was
a drinker. She was Scottish and liked a drop of whisky. I
had my first can of Tennent's when I was 12 – I liked it and
I never stopped."

Yana says the drink helped her escape her destructive
family background. "My mum was violent with her
boyfriends. I could see that violence in the home was one
way of getting things sorted." She continued drinking into
her teens. By the time she was 17 Yana had two young
children with a boyfriend who was hooked on drugs and

in and out of prison. He died when he fell from a 10th-floor window
during a burglary to find money to feed his addiction.

Shortly after her 18th birthday Yana received her first prison
sentence for assault and her children were taken into care. It was
the start of a vicious circle of violent offending fuelled by addiction. "I
lost count of how many times I was in prison," says Yana. "I tried to
mask everything with my aggression because I did not want people
to know that underneath I was vulnerable and fragile."

The turning point came in 2007 when she was jailed for three years
for beating up her mother during a crack cocaine-fuelled row.

"That was the time when I came to realise that I was no good. I was
sitting there in my cell for beating up my own mum and it made me
feel ashamed."

She made five attempts to get off drugs with the help of programmes
in prison but they all failed and it took a life-changing event before
Yana could break her addiction. "I got a call in prison to say that my
daughter had been hit by a car and she was in hospital in a coma. It
was a devastating moment ... I believed it was a direct consequence
of my drug using. I remember asking God not to take my daughter
as well as her father."

Sitting in the audience politely applauding their mother's success
are her son Anthony George and her daughter Shicara, who was
fortunate to survive the car accident.

Yana's journey from a history of violent offending and crack cocaine
addiction to proud mother was one of scores of harrowing stories
recounted by addicts at the weekend. For many of them the route
from addiction was a journey they didn't expect to survive.

Yana has been out of prison for six months and is working for the
Salvation Army and living in London. Turning to her children, she
says: "If it wasn't for you two I wouldn't be here today."

Photo by Susannah Ireland

'I couldn't look after my children': Spencer Coleshill, 40

He blames his early interest in drugs on his dyslexia and subsequent failure in school. It led directly to a lifestyle of drug-taking which inevitably ended up with a string of prison sentences for theft and burglary to support a heroin addiction. By the time his girlfriend had fallen pregnant and he became the father of twins he was out of control.

"I loved my children but I couldn't look after them because I didn't love myself," says Spencer.

Despite several attempts to get off drugs, it wasn't until he went on an abstinence programme that he was able to make any progress. Today he is married with two more children and is a chief executive of a national chain of garden centres. But even now he admits: "You can't ever stop working at the addiction. I have good days and I have bad days."

Photo by Susannah Ireland

'I got hooked on heroin in jail when I was 18': Marcus Paine, 37

He began experimenting with drugs soon after his parents separated when he was 14 years old. He started on lighter fluid and glues before graduating to cannabis, LSD and amphetamines. By 18, he was in prison for attacking a householder who had challenged him during a burglary. A judge called him a "one-man crime wave" and another described him as the "scourge of Europe."

It was during a spell in prison that he says he became addicted to heroin and a number of overdoses soon followed. "I was so near to the end that one day when I went to see my probation officer, she just burst into tears," remembers Marcus. It was only by joining a Rapt programme that he broke free from his addiction. He now works as a specialist sprayer painting luxury housing developments in London where he is trusted with the keys to the properties.

Next month Marcus and his partner are expecting their first baby. "I thought all those years of abuse had ended any chance of me having children."

Photo by Susannah Ireland

'When I got my hit, I forgot my crimes': Keith Wallace, 46

"Normally when I speak to this amount of people there is a judge present," says Keith Wallace, 46, a drug addict who has spent the best part of his life involved in crime.

Keith has been clean of drugs for more than four years and is now a successful desktop publisher. Nervously addressing a reunion of rehabilitated drug addicts in London, Keith says he can still remember the dark days when he thought he wouldn't ever break free from the cycle of addiction and crime.

"The first burglary I did was in a family home," he recalls. "I had been on a three-day bender and I could hardly stand up straight. But I went into their bedroom and there was a picture of the family. I had to turn it face down and then I burst into tears."

Keith sold the contents that he stole to support his crack cocaine addiction. "As soon as I got that first hit I forgot the whole thing."

The Independent, 4 October 2010

Education

Girls

Boys Teachers

Environment

University

Uniform Rules

Libraries

Success Rebellion

Schools

THE ISSUE: UNIFORM

Heads who send home pupils for clothing violations **may get results, but need to tread carefully to stay within the law**

SOME ISSUES:

Do you think it is important for a school to have a uniform?

Can insisting on a uniform have an effect on other parts of school life?

How strictly should a school make students stick to the rules?

If you were to be in charge of setting the uniform, what would you make people wear?

When headteacher Howard Lay chose to begin the school year by sending home 60 girls for wearing the wrong kind of trousers, he almost certainly knew what would follow: outraged parents, stroppy pupils and unwelcome publicity in the press. But heads who have made similar stands insist a tough approach can work.

In 2007, headteacher John Biddlestone sent home 36 pupils from Swinton High School in Salford when they turned up in non-regulation shoes. This year, it was a different story. "On the first day of term we inspected all our pupils – 1,000 of them – and there was not one single breach of uniform," he says. "So our policy has clearly been effective."

At Nunsthorpe School in Middlesbrough, head Debbie Clinton goes even further, claiming that her decision last year to send home 65 students was "a major turning point in the history of the school". Readers of the Northern Echo branded her variously "petty", "authoritarian" and "a control freak" after a top-to-toe crackdown on everything from coloured hair bobbles to patterned socks. But Ms

Clinton insists she has been vindicated: "It sent a clear message that disobedience would not be tolerated, and since then attendance has shot up, behavioural incidents have gone down, and we've had record exam results."

But headteachers who choose to exclude pupils over uniform issues need to tread carefully if they are to stay within the law. Guidelines allow schools to send pupils home to get changed, but this must be marked as an authorised absence. Only in the case of "persistent and defiant" flouting of the rules can a pupil be sent home for the day or excluded, and even then schools need to be sure that financial hardship is not at the root of the problem.

It is also important to be sensitive about cultural issues. Under the Human Rights Act, all pupils have the right to "manifest religion or belief". However, there are legal precedents where a school's policy on items such as jewellery or veils has been upheld because the act does not give people the right to manifest their beliefs "at all times". It's a complex issue, and it is important that uniform rules are clear, detailed and circulated to parents and pupils at regular intervals.

Of course, different schools take different approaches. In some parts of the world, such as Queensland,

Australia, it is illegal to remove children from lessons because of uniform transgressions, and there are plenty of heads and teachers in the UK who would agree with that principle.

"You need to keep a sense of perspective," says one deputy head. "You can't deny someone access to education just because their trousers are too tight or their socks are the wrong colour."

But heads such as John Biddlestone argue that if persuasion, negotiation and after-school detention have failed, they have little choice

but to send pupils home. "If you adopt a clear, consistent approach, uniform issues soon become a thing of the past," he says. "Once that happens, you're free to focus on what matters, which is teaching and learning."

TES Magazine, 8 October 2010

THE POLICY

- Uniform policy must be "fair and reasonable", and the uniform "affordable".

- Schools should publicise their uniform policy on their website.

- Pupils should not be punished for uniform issues linked to financial hardship.

- If a child is sent home to get changed, it must be marked as an authorised absence.

- Exclusion is only appropriate in the case of persistent offenders.

Budget cuts put more than 375 libraries under threat. We should be outraged, says Robin Ince (but keep the noise down)

Time for a quiet rebellion over library closures

Time for a quiet rebellion over library closures

SOME ISSUES:

Why are libraries important?

Why is it important that communities have access to libraries?

What do you use the library for?

See also:
Library fine?
p156, *Fact File 2011*

Rebellion can be messy, noisy and violent. But between 12 and 15 January, there was an act of rebellion that was quiet, ordered and fabulous to behold. It took place on the outskirts of Milton Keynes, not always known for the fabulous and rebellious.

The town of Stony Stratford is the site of the first great library revolt of the 21st century. The building is under threat of closure due to council budget cuts. As a joke, a local resident suggested that people should show their support in a fitting way - by getting out their library cards and borrowing every single book on the shelves. Through word of mouth and the internet, this joke became a reality and the shelves have been politely emptied: all the books - some 16,000 in total - are now on loan.

This very British uprising has occurred because upwards of 375 public libraries are under threat of closure as a result of the local authority funding cuts coming in April.

The readers are restless and it's no wonder, for, as the science educator Carl Sagan said in Cosmos: "The health of our civilisation, the depth of our awareness about the underpinnings of our culture and our concern for the future can all be tested by how well we support our libraries." When musing on his blindness, Jorge Luis Borges "imagined that paradise will be a kind of library".

Book worms
My first library was the mobile one that visited our village in South Hertfordshire every other Friday, where I borrowed books about the

adventures of multicoloured bears. Then it was the local library, where I repeatedly took out The Making of Doctor Who and Usborne books on life in ancient Greece. As an impoverished touring stand-up, I spent my days in the city-centre libraries of Manchester and Sheffield, poring over newspapers in search of fresh inspiration for whatever cellar gig I was playing that night. Now, I sit and wait under posters of

or how to make the perfect meringue. And what about people who don't have the internet at home - where do they go to get online? Why, the local library.

Then there's this argument: "Libraries are the preserve of the middle classes." I have (unscientifically) polled a few hundred people on this subject on Twitter. The replies came thick and fast from librarians and library

are packed with under-tens. For many, the first experience of the wonder of reading is browsing through the boxes of books or being enraptured by readings of the Charlie and Lola stories or Roald Dahl. The trip to the library can be a weekly highlight. They might stop being regular visitors when the hormones kick in and they become more interested in the mating rituals around the benches outside but they'll be back.

> *"The health of our civilisation, the depth of our awareness about the underpinnings of our culture and our concern for the future can all be tested by how well we support our libraries."*

cats in hats and potty-training princesses as my three-year-old son spends hours debating which books will be in this week's ration. Libraries are threaded through my life.

They are places where we can immerse ourselves in ideas or imagine other lives and worlds. (As Groucho Marx once said: "I find television very educational. The minute somebody turns it on, I go to the library and read a book.") Mass library closures are an ugly reflection on any country's culture; especially a country that declares it wants the best for its children and then hinders their learning.

I have heard many arguments for the closures from politicians and passers-by in the past weeks but none stands up to scrutiny. "Who needs libraries when you have the internet?" is the charlatan modernists' attitude. This misses the point. Books are an adventure.

There is a joy in going across a stacked shelf, flicking through the chapter headings and searching through the index in the hope that you will find the answer you need to whatever baffles you that day, whether it's something to do with the Napoleonic wars

users, aged between 16 and 78. True, the Downton Abbey screenwriter and authentic posh person Julian Fellowes has just appeared in a protest video for Somerset's libraries, but I had many responses from those in areas without herbaceous borders and farmers' markets; they, too, found their library a place of solace.

Among them was someone who mentored an Iraqi refugee at the local library. Another had been homeless; he used to spend days in the library, working out how to get out of that predicament. Those who had been "outsiders" at school told me about the libraries they used as refuges from aggression. Many said that they always joined the library when they arrived in a new town because it is the perfect place to get a sense of the community.

The revolution may not be televised but, at the very least, it will have a poster confirming its date on the library noticeboard.

Use it or lose it
Some claim that youngsters don't use libraries any more but that's just wrong: they

The final argument deployed against library closures is this: "Aren't there more important things to worry about?" Fine. In the struggle for existence, libraries may seem a low priority. But they are a sign that a society believes the life of the mind is important. If some are underused, the solution is not to shut them but to get people back inside them and remind them of why libraries are there.

You might not belong to your library now, but, one day, when you walk by a building site promising luxury apartments, where kids on tricycles once excitedly wheeled back with their new favourite book on dinosaurs, you will be sorry that it is gone.

Get out your library card and start borrowing again. If the Prime Minister really is a fan of the Smiths, then he knows this - there's more to life than books but not much more.

Robin Ince is the author of 'Bad Book Club' More details at: robinince.com

New Statesman, 27 January 2011

The class divide:
How to teach boys and girls

What does research that female pupils learn better in warmer classrooms mean for mixed-sex schools?

Michele Hanson

Research suggests that girls do better in warmer classrooms. Heavenly news for the Girls' Day School Trust, the group of 26 independent schools behind this finding, but what if we want to keep our girls and boys in the same classroom? It won't be easy, now that we have this temperature problem (24C for girls, 21C for boys) on top of all the other differences.

We have already been told that girls like a cosy, intimate, safe environment, boys like a big, brutish, perilous one; girls like to sit still, write neatly and work, without having to raise their hands, in a smallish, contained area, for an hour at a time, and like to relate the Fibonacci series to the bracts on a pine-cone; boys like to jump around, throw their pine-cones about, spread their equipment widely, and only work in short half-hour chunks; girls like a quietly spoken, friendly teacher on first-name terms; boys like a strict shouter, roaring "hands up", who avoids direct eye-contact.

I generalise, of course. In my years at the chalkface I came across a boy who liked to sit in a warm room quietly reading, but the other boys would quickly find him and smack his book into the air, so in the main, boys and girls do have conflicting requirements, and arrangements must be made.

Regretfully, the class will have to be divided – boys on one side, girls on the other. To avoid distraction, there will be a screen down the centre (teacher is visible from both sides) with fan heaters on the girls' side, which will contain alcoves, comfy chairs and sofas, and tables around which the groups of co-operative, collaborative girls may sit, while teacher mingles with them, quietly encouraging the girls, who though cleverer than the boys, have a lower opinion of their own achievements.

Meanwhile, on the boys' side, there will be an adjoining, sound-proofed and padded chamber, into which, after a short burst of competitive, unco-operative work, the boys can escape for some rough and tumble and bouncing on fart-cushions. Better still, this chamber could lead to a hazardous cliff edge, with abseiling facility, above an icy plunge pool to cool down the boiling boys. Then they can return calmly to their section of class, at the back of which an ex-army chappie will be standing ready to discipline any boy who isn't calm enough. That should do it.

The Guardian, 31 January 2011
© Guardian News & Media Ltd 2011

SOME ISSUES:

Does it matter what environment you learn in?

What conditions would make you learn more and enjoy learning more?

Do you really think boys and girls like such different styles of learning?

Are mixed or single sex schools or classrooms better?

Warm Encouragement Calm

Noise Competition Action

Environmental issues

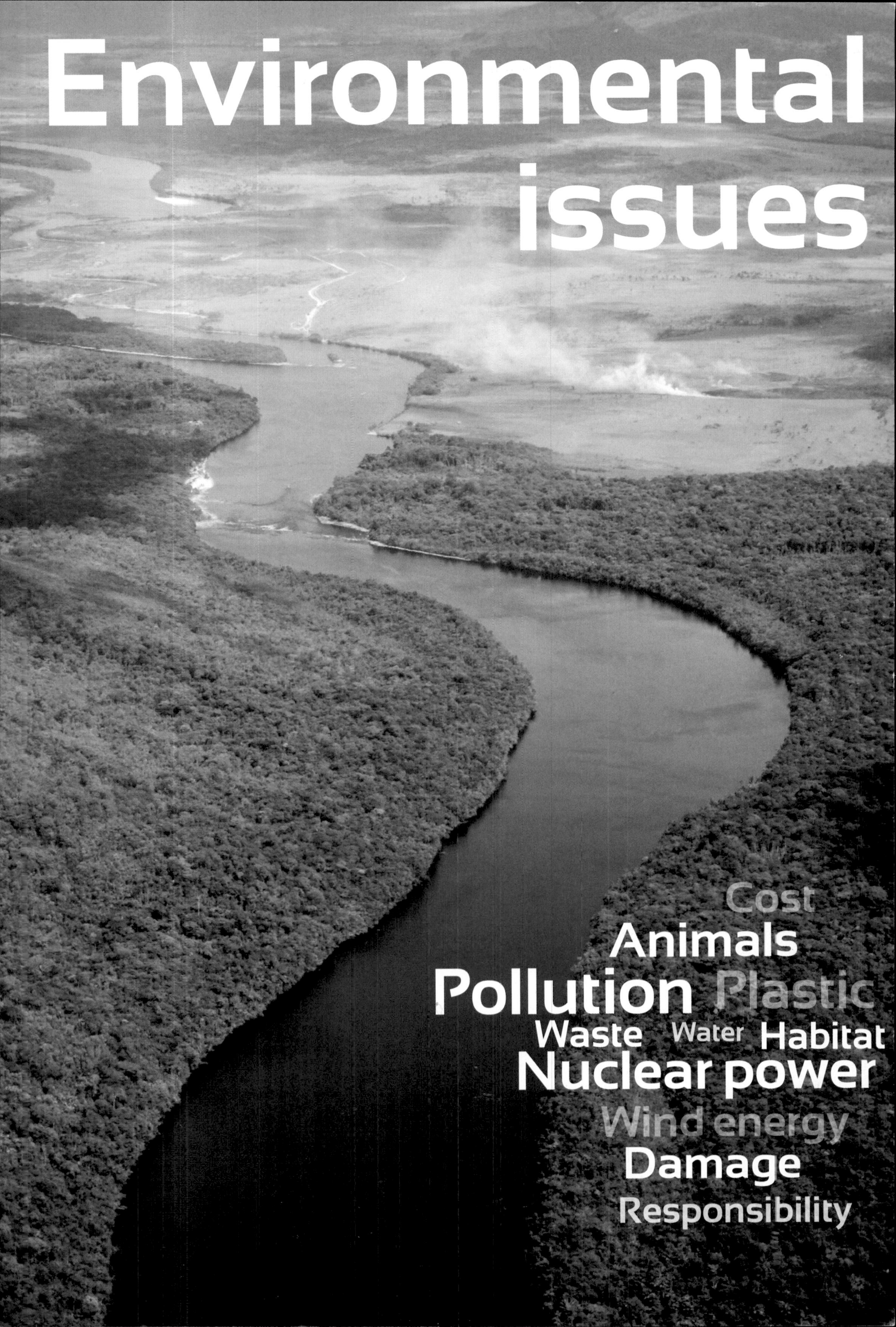

Cost

Animals

Pollution Plastic

Waste   Water   Habitat

Nuclear power

Wind energy

Damage

Responsibility

THE NUCLEAR DEBATE

ONLY A FEW MONTHS AGO NUCLEAR POWER WAS RECEIVING GREAT PUBLICITY. Some prominent environmentalists, such as George Monbiot, had given up years of opposition and were convinced that nuclear power was the only solution to global warming. Then came the Japanese earthquake and tsunami and the meltdown at the Fukushima nuclear plant. Suddenly countries were looking again at their nuclear programmes and delaying or cancelling them.

SO IS NUCLEAR POWER THE SOLUTION TO OUR ENVIRONMENTAL PROBLEMS OR A THREAT TO OUR VERY EXISTENCE?

Most environmentalists agree that global warming is the biggest threat facing the planet. It is a problem that is likely to grow as more nations develop their manufacturing potential and increasing prosperity brings a greater demand for products and power – specifically electricity.

Producing electricity through coal-fired power stations means also producing the chief greenhouse gas, CO2. We desperately need to reduce our production of this gas if we are going to reduce the threat of climate change – and we need to do this quickly.

The reason that nuclear power is favoured by some environmentalists is that they see it as the only possible way to reduce CO2 emissions in time to make a difference.

COMPARED TO OTHER FORMS OF POWER GENERATION, NUCLEAR PRODUCES RELATIVELY LITTLE CO2 In Britain, for example, using nuclear power currently reduces our CO2 emissions by somewhere between 7% and 14%.

THE TECHNOLOGY IS AVAILABLE NOW – it does not need years of research and experiment. Nuclear power stations are efficient – able to generate large amounts of electricity – and flexible, the power produced can be adapted to meet the demands of the weather or peak consumer times. A nuclear plant can work throughout the day and night without interruption.

ANY NATION WHICH HAS NUCLEAR POWER STATIONS HAS CONTROL OVER ITS OWN ENERGY RESOURCES. It isn't dependent on imported coal or gas, so other countries cannot threaten to interrupt its supplies or raise prices.

THE NEED FOR NUCLEAR POWER IS PRESSING.
Environmentalists often point out, with regret, that there is simply not enough time left for renewable sources of energy, such as wind, wave or solar power, to meet our energy

SOME ISSUES:

What do you think are the main pros and cons of nuclear power?

Does the thought of nuclear power worry you?

Are the possible environmental benefits worth the potential dangers?

demands and still slow down global warming. A new nuclear station, for example, would generate the same amount of electricity as about 3,000 wind turbines. Such renewable sources also have their own environmental costs. Those 3,000 turbines would cover hundreds of square kilometres, disrupt wildlife, destroy landscapes, annoy (certainly some) residents and use far more steel and concrete than a nuclear plant.

RENEWABLES ARE ALSO SUBJECT TO CHANGES IN THE WEATHER but above all, cannot be constructed quickly enough or work efficiently enough. The only solution, then, to climate change is the nuclear one.

Why then do other environmentalists still stand four-square against expansion of the nuclear industry? The answer comes in one word – danger.

WE STILL DO NOT KNOW HOW WE CAN SAFELY DISPOSE OF RADIOACTIVE WASTE FROM NUCLEAR PLANTS. It has to be looked after for several thousand years. We have 50 years worth of waste on our hands right now and currents costs of disposal are about £56 billion.

Given how dangerous radioactive material is, **THE CONSEQUENCES OF AN ACCIDENT COULD BE CATASTROPHIC.** An explosion and fire at the Chenobyl nuclear power plant in the Ukraine in 1986 released large quantities of radioactive contamination into the atmosphere. The Fukushima plant in Japan was more modern and better designed but still unable to stand up against the forces of nature. **ACCIDENTS CAN AND WILL HAPPEN**, we cannot plan against every single eventuality and when the outcome could be so dire, should we even take the risk? And the more plants there are the greater the risk.

THE SAME TECHNOLOGY THAT PRODUCES ELECTRICITY CAN BE USED TO PRODUCE WEAPONS – in the hands of rogue states this represents an enormous threat. Would any nuclear plant be safe from a terrorist strike like the 9/11 attacks in New York?

Even if all these risks could be set aside, **SOME ACTIVISTS CONTINUE TO QUESTION WHETHER NUCLEAR REALLY CAN DELIVER SALVATION FROM GLOBAL WARMING.** A new nuclear power station can take from 20 to 30 years to go from planning to generation of electricity. Nuclear uses uranium, a scarce resource which may run out in the next 30 to 60 years. There are also environmental costs in the mining and shipping of uranium.

SO, THE ENVIRONMENTAL DILEMMA REMAINS – DO WE OPT FOR AN EFFICIENT BUT RISKY NUCLEAR ROUTE OR THE SLOW BUT LESS RISKY RENEWABLES? It seems it must be an either/or – investment in nuclear power rules out investment in renewables and vice versa. And the third possibility for reducing CO_2, that we drastically limit our demand for goods and electricity, is seen as the least likely of all.

Sources: Various

The truth is hard to swallow

These are actually the stomach contents of a dead albatross as found by Chris Jordan who took the image

Our plastic waste

Chris Jordan is an environmental artist and photographer from Seattle. Since 2009 he has been working on a project based on the Laysan Albatross who live on Midway Atoll Island, a remote and isolated island in the South Pacific based midway between North America and Asia. The island, which has an area of only 2.4 square miles, is home to many different sea birds including 500,000 mating pairs of albatross.

The project, now called Midway Journey (which has its own website www.midwayjourney.com), began with Chris Jordan's startling images, and has now developed into a larger scale artistic and environmental project involving various artists and documentary makers.

Chris Jordan's images, which show the decomposing bodies of numerous albatross chicks and adults, are a shocking depiction of a real environmental tragedy. The images, taken at different states of decomposition, reveal the dreadful reality of where exactly our daily waste is ending up. How is it that birds living on a tiny island in the middle of the South Pacific are dying because of our wasteful lifestyle?

The plastic pollution cast aside by our society is not only washing up on coastlines all over the world, it is swirling in the middle of the Pacific Ocean as part of the Great Pacific Garbage Patch and is now, unfortunately, beginning to be mistaken by seabirds for food.

Albatross parents, with chicks to feed, can travel for thousands of kilometres for up to two weeks at a time, collecting food for their young. They source food floating on the surface of the sea, such as fish eggs or top floating squid, and swallow these to return them to their young.

SOME ISSUES:

Do you know what happens to the plastic you throw away?

How do you think plastic waste is ending up in the oceans?

What should be done about this issue?

Is it fair that nature should suffer for our daily waste?

When they get back to their young, the parents regurgitate the food they have gathered straight into the stomachs of their young.

Due to the large amount of plastic pollution in the ocean, parents are unwittingly collecting plastic bottle tops, lighters and other such waste, and returning to deposit these straight into their babies' stomachs. A natural act of parental care is killing tens of thousands of albatross chicks a year, on this island alone, because of our waste. The chicks, and in many cases the adults too, die of toxicity or choking or eventually dehydration and starvation – because their stomachs are so full of plastic they can no longer accept any more food.

Chris Jordan's images are a stark depiction of the massive environmental impact that our daily waste is having on the world around us. Not a single piece of plastic seen in any of these images has been added, arranged or altered. They are the actual stomach contents of the deceased birds found on that island which is 2,000 miles away from the nearest continent.

From this

Laysan Albatross protects its egg

To this

One of Chris Jordan's images from Midway Island of an albatross killed by plastic waste

Photo courtesy of Chris Jordan

Our waste

Parent albatrosses accidentally scoop up plastic waste in the ocean and feed it to their young. This causes them to die of choking, toxicity or eventually starvation and dehydration

Photos courtesy of Chris Jordan

Their loss

Tens of thousands of albatross chicks are dying each year on this island alone as a result of our plastic pollution. The island is 2,000 miles away from the nearest continent, and yet the waste of the world is swept up on its shores daily

Chris Jordan images used are part of the 'Midway: Message from the Gyre' set, courtesy of Chris Jordan. There are more images available to see here: www.chrisjordan.com

A British Noah's Ark

Britain's climate could provide a 'Noah's Ark' for species affected by global warming in their own habitats. Roger Dobson explains

A word of warning for any rabid anti-immigrationists out there; a new kind of migrant may soon descend upon the shores of Britain searching for the chance of a better life.

These permanent incomers will not be fleeing political, economic or religious oppression, but escaping climate change and avoiding extinction.

According to new research, the British Isles could become a vast living ark, or ARC – assisted regional colonisation area – where animal and plant species threatened by climate change would begin a new life.

The Iberian lynx, Spanish imperial eagle, de Prunner's ringlet butterfly, and the Caucasian wingnut tree, are among the potential species listed for rescuing and moving to Britain, which, researchers say, is ideally placed to become an ARC.

Professor Chris Thomas, a conservation biologist at the University of York, says: "There is an urgency about this and we need to develop a long shopping list of species that could be located here and monitor them so that action can be taken when needed. This kind of translocation is the only realistic conservation option we have for species that cannot otherwise escape the threat of climate change.

"The later it is left, the harder and more expensive these translocations to the ARC will become. The only viable option to maintain populations of many of these species in the wild is to translocate them to other locations where the climate is suitable, and Britain is ideal."

Climate change poses a real threat to animal and plant species. While the challenges to large mammals, like the polar bear and panda, have been well documented, many thousands of diverse species are threatened globally.

Some are equipped to adapt to a warmer world and some are able to naturally migrate, but for many others, survival will be a challenge with a

SOME ISSUES:

Is it right to play with nature in this way?

What problems do you think this might cause?

Is this the best solution to the issue of extinction?

For a discussion on conservation in zoos, see **Dartmoor Zoo's battle for survival,** p23 and **The safest place for an animal is its natural habitat – not a zoo,** p26

very real threat of extinction. There's evidence that some species are already shifting their distributions towards higher latitudes and elevations, but many others are unable to cross natural and human-created barriers.

Those animals that are native to the summits of single mountain ranges, for example, like the climate-threatened golden bowerbird in the mountains of Queensland, face huge hurdles. In order to migrate the birds would have to descend and pass through hostile environments, and it is unlikely that they would spread across hot lowlands in order to set up home in cooler areas. If they had been capable of that, they probably would have already done so. It has been estimated that unless something is done, 20 to 40 per cent of species could disappear with climate warming.

One strategy to deal with the emerging crisis is assisted colonisation, the idea of moving plants and animals from the area where they are threatened, to a safer environment – like parts of the UK.

Such translocations, have been carried out on a small scale, for more traditional conservation reasons – and many have been successful. Scientists in New Zealand and Australia have developed a successful strategy of establishing endangered species on offshore islands where predators, like rats, are not present. A population of captive-bred dibblers, an endangered marsupial from Western Australia, was successfully moved to a predator-free island two decades ago, and the movement to another island of Gilbert's potoroo, an endangered Australian mammal, has also worked.

The Georgia Plant Conservation Alliance is working on trying to establish the Torreya taxifolia, which is native to Florida, in the Appalachians to protect the ancient and endangered tree from fungal pathogens in its native areas. Attempts are also underway to move a population of endangered Bermuda petrels

to an area where hurricanes and sea-level rise pose less of a risk.

While many of these one-off projects have been carried out successfully, the sheer number of species at risk worldwide in various climate-change scenarios means that an overall strategy is needed to co-ordinate the exodus from the threatened areas.

Although the concept of rescuing species and translocating seems an attractive one, it is not without its challenges. Immigrant species could become pests or disrupt ecosystems in their new homes, they could become victims of predators and they may bring new diseases or parasites.

Thomas, who makes the case for an ARC strategy in the scientific journal Trends in Ecology & Evolution, accepts that translocation could cause problems, but says it needs to looked at globally. "In general, most species on Earth are restricted to small geographic areas," he says. "In Britain we have very few species that are unique to this country.

"We rightly invest in conservation in Britain, but we spend not to prevent global

Researchers say the establishment of the Iberian lynx in Britain would represent a great contribution to world conservation... rabbits, its main prey, are abundant in southern Britain

extinction, but to try and keep species in our own country. The red squirrel is an example. Even if it disappeared from Britain, it would not be extinct at a global level.

"Although introduced species can cause changes to the distributions and abundances of indigenous species, they do not normally bring about species-level extinctions. While some native British species have declined and become more localised, to the best of my knowledge, no native species has disappeared as a result of non-native species – other than humans – establishing in Britain."

He adds: "Britain contains few native species, has its vegetation heavily modified by humans and appears almost immune to extinctions from introduced species. It therefore represents an ideal destination for species displaced by climate change."

The Independent, 29 March 2011

Animals that could be brought to Britain

1. Iberian lynx (Lynx pardinus)

The most endangered cat in the world, it lives in the Iberian Peninsula. It is descended from lynx that lived more widely in Europe before the late Pleistocene arrival of the now-widespread Eurasian lynx. Researchers say establishment of the Iberian lynx in Britain would represent a greater contribution to world conservation than re-introducing the Eurasian lynx. Rabbits, the main prey of Iberian lynx, are abundant in southern Britain.

2. Spanish imperial eagle

An extremely rare eagle that is native to Spain and Portugal, it is a large – up to 33in in length – dark brownish-black bird with prominent white wing marks. It is potentially threatened by climate change. Rabbit, its main prey, is found in abundance in Britain.

3. Provence chalkhill blue (Polyommatus hispanus)

A butterfly found in northern Spain, southern France and northern Italy, it is currently at serious risk of extinction from climate change and researchers say the climate in southern England is predicted to become suitable. The host plants of the butterfly already grow in southern England.

4. de Prunner's ringlet

A butterfly native to southern European mountains, it is threatened by climate change. Projections suggest that England represents a considerable portion of its potential new range – and the larvae feed on types of grass already common in Britain.

5. Iberian water beetles

Many of the 120 water beetle species native to the Iberian Peninsula that occupy streams in one or a few mountain ranges are under threat from increased droughts.

6. Pyrenean desman (Galemys pyrenaicus)

A distinct semi-aquatic insectivorous mammal that lives in streams in the Pyrenees where it is threatened by climate change. Establishing populations in streams in western Britain might be feasible.

Family & relationships

Separation
Homosexuality
Fostering Mothers
Fathers Equality
Marriage Love
Abuse Divorce
Happiness

Marriage keeps us happy - don't let laws erode it

Sebastian Shakespeare

SOME ISSUES:

Is marriage still important?

Do you think unmarried couples should have the same legal rights as married couples?

If couples can get divorced, is it really a commitment at all?

For a contrasting view see **All love is equal,** p77

See also:
For better, for worse, p61, *Fact File 2010*

Unmarried couples should enjoy the same legal rights as those who have tied the knot, says the country's most senior family judge, Sir Nicholas Wall (married with four children). Millions of unmarried couples should be able to share property and money if they split up.

On the surface this seems fair and equitable - but won't it discourage people from marrying altogether? Sir Nicholas Wall insists it won't undermine marriage, but how can he be so confident? Marriage as an institution is already on the way out and less popular than ever. It remains stubbornly in decline.

Fewer of us are doing it and more marriages end in divorce than ever before. One in six couples are unmarried, and that figure is expected to rise to one in four in 20 years' time.

Once again the real winners in this scenario will be the lawyers. Sir Nicholas's proposal

Won't it discourage people from marrying altogether?

is a gold-diggers' charter. And it will be a legal quagmire. How long will you have to cohabit with someone before you can have a claim on their estate? A year? Two years? The cut-off date will be totally arbitrary. Individuals will no longer notch up partners on their bed posts. They will be encouraged to change their bed posts every two years.

Sir Nicholas claims women cohabitees are particularly disadvantaged. But if a woman lives with a man and he refuses to get wed, she can always up sticks and leave. It's not as if she is compelled to stay with him. What surprises me is the number of people who stay together without marrying: is it because they are waiting for somebody better to come along before they decide to commit?

Marriage is the solvent of society (be it a civil marriage or a church blessing) and should be encouraged, not discouraged. If people are not prepared to commit to each other, why should they be entitled to the same rights? It would be a shame if marriage became simply a middle-class indulgence, like organic food.

Marriage improves your longevity, mental health and lifestyle choices. Only last month, a study published in the British Medical Journal showed that committed couples live longer than singletons and that having lots of sexual partners can shorten your life span.

Society still values marriage (just), as do our political leaders. "I know from my own life that a happy marriage and healthy children matter more than anything else," said Nick Clegg last year.

From 2012 David Cameron has pledged to introduce a happiness or GWB - "general

> *It would be a shame if marriage became simply a middle-class indulgence, like organic food.*

> *If people are not prepared to commit to each other, why should they be entitled to the same rights?*

well-being" - index which will measure people's quality of life and not just their economic prosperity. If Cameron is so keen on our collective happiness, he should not allow the judiciary to erode further the institution of marriage and line the legal profession's pockets under the fig leaf of fairness. That is a recipe for unhappiness all round.

London Evening Standard,
4 February 2011

All love is equal – but not before the law

SOME ISSUES:

What do you think about the fact that same sex couples are banned from having an actual marriage in the UK?

Why do you think this is?

Is it fair?

What do you think about same sex marriage?

Why might a heterosexual couple choose a civil partnership?

For a contrasting view see **Marriage keeps us happy – don't let laws erode it**, p75

For updates on the Equal Love Campaign see **equallove.org.uk**

10th Anniversary of World's First Legal Gay Marriage

Exactly 10 years ago, the Netherlands became the first country in the world to legalise same-sex marriage. A group of Dutch gay rights activities had campaigned for the change in law from the mid-1980s onwards, and, following the introduction of registered partnerships in 1998, the right to marriage equality was finally won in 2001. According to the Netherlands Central Bureau of Statistics, between 2001 and 2009, 13,460 same-sex couples in the country enjoyed their equal right to marry. The landmark ruling kick-started a global trend, and same-sex marriage has since been legalised in South Africa, Argentina, Portugal, Spain, Belgium, Sweden, Norway and Iceland, plus seven US states and Mexico City.

However, this global shift towards equality represents a stark contrast to Lesbian, Gay, Bisexual, Transgender, Intersex (LGBTI) marriage rights in the 80 countries where same-sex relationships are illegal. In 2005, Uganda amended its constitution to become the first African country to ban same-sex marriage. The extent of the persecution of Ugandan gays was recently highlighted when, on 26 January 2011, committed LGBTI rights activist David Kao was found bludgeoned to death in his house. He had received homophobic death threats and had been named by Uganda's tabloid Rolling Stone in an article that called for gay people to be killed.

In January 2009 a bill to ban 'same gender marriage' was approved by the Nigerian House of Representatives. At a public hearing later that year, international human rights groups testified against the bill, and it is yet to come to a final vote. According to Human Rights Watch, the law would punish people of the same sex who live together 'as husband and wife or for other purposes of same sexual relationship' with up to three years of imprisonment. Anyone who 'witnesses, abets and aids' such a relationship could be imprisoned for up to five years.

In Britain despite the legalisation of civil partnerships in 2005, gay couples are still banned from civil marriage and, simultaneously, heterosexual couples are banned form civil partnership. The Equal Love Campaign, led by LGBT rights activist Peter Tatchell, is mounting a legal bid to end this discrimination. In February, the campaign organised eight couples – four gay and four heterosexual – to file a joint legal application to the European Court of Human Rights. They are asking the court to declare the twin bans on same-sex civil marriages and opposite-sex civil partnerships illegal. 'These bans are a form of sexual apartheid,' says Tatchell. 'There's one law for gay couples and another law for heterosexual partners. In a democratic society, we should all be equal before the law.'

The Equal Love Campaign has drawn inspiration for their fight from the pioneering Dutch example. 'The legalisation of same-sex marriage by the Netherlands was a truly historic, trail-blazing world first,' Tatchell says. 'The symbolic significance was immense. It showed that gay marriage was possible and achievable.'

Anna Webster
New Internationalist, April 2011

Children and divorce: the father's case

Family law has to move on from 1950s notions about gender, says a father who is going through the trauma of divorce

SOME ISSUES:

Why do you think divorce courts prefer children to stay with their mother?

Do you think this is fair?

What effect do you think this would have on the children?

If men and women share childcare, then should they share custody if they divorce?

www.fnf.org.uk
www.fathers-4-justice.org

Entering the world of family law feels like shooting back in time, a breakneck journey from 2010 into the 1950s.

In that 2010 world outside, my wife works no less than I do and childcare is shared – the very model of the professional, liberal set-up, with no room in the house for a gender convention. In family law, however, you sometimes wonder if there's anything but.

Setting about the soul-numbing bureaucracy of divorce, I was discussing with a solicitor the future of our young child. My wife had filed her initial set of forms, asserting how he would "reside" with her, although there was talk that she would be generous in considering the access I would have – a detail that more than any other sent my head spinning. "Access" to my son, I figured, was not a gift that was anyone's to give.

It was when I asked what seemed to me to be obvious questions – what if I wanted

The default, whatever the home set-up, is born of some notion of the sacred bond between mother and child.

By contrast, the role of father, it seems, can be discharged in a weekend visit once a fortnight.

My own very close relationship with my dad was shaped by daily tenderness, and daily banter.

something different; shared care or to be the primary carer (my wife's position) – that things took a real tumble into the irrational. "That's not done", "it's really difficult", "the presumption is always with the mother", lawyers told me. (I consulted a few.)

But why? What's the rationale?

The truth is that the system doesn't worry overmuch about a rationale. No arguments are made on behalf of mothers because they don't need to be. So while it might be more understandable to award "residence" to a mother if the household has been divided along 1950s lines, you don't really hear about degrees of entitlement.

The default, whatever the home set-up, is born of some notion of the sacred bond between mother and child. (To make myself feel better, I sought comfort in scientific research, hoping that there were good reasons in favour of the mother. But beyond the very early stages of the child's life, there don't appear to be.)

By contrast, the role of father, it seems, can be discharged in a weekend visit once a fortnight. (My own very close relationship with my dad was shaped by daily tenderness, and daily banter.)

So, faced with this implacable convention, the onus is then on you, as the father, to make something of it.

Do you want to? You're already pretty raw about the divorce: how will our stupidity and mistakes affect our son? And it's not a competition of pain – you accept that your wife feels as wretched too.

But if the mother is not open to private discussions about child arrangements, the father then has to decide if he wants to press what lawyers tend to describe as "the nuclear option".

Which gets straight to the imbalance: if a mother wants to be primary carer, it's "natural", the norm; if the father wants the same, it's the "nuclear option". Faced with this lack of reason, I admit to being overcome, at times, with despair as if trapped in some rare condition where you mouth words and nobody hears a thing."

Let's imagine how things might be otherwise. Imagine all that we judge right and proper in the outside world – in employment protocol, say – applied to family law. If the parents don't agree on childcare arrangements, they would have to submit to some gender-free assessment: who's the better "candidate"? Now this is a horrible analogy, would be a horrible test – but preferable, surely, to simply assuming that the answer is always the mother.

In truth, the mother might be the "better" option in most cases, and many men might not be interested in being primary carers. Fine. But those who are should have a fair hearing.

In the few months since I sank into the process, there's been a perceptible shift – reason has started to gain a deal of ground on convention. Lawyers are now more optimistic about your chances as a father. The work of Families Need Fathers, the intervention of Louis de Bernières, the early word from the family justice review, all are changing the mood music, I'm told by lawyers. This, in turn, means more men are asking to be primary carers. Now we are beginning to feel we have a chance.

The father lives and works in London

The Observer, 26 September 2010
© Guardian News & Media Ltc 2010

Experience:

I'm proud my mother left me

Michele Gorman

I remember the meal exactly: steak, mashed potatoes and buttery corn on the cob. All my favourites. Mid-chew, my father calmly announced, "Your mother and I are separating. She's moving out." With a mouthful of potato I became the product of a broken home. And with those words my father became a full-time parent to two young girls, aged seven and 11.

It was impossible for my little sister and me, on that night, to reconcile the happy family life we knew with the reality that it was breaking up. But the truth was my mother didn't love my father, and hadn't done for many years.

That's not to say the marriage was loveless. My father deeply loved my mother, enough for both of them for a while. Desperately, he used words he hoped would convince her to stay. If she wanted out, he told her, she'd have to be the one to leave. He knew he had society on his side.

This was the late 70s. Women did not leave husbands without stigma. My sister and I weren't even aware of these taboos. We grew up in a small town where all our friends' parents were married, to their first spouses, as were all our neighbours, cousins, aunts and uncles.

But my mother knew she had to leave, and so she explained to us until she was sure we understood. "I'm unhappy being married to your father," she said, "and I'm making him unhappy. That isn't good for either of us, and it isn't good for you two either."

It was her family's reaction that left the deepest scars. Mothers do not leave their children, they told her with their silence

The message was consistent, and clear. She wasn't leaving us. She was leaving her husband. We had the choice to go with my mother. We chose not to. My mother's new place would be just three miles away but I wanted my friends around me, and the familiarity of the home I'd grown up in. Besides, on a practical level, I didn't see how the school bus would know where to find me if I moved. (I'd had similar concerns about Father Christmas years earlier when we went to my grandma's for Christmas Eve.) My mother must have been devastated by our choice, and overwhelmed at the enormity of what she

SOME ISSUES:

Is it right to leave your partner if you no longer love them?

Does that change if you have children?

Why is there more pressure on women to raise their children than on men?

See also:

For better, for worse, p61, *Fact File 2010*

Family matters, p73, *Fact File 2011*

www.itsnotyourfault.org

was doing. Recently she told me about the first night in her new place. She stood in the bathroom, looking in the mirror, and heard a noise It was high-pitched and terrifying. Then she realised the sound was coming from her.

My mother knew she'd made the right decision but was unprepared for the consequences. The neighbours stayed neutral at first but social invitations quickly dried up. Long-time friends snubbed her at the supermarket. Dad was the wronged party, in their eyes, left to care for the abandoned waifs. They didn't see the pans of lasagna, our favourite food, dropped at our door because she knew the way we liked it. But it was her family's reaction that left the deepest scars. She was judged and convicted in absentia. Mothers do not leave their children, they told her with their silence. Her brother still doesn't speak to her. Her father broke off all contact for more than 15 years, though eventually

They didn't see the pans of lasagna, our favourite food, dropped at our door because she knew the way we liked it.

they rebuilt a close relationship. Many aunts, uncles and cousins also believed my mother was an abomination, and most of those living still hold a grudge. Her decision cost her almost her entire extended family. Their condemnation was misguided.

My relationship with my mother didn't change when she left because we saw and talked to each other so often, and as a working mother we'd never seen her during the day anyway. We stayed at her place regularly – it was another home to us.

My mother and I are extremely close. I have no doubt that if she'd stayed in the marriage we'd have a different relationship today; I would have grown up with someone miserable and frustrated. As it was, my mother wasn't afraid to make a

horrendously hard choice, for her own good and the good of her family. She always says she wasn't meant to be a wife. She's too independent to be happy in that role.

That sense of independence is something she passed on to my sister and me. And she managed to do it without seeming bitter about relationships. She became a stronger person because she was brave enough to leave. My sister and I grew up on many mantras from my mother but I think the most important is: f you don't like something about your situation, see how you can change it. She taught me that it's better to be judged by others as unconventional than to judge yourself a coward.

The Guardian, 17 July 2010
© Guardian News & Media Ltd 2010

Fostering prejudice

Anti-gay couple cannot become foster parents

A Christian couple have been banned by judges from fostering children because of their views on homosexuality.

Owen and Eunice Johns, both in their sixties, cared for about 20 children in the 1990s, after their own children had grown up. After a break from fostering to run a catering business, they reapplied in 2007. In the intervening years equality laws had been introduced which meant that their views on homosexuality barred them from fostering a child.

If the issue of homosexuality came up, Mrs Johns told the social workers, "we would sit down and talk to the child to find out where it is coming from. They said, 'No, you would have to tell the child it is all right to be homosexual because there are too many children that are confused with their sexuality.' We thought, yes, but at eight?" The Johns were offered a re-education programme but felt that they could not abandon their religious standpoint. "Our Christianity is our lifestyle. We can't take it on and off."

The social worker's report on the Johns described them as "well-meaning" and "kind and hospitable people who would always do their best to make a child welcome and comfortable" but also that they held views on same-sex relationships which "are not in line with the current requirements of the national standards, and which are not susceptible to change". Believing that they held "normal, mainstream, Christian views", the Pentecostal Christians went to the High Court – but judges backed the ban and said gay rights laws "should take precedence" over laws on religious bias.

Ben Summerskill, head of gay charity Stonewall, hailed the verdict and said: "We're delighted the landmark decision has favoured 21st century decency above 19th century prejudice. In any fostering case the interests of 60,000 children in care should override the bias of any prospective parent."

Mrs Johns, 62, said after the London hearing: "All we wanted was to offer a loving home to a child in need. "We have a good track record as foster parents. But because we are Christians, with mainstream Christian views on sexual ethics, we are apparently unsuitable as foster parents. We are prepared to love and accept any child. All we were not willing to do was tell a small child that the practice of homosexuality was a good thing."

What the blogger says:

The best response to the news that "Anti-gay Christian couple lose battle to become foster parents" was: "Good. I have a LOT of religious tolerance but only for tolerant religions," by random blogger Chris Horner. I couldn't have put it better myself!

The news that Eunice and Owen Johns, a Christian couple morally opposed to homosexuality, lost a High Court battle today over the right to become foster carers, is indeed a landmark. When you see the picture of Mr and Mrs Johns, and read that "All we wanted was to offer a loving home to a child in need. We have a good track record as foster parents", you do feel a slight twinge of sadness for the child who has missed out. As they say "a vulnerable child has now likely missed the chance of finding a safe and caring home at a time when there are so few people willing to

SOME ISSUES:

Do you agree with the main article or the other side of the argument?

Why?

Is it better for a child to be fostered even if the parents are not tolerant of different beliefs and sexualities?

What effect could this have on the child if they were in fact gay?

Was the court ruling right?

See also pages 152-155 for other discussions of clashes between religious beliefs and tolerance

You cannot place a child with people simply because they are better off than where they came from

foster or adopt." Let's face it, any care, is better than no care at all – isn't it?

Well it depends on the type of care, surely. The Johns say "We are prepared to love and accept any child. All we were not willing to do was to tell a small child that the practice of homosexuality was a good thing." So, what if the child in their care was homosexual? What sort of care would it receive?

I'm not suggesting that the Johns would have acted cruelly. Unless of course you think it is cruel to tell a child that a fundamental part of the way they are, is wrong. Oh wait, that is quite cruel isn't it?

On the other hand, what if the child in their care was not homosexual? They would have had a perfectly normal upbringing. Normal – like the many other millions of children raised in households, where prejudiced and bigoted views are held and seen as acceptable. They, in turn, could have gone about their life, thinking that homosexuality was not a good thing; spreading the Christian message of love and tolerance with every back-handed comment, rolling of the eyes, and 'gay' joke they shared with friends. And so the cycle goes on.

Oh it's ok, these are proper homophobes, but at least he isn't getting a beating

While there are many millions of children raised in families with discriminatory beliefs about sexuality/race/gender and so on, this is certainly not to be encouraged. You cannot place a child with people simply because they are better off than where they have come from "Oh it's ok, these are proper homophobes, but at least he isn't getting a beating". I hope that Mr and Mrs Johns, like Peter and Hazelmary Bull – the Christian hoteliers ruled to have acted unlawfully by refusing a room to civil partners Mr Hall and Mr Preddy in 2008 – will reflect on this.

The Johns have said "We feel excluded and that there is no place for us in society". There are many homosexual people who can understand that sentiment exactly.

Blog: 1 March 2011, annelouisekershaw365.com
Other sources: various

Photo: DAVID JONES/PA Archive/ Press Association Images

The other side of the argument

People often say to foster parents "You must be a saint!" But after the recent judgement in the high court it seems that even a saint would struggle to pass stringent tests that now prevent many ordinary folk from offering a loving home to a needy child.

If the same criteria were applied to natural parents the human race would probably die out. How many parents could claim to be tolerant and advocates of diversity and equality. When faced with a child whose life choices completely contradict their beliefs, would most "sit down and talk to the child" as the Johns promised? Or would they lay down the law, saying "not in my house"?

No wonder there is a shortage of foster parents. You can be banned for being a smoker, too old, too fat and now too religious! Another rule imposed by social workers is that children's ethnicity counts more than their need for a stable family. This ruling by the judges will have worsened the shortage of black fosterers – as many families of Caribbean origin are more fervent Christians than church-going whites.

Social workers, who were fooled by chocolate smeared over Baby P's bruises before he was killed, now take even more children into care. This decision surely dooms them to stay there, rather than be fostered with experienced, stable, caring people. Wouldn't any child be better off in a warm loving home – even if it is a bit old-fashioned?

Wouldn't any child be better off in a warm loving home – even if it is a bit old-fashioned?

I sent my abusive father to jail – this is my story

Siobhan Pyburn

I don't remember exactly what age I was when my father, Bill, started abusing me. It first happened in a caravan on some land that he owned. He began by asking me some questions about sex, curious to know how much I knew about it. He closed the door, and locked it, to make sure that no one would know, and the first incident occurred... one of many. Afterwards, confusion was the first thing I remember feeling. What the hell did he just do? Then, we went to the shops and he bought me fish and chips. He said something to the effect that it was for me being such a good girl. I didn't understand that he had committed a crime, I barely realised he had violated me in any way. I was too young to have set up proper personal boundaries, and he was my father, so I trusted him.

From there, incidents happened every weekend, whenever I'd get taken to his land, and his caravan - and he'd always 'reward' me, with chocolate or a computer game or something similar. If I asked for anything, he would always abuse me first so that I 'earned' it. He called the abuse 'itching'.

The incidents progressed and happened elsewhere, such as when I was at home. Sometimes he'd offer me gifts if I let him abuse me, and because I was too young to understand, I obliged, and thought that there wasn't anything wrong with it. Daddy would never hurt me, right? I entered puberty and realised that it wasn't normal, that it wasn't what all the dads did to their children and that - I thought - it was far too late to stop it. After all, I'd let it happen, I was to blame. He always

SOME ISSUES:

Can you understand why Siobhan didn't tell anybody about the abuse straight away?

What help and support do you think should have been provided for Siobhan once people were aware of the abuse?

How can more people be encouraged to speak out about abuse?

For more information or support go to:
www.nspcc.org.uk
www.the-phoenix-project.co.uk

> I was too young to have set up proper personal boundaries, and he was my father, so I trusted him.

I was convinced that I would be disowned from my family if I ever told anyone about the abuse.

enforced that way of thinking, and would tell me regularly that if I told anyone, 'it would incriminate us both'. He also said he might commit suicide, and that I'd never see him again. I began to loathe him. I wanted him to die.

Bill was diagnosed with prostate cancer around that time, and after the operation (which he survived with flying colours, as well as fighting off MRSA) the incidents got worse because he made me do things that he said would help with his 'condition', during his recovery. At school, I had started a relationship with a boy and wanted to see him on the weekends, and Bill used that to get more sexual favours from me. I used to look at my boyfriend across the classroom and think 'If only you knew what was happening to me...'

I was convinced that I would be disowned from my family if I ever told anyone about the abuse. I felt like I was a prostitute, cheating on my boyfriend. I was very insecure and always thought of other girls as being better than me in every way, because they were 'pure', and I was not. They were whole, and I was fragmented. And I became obsessively needy and clung to my boyfriend, telling myself that I needed to spend as much time as I could with him, because he was my escape.

SPEAKING UP

When Bill took me and my brother up to see my Mum and second brother (who lived away from me) over the holidays, my life changed forever. He never stayed with us when we were with mum because my parents always argued, so he left us there and went back home. My mum mentioned child abuse in passing in a conversation we were having about something else. Whenever she would steer the conversation elsewhere I'd bring it back to the subject until she asked me "Why are you asking me about this? Your Dad isn't doing anything to you, is he..?'

When I nodded, she was shocked, and left the room without saying a word. I couldn't believe the words had come out of my mouth, and I knew from then that everything was about to change. The next night, she told my brothers, who called the Police. I remember Mum waking me up in the early hours of the morning, and leading me into the living room, where my brothers gave me a hug, held my hand

and said nothing. I felt numb. The police arrived at 5am Christmas day to conduct an initial interview, and a week later I was doing my video interview at the station. Bill was still back at home, oblivious that I'd somehow found the strength to disclose. When I was told that he'd been arrested, I wished that I could have been there when they did it.

I stayed with my Mum and out of school for a number of weeks, and they were some of the worst times of my life, despite it being the beginning of the end of my abuse. I felt isolated, alone and, for a time, suicidal. I didn't know what was going to happen next, and felt like the rug had been pulled out from under my feet. It was also when I began to replay everything that had happened to me, and realise how badly I'd been exploited. I rang my boyfriend and told him, in a very long and emotional phone call, about being abused, and the part that he had played in it, without ever even realising. Although he and his family were all very supportive of me, we fell apart a few months later, and I felt that it was a necessary loss, as the relationship had been so tied up with my abuse.

Bill got evicted from our house, and Mum sold it. I moved to a new home with my brothers, and started at a new school for year 11. I remember having this glorious feeling of a fresh start, and I made new friends. When I got told over the phone, that Bill was going to go on trial for what he had done, I was happy. It was a long wait for the trial, and it was delayed for a few months, but finally took place in early 2007.

THE TRIAL

The trial lasted for a week, although I was only required as a witness for one day. Because I was underage, I was taken into a separate room from the rest of the court, and

> "You, who are meant to be one of the most important and trusted people in your daughter's life, used her young body for your own sexual gratification. If there was anyone from whom that poor girl should have been protected, it was you."

communicated via a video link. Bill's defending barrister asked me intrusive and graphic questions, and scraped the barrel to find any excuse that might vaguely imply that I was lying about the whole thing. It was his job to try and win the case for him... I just wonder if he slept well that night.

Mum and I stayed home on the day of the verdict. Mum prayed all morning that I'd get justice. We got a call at about 3pm to say that Bill had been proven guilty on 13 counts of indecent assault, and we cried. It was very emotional, and I was so relieved. We won. The sentencing took place, and I attended it in person. I saw him, and he saw me, and I saw him get sent away by the Judge, whose words I'll never forget: "You, who are meant to be one of the most important and trusted people in your daughter's life, used her young body for your own sexual gratification. If there was anyone from whom that poor girl should have been protected, it was you."

He received a sentence of three years, and was released after eighteen months for good behaviour. Is there a need for penal reform? I think so.

A NEW LIFE
When the abuse ended, my life began, all over again. At the time of writing I am 19, and to strangers I probably seem like an 'ordinary' girl. There's no need for any more people to know about my abuse because it's in the past; every time that someone new does find out about it, however, they always express their surprise that someone as 'grounded' as me could ever have come from something as traumatic as that. It pains me to think about all the children – and adults - who are still at the stage before their disclosure. Whilst every case is individual, I don't believe that anyone can understand the kind of negative emotions that a victim goes through better than someone who has been through it themselves. It's high time that people become more aware of how much of a serious and common issue this is.

I want to help create a society where children are

regularly reminded that they can go somewhere that's safe and confidential to disclose to someone who will take them seriously if they are being abused by anyone, anywhere. And I want the perverted perpetrators who get kicks out of abusing children to be made fully aware, by this society, that they can't escape justice so easily anymore. Support for children and general awareness of the issue is a lot better than it was 30 years ago; but it can be a lot better still. It sounds so simple, but to assume that adult survivors feel that their abuse was not their fault would be a mistake. We know, intellectually, that it wasn't our fault – but few of us actually feel it. And that lingering sense of guilt is instrumental in preserving the potentially lifelong self-torture that many of us endure.

What I'm saying is... Anyone who has been sexually abused needs copious amounts of reassurance that it was not their fault. We need to feel that society's got our backs, and that can be achieved through regular contact with the appropriate support services who are available, yet so little known: no counsellor came to my rescue when I was at school immediately post-disclosure, when all the teachers knew why I had been absent. I organised my own help.

My abuser got a ridiculously lenient custodial sentence that, to my mind, does not equal the immense level of pain that he caused. What do you suppose that did for my sense of guilt?

On the flipside, now that I am an out of the closet survivor, able to transform my experiences into something positive in order to help others – and now that I have received significant recognition for doing exactly that – what do you think that did for my sense of feeling like the abuse was my responsibility? It has blown my mind in every positive direction. For every iota of recognition I get, that sense of guilt gets pushed a little further out of my mind. I want every survivor to experience that.

Let it be known, that disclosing about my abuse was the best thing I ever did.

Source: Phoenix

Financial issues

Wages
Money Struggle
Inheritance **Students**
Donations
Lending **Poverty**
Tax **Charity**
Borrowing

"I'm giving £1m to charity on an ordinary salary"

SOME ISSUES:

What is the most effective way to persuade people to give? And the least?

Is it right that we should live more basically in order to help others?

How much would you give to charity?

Should we give as much as we possibly can to charities?

See also:

The Charity section of *Fact File 2011*, p36-43, all about how much people give and how they give it

www.givingwhatwecan.org

As an academic at Oxford university I don't have an enormous salary, but even so I have made a pledge to donate £1m to charity over the course of my working life.

It wasn't an easy decision, but I chose to do this after realising just how much more good my money could do for others than for me. I'm a research fellow in ethics, and my thoughts on the ethical issues around global poverty have had a dramatic impact on my personal behaviour.

The philosopher Peter Singer – a fellow Australian – said that the money we spend on luxuries could be used to save people's lives in developing countries if we so wished. How then can we justify choosing the luxuries? This is a strong argument, and quite confronting. So I asked myself what standard of living is justifiable. How little could I live on? The figure I came to is around £10,000 a year, including rent, clothes, food and holidays.

I'm happy to continue the relatively frugal lifestyle I had as a graduate student – it's certainly much better than what most people in the world can afford. I have a nice place to live, a good computer and phone. The things that are most important to me cost

I calculate that the money I give away can save between 2,000 and 10,000 lives

So I asked myself how little could I live on?

very little: such as spending time with my wife and friends, reading books and listening to music.

I am 31 so I can expect to work for another 35 years. My annual salary over that time will average about £45,000. After tax this should allow me to give away an average of £30,000 a year – amounting to slightly more than £1m by the time I retire. Last year I earned £25,000 before tax and gave away £10,000 of it. I also managed to save some money towards buying a house with my wife, which we will live in, then eventually sell and give away the proceeds.

I do my giving at the end of each year. I've researched which charities are the most effective and this has led me to support those fighting tuberculosis and parasitic infections in the developing world.

I calculate that the money I give away can save between 2,000 and 10,000 lives (taking into account the total cost of medication, delivery, and administration). Compared to this, the benefit that I would get from spending the money on myself is clearly quite insignificant. Indeed, there are strong arguments that by donating to the most cost-effective charities your money goes more than 10,000 times as far as if you spend it on yourself.

I'm not doing this alone. I've started an organisation called Giving What We Can, which has 64 members (including Peter Singer). Each of us has pledged to donate at least 10 per cent of our earnings to wherever we think it can do the most good. My wife Bernadette, an NHS doctor, has supported this from the beginning and will give away everything she earns over £25,000.

As a couple we don't think that what we're doing is really all that sacrificial. We are still left with a joint income that is exceptionally high by world standards. We are donating about a third, but not having to give up the things that really matter to us. In fact it is probably improving my quality of life. It's not that it gives me a warm glow, but it does give me a certain peace with myself, and a sense of purpose.

Some people suggest I should first make huge amounts of money. My answer is that by doing it my way I have attracted others to join me – and our collective giving will be far more substantial

Last year I earned £25,000 and gave away £10,000

than anything I could have made on my own. Together, the members of Giving What We Can have pledged to donate £14m over the course of our careers, which should save between 30,000 and 100,000 lives. I'm not sure I could have made that much for charity by playing the markets.

Toby Ord, as told to Cole Moreton

Financial Times Magazine, 28 January 2011

I blew my million-dollar inheritance
Alex Lasarev

SOME ISSUES:

How do you feel about the writer's upbringing?

What about his attitude towards his mother's death?

Did it matter that Alex wasted his money?

See also:
Spend or save,
p82, *Fact File 2011*

When I was three, my father left home and I lived with my mother in a suburb of Toronto. She knew nothing about raising a child; she could barely look after herself – she would dress me in the cheapest clothes imaginable and my shoes were so ill-fitting it would hurt to run; every day it was agony just walking to school. And if I wanted any toys, I had to save up from what I earned on my paper route and buy them for myself. I was the school freak, tormented by the other kids.

My mother also suffered extreme mood swings. Periods of calm were few and far between, and often the scariest, because they heralded the storm I knew was coming. At 15, I ran away. I returned home several times afterwards, in the hope that things would change, but they never did and eventually I left permanently, splitting my time between youth hostels and the streets.

I was 18 when everything did change. Out of the blue I got a call from one of my mother's oldest friends. She got straight to the point: "Your mother's dead, Alex," she said. My mother had committed suicide. She was 51.

I cried uncontrollably at the funeral, yet my grief was matched by a sense of liberation and relief: in a way, the nightmare was over.

Living the way we had, I had no idea I was due to inherit a substantial sum. My mother was a talented violinist and played professionally, yet she spent nothing. She squirrelled away everything, investing much of it in property. It was only when I began opening her mail that I realised there were bank accounts in our joint names containing well over $1m. This, together with other assets, including one very valuable violin, had made me a millionaire overnight. I went from living in squalor to becoming a very rich teenager. Sudden inheritance puts you n a cocoon; it makes you fee invincible. I remember being in a cab with a cheque for $75,000 tucked in my back pocket. I thought I was Superman.

My lifestyle changed instantly. I moved out of the hostel and into a luxurious penthouse. I was too young and immature to handle such wealth. I soon found out that, with money in your pocket, everybody wants to be your friend. In my naivety, I helped out anyone who asked. Even close friends asked to borrow money and became greedy. One even forged a cheque in my name and then denied it.

> ## Sudden wealth puts you in a cocoon; it makes you feel invincible. I thought I was Superman

Some of my foolishness makes me laugh now. In 2001, I meant to buy $10,000 worth of shares online, but I typed in an extra "0" by mistake. The bank automatically put the payment through. A week later, the stock collapsed and I lost $50,000 overnight. Then I bought a sports car for an ex-stripper whom I'd recently met; she didn't hang around long.

I wish I could say it all went on drugs and women, but only a tiny fraction did. The rest went on limo rides and clothes, loans to friends and business ideas that didn't work out.

At 20, I hit my lowest point. I knew something was wrong. Depression gripped me and I couldn't function. It took a course of antidepressants and watching HBO (*Home Box Office, American premium television network*) for a few weeks to kick me out of it. Once I'd recovered, I plodded along, blowing the rest of my fortune over the next four years.

I had gone from living on the streets to being wealthy and then losing it all, including my penthouse. I had returned to where I'd started.

So I focused on the only thing that had ever really made me happy: comedy. I had tried stand-up before my mother died, and liked the feeling of freedom it gave me. I had a friend who was a stand-up in London and decided to visit him. I started doing shows almost every night and began to work at the craft.

It was a revelation. I also started going out each day and doing what scared me the most – talking to strangers. All the confidence that had been beaten out of me as a child was being discovered again.

Now, I travel around the world performing comedy, and also work as a confidence coach helping people overcome their own fears. I wouldn't change a thing that's happened. In a way, I suppose, I'm living the childhood I should have had 25 years ago. Better late than never, I suppose.

The Guardian, 19 June 2010
© *Guardian News & Media Ltd 2010*

time to stop glossing over these artful tax dodgers

Sharon Owens believes in paying her taxes and wants the big money earners to do the same

I've never supported direct action because I've always felt that setting fire to cars and throwing gloss paint over office windows only adds to the general misery of any given situation. But the way things are going, some might say that direct action is inevitable.

Now let me begin by admitting I'm not very good with money. After I graduated from art college, I spent eight years dithering over various ideas for a children's book. Then I turned to writing popular fiction. For the first two years that I worked as a writer, I earned precisely nothing, because I wrote a play that wasn't commissioned and a book that was never finished.

After that, I spent a year writing a novel for which I received an advance of £345. Then I had six good years, but even so I lost more than 60% of my novelist's income to tax, national insurance contributions, primary publisher's commission and their sub-agent's fee.

I don't mind admitting I couldn't have worked as a writer at all if my husband hadn't had a steady job and if our mortgage hadn't been quite reasonable. Still, I was never really in it for the money. I'm not a worldly person. My only luxuries are tea, crisps, glossy magazines and the occasional tin of Farrow & Ball estate emulsion*.

But the news that Barclays Bank paid only 1% in corporate tax last year has really depressed me. During my chequered career, I have never, ever slipped so much as a short story fee of £200 under the radar. I wouldn't be able to sleep at night if I knew I was wilfully concealing income from the Inland Revenue. I believe in paying my way in society.

But why is the Government announcing a sharp crackdown on benefits and a massive cut in public spending, while allowing major corporations and the super-rich to get away with tax avoidance on a grand scale? It may be legal, but it isn't very nice at a time when ordinary people are literally dying on hospital waiting lists.

I happen to know that Barclays Bank currently charges individual customers £12 for a late payment on a credit card statement. And I don't think there's a pre-fine investigation to ascertain whether a payment was late because the cheque was actually posted late, or because

SOME ISSUES:

Do you agree with the student protests?

What type of protest do you think is acceptable?

Is violence ever acceptable?

For more discussion of a widening pay gap see **Fair play on fair pay, p 191 & Prospects for young people left trailing by a self-perpetuating elite, p194**

I've never supported direct action because I've always felt that setting fire to cars and throwing gloss paint over office windows only adds to the general misery of any given situation.

the cheque perhaps languished in the sorting office for a few days. They just fine you and that's it.

So what can individuals do if they disagree with any interest charges levied as a result of a grey area late payment? Not a lot. What can individuals do about service charges and fees and fines and interest and VAT and all the rest of it? Not a lot. Well, I've been lax about money for far too long. From now on I'll be on top of my finances.

I'll pay bills with weeks to spare. I'll look for special offers. I'll query anything I don't like the look of. I'll switch suppliers if they put me on hold for half the morning. I don't think I'm at the stage of flinging gloss paint, but I know some people who definitely are. I know some people who will certainly be homeless if they lose their tax credits allowance.

I know some people who are in despair because their rent is so high they can barely afford the bus fare to work any more. I know some people who can only buy clothes from charity shops. Basically the majority of people I know are already living close to the poverty line and cannot afford any rise, however small, in the cost of housing, food, fuel, transport, or utilities. And yet the super-rich can go on registering their business interests in foreign tax havens. They can practise tax-avoidance. They can put vast sums of money in trust funds.

They know all the tricks of the trade and they have all the connections necessary to make it happen. I just hope they know what they're doing. Ordinary people have had enough. People who work can't afford a tax-hike. People who are sick can't afford a cut in benefits. The small-scale self-employed are disgusted by Barclays Bank's paltry 1% corporation tax.

I hope we won't see civil unrest in the months and years to come. Perish the thought! But many ordinary people may feel they have nothing left to lose.

Can of Farrow & Ball, anyone?

Belfast Telegraph, 24 February 2011

* Farrow & Ball is a high quality paint company producing expensive, classic paint in traditional colours

A demonstrator kicks the windows of Millbank Tower, in Westminster, central London as students and teachers gathered in central London to protest against university funding cuts and Government plans to charge up to £9,000 per year in fees from 2012.
Photo: Dominic Lipinski/PA Wire/Press Association Images

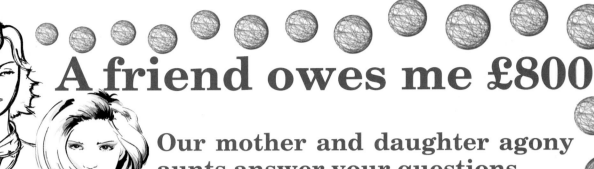

A friend owes me £800

Our mother and daughter agony aunts answer your questions

Dear Vicki & Octavia,

A friend of mine owes me £800. I lent her the money last year to help with rent when she was made redundant; she said she'd pay me back when she got a job. Nine months later she has only found temp work and is staying with relatives. She's feeling demoralised, but I need the money. What can I do?

VICKI She hasn't got it to give you. People without money can only pay back an overdue debt by borrowing £800 from somebody else in order to give it to you. You can ask her to do that. You can't make her do that. Debt-collecting is desperate work: look at Vinnie Jones's character in Lock, Stock and Two Smoking Barrels. Ordinary nice people like you and me don't really employ head-squished-in-car-door methods with equanimity. If you really do need payback, you can whine, beg, call her daily and weep and wail on her family's doorstep, with the aim of flushing out someone prepared to come to her aid.

OCTAVIA 'Never a borrower or a lender be,' Granny told me, only slightly misquoting Polonius. I never took heed, and take and offer loans with what she'd have termed gay abandon. What I did learn is: never lend what you can't afford to lose. Lending to friends is like playing the stock market with no hope of profit – you only lose or break even. You can't ask for it back in a block without being a right meanie, but you could get her to set up a weekly standing order for £20 and look forward to it trickling in over the next 10 months.

Stella Magazine,
22 August 2010
© Telegraph
Media Group
Ltd 2010

SOME ISSUES:

What would you suggest to the person writing for advice?

Do you think it is ok to borrow or lend money between friends and family?

Can you impose a time limit on a loan to a friend?

Who has given the best advice here?

Food & drink

Health
Obesity Diet
Food miles
Supermarkets
Environment Insects
Cost Eating disorders
Locality Nutrition

FOOD RULES

For twenty-five years, Michael Pollan, award-winning author, journalist and campaigner, has been on a serious food mission – he wants us to eat real food.

He's been writing books and articles about the places where nature and culture meet: on our plates, in our farms and gardens, and in the built environment.

He is the author of four bestsellers, the most recent of which, Food Rules: An Eater's Manual (2010) is, in effect, a compact version of his previous work.

It is made up of 64 simple and deliberately catchy rules ("The whiter the bread, the sooner you're dead") which encourage you to eat a healthier diet made up of real, honest, proper food. The rules are intentionally basic and easy to follow, for example "Don't eat anything your great-grandmother wouldn't recognise as food."

Despite our obesity epidemic making us eager to buy anything that claims to be "low fat" or "light" Pollan recommends: "avoid food products with the wordoid 'lite' or the terms 'low-fat' or 'non-fat' in their names." His reasoning is that when food companies remove the fat from products, they often also remove a lot of the taste. To overcome this, they will increase the sugar or artificial sweetener in a product to replace the lost flavour. This sugar, and yes, even the artificial sweetener, is often just as calorific and even more damaging to your health.

Pollan notes that since Americans – and therefore the rest of the western world – began producing and eating low-fat food products, we've actually been consuming up to 500 extra calories a day. Quite the opposite of what we intend when we buy the low-fat option.

Pollan has based his rules on two facts, that are not open to argument. Fact one is that people who eat what he labels as a western diet ("lots of processed food and meats, lots of added fat and sugar, lots of everything except vegetables, fruits and whole grains") end up suffering from very western illnesses such as obesity, cardiovascular disease, type 2 diabetes and cancer.

Fact two is that people who eat non-processed diets, and more traditional foods, tend not to suffer from these diseases. Even certain indigenous people, who, according to western food scientists, eat far too much fat, carbohydrates and protein, still avoid these illnesses.

His overall opinion, based on these two facts, is that human beings can survive and thrive on a variety of different diets, with one major exception: the highly processed food diet most of us in the west are now eating.

SOME ISSUES:

What do you think about some of Michael Pollan's food rules?

Do you think processed food is bad for you?

How much of the food you eat do you cook from scratch?

The world of processed food is a business person's dream, "You can tweak it, reformulate it and reposition it ad infinitum. And every time, you make money."

Pollan explains that the more food is processed the more profitable it gets for food production companies, and the less healthy, and potentially more damaging it gets for us. Yet the producers try to blind us with science. We don't talk about food anymore but about omega 3, antioxidants and added fibre. Food, in its natural state, has all the nutrition in it we need. The food companies would have us believe that we are getting better and healthier food through their processing. What we are really getting is highly industrialised and modified food that is damaging our health. Yet as we stand and chat about the added bifidus digestivum we are playing right into their hands.

Pollan says that the world of processed food is a business person's dream, "You can tweak it, reformulate it and reposition it ad infinitum. And every time, you make money." This explains rule 11 "Avoid foods you see advertised on the television"– because only the largest food manufacturers can afford advertising and more than two thirds of TV food ads promote processed foods. Choosing not to buy 'foods' advertised on TV means you are likely to avoid eating what Pollan calls "edible foodlike substances". Let's face it, when did you last see an advert for a tomato, apple or orange, or just plain, unprocessed meat and potatoes?

Although processed food is seen as convenient, and a cheap and easy way to eat in today's hectic world,

Some of Michael Pollan's Food Rules:

The whiter the bread, the sooner you're dead

Don't eat anything your great-grandmother wouldn't recognise as food

Avoid food products containing ingredients no ordinary human would keep in the pantry

Avoid food products with the wordoid 'lite' or the terms 'low-fat' or 'non-fat' in their name

Don't get your fuel from the same place your car does

the prospect of living with the diseases associated with it, removes the convenience somewhat.

Pollan is optimistic, about his campaign. "It's too soon to say whether radical change is possible – the real challenge, in the end, is finding ways to make money selling simple foods. But if this movement does what most movements do – shifts the centre just a few degrees – then that will already be progress. I won't be discouraged."

Following his simple eating rules is a great place to start.

http://michaelpollan.com

Sources: Various

We – the population of the world – consume meat and milk in larger amounts than ever before. Our numbers are increasing and as developing countries begin to prosper, their diets become increasingly 'western' – high in dairy and meat products.

So far, so delicious. But the animals we keep to (literally) feed our demands produce nearly 20% of all the greenhouse gases created by human activity. So while feeding our faces we are stoking up global warming. Is it time to look for a less polluting protein source?

This is where the insects wriggle, hop and crawl in to the argument. They can feed us without costing the earth – provided that we can bring ourselves to consume mealworms at meal times.

Why are insects so much better for the planet? It starts with the fact that they are cold-

Overcoming the 'Yuk!' factor

Bugs for breakfast, locusts for lunch, termites for tea – could you overcome the yuk factor to save the planet?

SOME ISSUES:

Considering the greenhouse effect, do you think we should reduce the amount of meat we eat?

Would you consider eating insects to help the environment?

Do you think we could actually like eating insects once we got used to it?

blooded. Unlike cows and pigs, they don't need to use up food energy, to keep their bodies at a fairly constant temperature. So more of their food intake goes towards their growth.

They also give out less of the polluting, warming greenhouse gases. For example the migratory locusts (Locusta Migratoria) produce 18 grams of carbon dioxide for every kilo of weight they gain while pigs produce anything from 80 to 1,130 grams. Emissions of other greenhouse gases, such as methane and nitrous oxide are also much lower. Compared to conventional livestock, insects can produce the same amount of protein with only 1% of the greenhouse gases.

The researcher who provided these figures was Professor Arnold van Huisof of Wageningen University, Netherlands, a highly rated institution in the field of food science and technology. He argues that farming mini-livestock (commonly eaten insects such as locusts, crickets and mealworms) produces more protein per bite than cattle with less cost, less water consumption and less pollution. But the professor knows that getting western adults to eat them is no easy task. "Only tasting and experience can make them change their minds," he says. So, with the help of a master chef, he gives cookery classes, tastings and talks using bugs farmed in Holland. "It is very important how you prepare them, you have to do it very nicely, to overcome the yuk factor."

The nations who are squeamish about eating insects are in the minority. According to the Food & Agriculture Organization of the United Nations there are 1,462 species of edible insects on record and insects are eaten, by choice, in 80% of nations. The FAO are committed to boosting the practice especially since a growth in insect eating could also provide jobs and protect forests where many wild insects are collected.

But will it catch on here? Paul Cook, who supplies produce such as ostrich, crocodile and rattlesnake meat also sells exotic insect snacks such as chocolate covered scorpions and worm crisps. He doesn't think we are ripe for the changeover from four to eight (or more) legged creatures. "They are in the fun element ... But I can't see it ever catching on in the UK in a big way," he says.

Yet we are not that far from it. We find sea creatures, such as prawns, mussels and crabs mouth-watering so why do their land-based cousins - woodlice and spiders - fill us with horror? It may be all in our minds.

In answer to the question "What do insects taste like?" the nutritional adviser for the *Insects are Food* website said: "Insects taste the way that people expect them to. If insects were delicious then we'd all know it and we'd eat them, since we like delicious food. Whereas if insects are perceived, however incorrectly, as disgusting, the chances that they'll be deemed delicious are pretty low."

So if we could change our frame of mind, we could change our taste buds too, and in the process, reduce the amount of greenhouse gases we produce. But in the meantime, despite the environmental arguments, you are not likely to find Pizza Locusta Migratoria at your local takeaway any time soon.

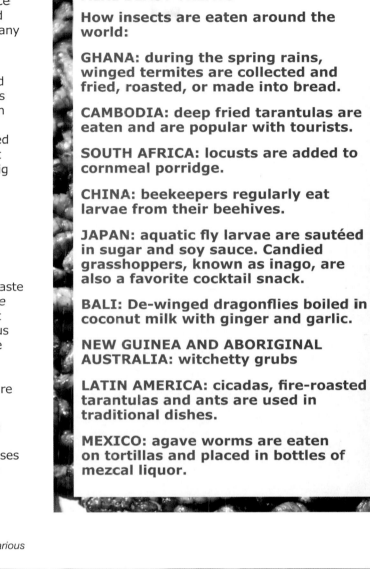

MINI BEAST TREATS

How insects are eaten around the world:

GHANA: during the spring rains, winged termites are collected and fried, roasted, or made into bread.

CAMBODIA: deep fried tarantulas are eaten and are popular with tourists.

SOUTH AFRICA: locusts are added to cornmeal porridge.

CHINA: beekeepers regularly eat larvae from their beehives.

JAPAN: aquatic fly larvae are sautéed in sugar and soy sauce. Candied grasshoppers, known as inago, are also a favorite cocktail snack.

BALI: De-winged dragonflies boiled in coconut milk with ginger and garlic.

NEW GUINEA AND ABORIGINAL AUSTRALIA: witchetty grubs

LATIN AMERICA: cicadas, fire-roasted tarantulas and ants are used in traditional dishes.

MEXICO: agave worms are eaten on tortillas and placed in bottles of mezcal liquor.

Sources: various

From here to eternity: 340 mile journey for clotted cream made two miles away

Supermarkets take pride in stocking local produce but distribution is 'complicated'

Steven Morris

More than a century ago Thomas Rodda began to sell his cream at markets in Cornwall, travelling as far from his farm as his horse could manage. Today a tub of Rodda's Cornish clotted cream on sale at Tesco in Redruth, two miles from the creamery in Scorrier, has been driven at least 340 miles to get there.

Rodda's great great grandson, Nicholas Rodda, admitted today that his forefathers would have been "surprised" that the cream was sent up on a Tesco lorry to a distribution centre in Avonmouth, near Bristol, one day, only to be sent back to the far south-west of England the next.

"It does sound crazy but it does make sense," said Rodda, the managing director of a company that makes 80m dollops of clotted cream a year. "It's complicated."

The issue was highlighted this week by the curious case of Ginsters, based in Callington (population around 6,000) in south-east Cornwall.

But its pasties – some destined for the new Tesco next door – are taken by lorry to Avonmouth before being moved back to the supermarket's shelves, a round-trip of at least 250 miles.

Many Callington residents, small-scale food producers and campaigners against "food miles" express bafflement and frustration.

But it goes further. Ginsters sends consignments destined for

SOME ISSUES:

Do you think it is wrong for food made locally to travel so far?

Would you be prepared to miss out on certain foods in order to help the environment?

See also:
Should I become an ecotarian?
p78, *Essential Articles 12*

other supermarkets by the same circuitous route. Pasties sold at the Co-operative store in Callington a mile from the factory have travelled to Portbury, near Bristol, and back – another round-trip of 250 miles.

Other producers who pride themselves on their local credentials also send their products on long journeys.

Cornish Country Larder makes St Endellion Cornish brie near Newquay, north Cornwall. It is sent to its depot in Taunton in Somerset and moved on to the Tesco distribution centre at Avonmouth before being transferred to where it has been ordered – including stores in Cornwall.

One route for Cornish sardines starts with them being landed at a port in south Cornwall before being driven inland to a processor on an industrial estate. They are moved up to a distribution centre outside the county before being sent back to stores in Cornwall.

When the Guardian bought sardines from a Tesco store, an assistant said they would have been landed about three days before they arrived on the fish counter. If they had come direct from port to shop it would have taken about 45 minutes.

Small pasty makers in Callington said they were amazed at the odyssey which Ginsters pasties were making.

"It seems an odd way of doing business," said Ann Arnold, of the Pasty Stop Bakery, where they make 300 pasties a day in a room above the shop. Their journey to market consists of carrying them down

"It seems an odd way of doing business," said Ann Arnold, of the Pasty Stop Bakery, where they make 300 pasties a day in a room above the shop. Their journey to market consists of carrying them down the narrow staircase

the narrow staircase. The journey is even shorter at the nearby Cornish Bakery, whose pasties make a trip of about a metre from the back room to the front counter.

Elaine Ead, the owner of the Chough Bakery in Padstow, north Cornwall, and a committee member of the Cornish Pasty Association, said she was frustrated by the sight of lorries trucking up and down the motorways. "We have to have a think about how food is produced and distributed," she said.

Tim Lang, the professor of food policy at City University London, who coined the phrase "food miles", said: "At one level it's completely absurd but it is alas the reality of modern logistics, which is based on cheap oil, the motorway system and mass production. If people don't like it they are going to have to be prepared to pay more for a more sustainable system of logistics."

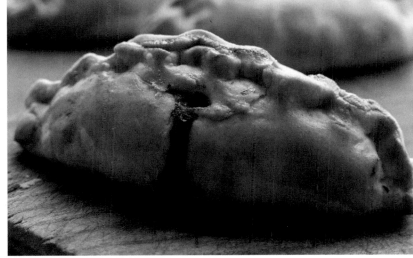

To learn that Cornish goods are being taken on tours of Britain to end up being sold in branches of Tesco right next door to where they were made tells us that, for all the claims of being green, UK plc has a very long way to go

Andrew Sims, policy director of the New Economics Foundation thinktank, said: "We do not pay the real environmental price for producing and transporting goods. It is economically inefficient and a market failure.

"To learn that Cornish goods are being taken on tours of Britain to end up being sold in branches of Tesco right next door to where they were made tells us that, for all the claims of being green, UK plc has a very long way to go to become environmentally efficient and responsible. It would be funny were it not for the sad waste of resources."

Tesco and the Co-operative insist their distribution systems are the most efficient and environmentally friendly ways of moving goods around.

A spokesman for the Co-operative Group defended regional depots. "If each individual supplier delivered directly to our stores, that would result in tens of thousands of extra vehicles on the road and not only significantly increase our carbon footprint but also add to traffic congestion."

Distribution centres were, said Tesco, the most efficient delivery network. "If it were more efficient to make separate deliveries to local stores from national suppliers, we would do so. But with more than 2,000 stores in the UK and an average Tesco superstore carrying 40,000 different lines, a centralised distribution system is more practical and efficient," a spokesman said.

He added that the company had cut the number of lorry journeys by investing in technology and other measures.

Ginsters, which is praised for using local ingredients, is upset at the criticism. Spokesman

Consumers would have to come to terms with very limited choice if producers delivered only locally, File said. "There would be no fresh fruit, no fresh vegetables out of season."

PASTRY BASE

Ginsters prides itself on its Cornish connections. Based in Callington (population around 6,000) in south-east Cornwall, it employs 700 people who help make around 3m pastries a week.

It has grown steadily since the 1960s when the Ginster family converted their egg-packing plant into a small bakery. Since 1977 Ginsters has been part of Samworth Brothers, the Melton Mowbray-based seller of pork pies, sandwiches and other goods, which has 7,000 employees in Leicestershire, Cornwall and Milton Keynes.

Pork pies packaged under the Ginster label are made in Leicestershire. One of Ginsters' favourite slogans is "Keeping it local". All of its beef is British and 65% comes from Jaspers, whose abattoir is five miles from Callington. Ginsters sources around 70% of its vegetables from Cornwall, much of it from Hay farm in Antony, 18 miles away.

A fifth of its flour is made using wheat from Cornwall. Ginsters has a fleet of 150 vehicles, delivering to service stations, convenience stores and small supermarkets. It uses Samworth Brothers trucks to get its pasties into some supermarket distribution systems.

Larry File said there would be "mayhem" if every producer tried to deliver to every store in the country.

Consumers would have to come to terms with very limited choice if producers delivered only locally, File said. "There would be no fresh fruit, no fresh vegetables out of season."

Back at the creamery, Nicholas Rodda said sending its products out on supermarket lorries meant it could get its products out of Cornwall. "We're so far from the marketplace. It's a tremendous logistical feat to get our cream to Scotland, Norfolk and Wales the following morning."

And, of course, back to Cornwall.

It would be funny were it not for the sad waste of resources

The Guardian, 3 September 2010
© Guardian News & Media
Ltd 2010

The woman who only ever eats Monster Munch

We all enjoy the odd packet of crisps, but for Debbie Taylor they are breakfast, lunch and dinner. In fact, she only eats beef flavour Monster Munch

By Lauren Taylor

Bizarre as it sounds, Debbie, 30, has eaten nothing but crisps for 10 years, and for the past two, beef flavour Monster Munch have been every meal. Friends and family have tried to persuade her to have a more varied diet, but Debbie insists she can't eat anything else. Meals out, Christmas dinner, barbecues, even eating the food she cooks for her family are all off-limits.

Debbie takes crisps to restaurants. And when her boyfriend Gerald Whittington, 55, took Debbie and her son Luke, 10, for a holiday in Spain, he even had to pack a separate suitcase for her Monster Munch! Hotel chambermaid Debbie from Harlow in Essex, eats six small packets a day or two large bags. She says: "I know it must seem strange but it works for me – I love Monster Munch!

"Gerald and my family have tried everything to get me to eat other food but I'm so used to crisps now there is no way I could tuck into a pizza or fish and chips." Despite her cheery attitude, Debbie's severely restricted diet is likely to be an after-effect of the eating disorders that plagued her from a young age.

After being bullied as a child for being overweight she suffered from anorexia and bulimia from the ages of 14 to 17 and her weight plummeted

SOME ISSUES:

Do you think it is possible to stay healthy eating only Monster Munch?

What would you do if someone you knew developed an eating problem like this?

Should the doctors do something about it?

And what about the family? Should they do something about it? What could they do?

See also:
Anorexia admissions,
p105, *Fact File 2010*

Photo: Mirrorpix

"I worry about the damage to her bones, she's not getting any kind of vitamins, protein or calcium. I think what she needs is a psychological change, it's a state of mind."

Night after night Debbie Taylor lovingly prepares dinner for her family then, as they tuck into their meal she reaches into the kitchen cupboard for a packet of Monster Munch

to 7 stone. She finally overcame those eating disorders, but her eating habits never returned to normal. Instead she went through phases of only eating one specific food. From the ages of 17 to 19, she only ate peanuts and over the next few years she gradually moved on to bread sprinkled with salt.

Pregnant at 20, she craved a variety of foods and ate properly for the first time in years. But as soon as she gave birth to son, Luke, she fell back into her old eating habits. For the next eight years she only ate Walkers crisps and for the past two years beef flavour Monster Munch has been the only meal she could stomach. Even when she started seeing Gerald in 2003, she couldn't change her diet and it caused awkward situations in their relationship's first months.

Debbie says: "Gerald wanted to take me out to dinner or cook for me at home but, whatever he

did, I couldn't eat anything. "At first he was really concerned about my health and I suppose it must have been embarrassing when we went out to eat in restaurants and I would only have Monster Munch." Since then Gerald has tried everything to encourage Debbie to eat a more varied diet.

He says: "It used to scare the living daylights out of me when we first got together, I worry about the damage she's doing to her body.

"I worry about the damage to her bones, she's not getting any kind of vitamins, protein or calcium. I think what she needs is a psychological change, it's a state of mind."

Debbie doesn't take any vitamin supplements and hasn't eaten anything green since she was a child, but nonetheless she insists she feels fine. She says: "Doctors don't understand. I've never been referred to a specialist or given any help. They think I'm just fussy and should change."

And Debbie admits she would like to eat normally some day. She's embarrassed when she pulls out her bright yellow packets in a restaurant and would love to eat a normal dinner with her family. She says: "When I have tried to eat something else my body isn't used to it and I simply can't eat or, if I co, it makes me sick."

For Debbie and Gerald, weekly trips to the supermarket attract confused looks from other shoppers. The couple take separate trolleys around the shop and Debbie clears the Monster Munch from the shelves. She says: "People do look at us funny when I put so much Monster Munch into my trolley. We usually add some sweets and Coke in that trolley for Luke – sometimes the cashiers ask if we're having a party!"

Beef flavour Monster Munch was only available in a multi-pack until last year so the couple used to throw away huge quantities of the other flavours. Now however they come in separate bags and she only spends £4 a day on her food.

At Christmas, Debbie prepares and cooks all the food, but when her family sit down to their roast dinners, she heads for the cupboard for her crisps.

"I worry that I overcompensate by cooking big meals for Luke and Gerald, I probably make far too much food, but Luke doesn't seem to have picked up my bad habits yet. Thankfully, he's got a healthy appetite. I'm a good cook and really enjoy preparing meals, I just can't stand the thought of eating them myself and the smell makes me feel sick."

In 2008, Gerald persuaded Debbie to go on a plane for the first time and the family flew to Barcelona. She says: "I was terrified of flying but also very worried that I wouldn't find any Monster Munch in Spain. Gerald reassured me we'd find some but we never did. Luckily, we found BBQ crisps so I managed to live on those for the week."

So when the family went on holiday to the Spanish island of Fuerteventura last July, Debbie wasn't prepared to take any chances – she packed a separate suitcase full of Monster Munch. "Just imagine if our bags had been searched going through customs!" she shudders.

Debbie's weight fluctuates and her wardrobe is full of clothes that are too big her for slight frame. At 5ft 3ins, she looks to be around a size 10 or 12,

but she hides her figure under shapeless clothes and never buys new outfits.

Gerald is always telling her she is beautiful but she refuses to believe him, avoids the mirror and won't even consider wearing a swimsuit on holiday. Although she's aware that her insecurities probably stem from her childhood weight problem and the cruel taunts of the bullies at school, she still can't pinpoint any reason for her current diet.

She insists she doesn't know her size and, unlike her teenage years, doesn't any longer obsess about her weight or starve herself. "When I'm hungry I eat a packet of crisps. I don't try to diet, Monster Munch is just what I feel like eating. But I do realise it's just another eating disorder. It's probably a branch of my anorexia and bulimia in my teens.

"I would like to change, I just don't know when it's going to happen and what it's going to take. I worry about the future, I would like to eat normally but I don't know how to get there." She recently discovered the term 'selective eating disorder' to describe her eating habits when she searched the internet for people similar to her.

Debbie says: "I know people must think it's strange but it's not hurting anyone else and my heart hasn't stopped yet. So until it causes me serious problems I'll happily go on eating my favourite crisps.

"I can't imagine life without Monster Munch!"

The Daily Mirror, 2 July 2010

Debbie doesn't take any vitamin supplements and hasn't eaten anything green since she was a child, but nonetheless she insists she feels fine.

Gender

Female
Work **Sexism**
Perception Media
Male Children
Achievement
Success Government
Abuse

Gender unknown!

> "Girls are told they are cute in their dresses, and boys are told they are cool with their toy cars. But if you give them no gender they will be seen more as a human and not a stereotype as a boy or girl."

It's not unusual for couples to decide whether they want to know the sex of their baby before birth. It is unusual, however, not to reveal the gender for more than two years, yet this is what a Swedish couple have decided to do to protect their child from gender stereotypes.

The toddler, known as Pop to protect her/his identity, has reached two and a half with only a few people knowing the sex. Pop makes the decision on what to wear each day – choosing both dresses and male style pants – and has hairstyles that are sometimes masculine and sometimes feminine.

The parents are convinced that gender is created by the way society treats boys and girls. "We want Pop to grow up more freely and avoid being forced into a specific gender mould from the outset," Pop's mother said. "It's cruel to bring a child into the world with a blue or pink stamp on their forehead." By not disclosing Pop's sex, and not even using he or she when referring to the child, the parents are hoping that people will not be able treat Pop in the way they would usually treat a boy or girl.

A Swedish gender equality consultant Kristina Henkel, interviewed in an English language paper says Pop's parents' experiment might have positive results. "If the child is dressed up as a girl or boy, it affects them because people see and treat them in a more gender-typical way," Henkel explains. "Girls are told they are cute in their dresses, and boys are told they are cool with their toy cars. But if you give them no gender they will be seen more as a human and not a stereotype as a boy or girl."

However Susan Pinker, an internationally published psychologist and journalist, has voiced her disagreement. "Ignoring children's natures simply doesn't work," she says. In her opinion males and females differ from birth because hormones present before birth will affect the way children of different sexes feel and behave. She says that child-rearing should not be used to prove a point.

Henkel, on the other hand, says that avoiding gender stereotypes can allow children to build character as individuals, not hindered by notions of what they should be as males or females. This belief is clearly shared by Pop's mother when she says, "I believe that the self-confidence and personality that Pop has shaped will remain for a lifetime."

Sources: Various

SOME ISSUES:

Do you think we treat people differently depending on their gender?

How do you think this could affect babies and children when growing up?

Do you think this is a good experiment?

How do you think it might affect the child, in positive and/or negative ways?

Keeping up appearances

A new study demonstrates that how women musicians dress alters the perception of how they play
Ben Goldacre

Everyone likes to imagine they are rational, fair, and free from prejudice. But how easily are we misled by appearances? Noola Griffiths studies the psychology of music, and she's published a cracking paper on how what women wear affects your judgment of their performance. The results are predictable but the context is interesting.

Four female musicians were filmed playing in three different outfits: a concert dress, jeans, and a nightclubbing dress. They were also all filmed as points of light, wearing a black tracksuit in the dark, so that the only thing to be seen – once the images had been treated – was the movement of some bright white tape attached to their joints.

All these violinists were music students, from the top 10% of their year, and they were vetted to ensure comparability: they were all white Europeans, size 10 dress, size 4 or 5 shoe, and aged between 20 and 22.

They were even equivalently attractive, according to their score on the MBA California facial mask, which seems to be some kind of effort to derive a numerical hotness quotient from the best fit of a geometric mask over someone's face. I'm not saying that's not ridiculous, I'm just saying they tried.

In fact they did better. All the performances were also standardised at 104 beats per minute, so the audio tracks from each musician could be replaced with a recording of a single performance, recorded by someone who was never filmed, for each of the various pieces in the study.

For technical proficiency, performers in a concert dress were rated higher than if they were in jeans or a clubbing dress

This meant there was no room for anyone to argue that the clothes made the musicians perform differently, and when the researchers checked in a pilot study, nobody watching the clips had spotted the switch.

Then they got 30 different musicians – a mixture of music students and members of the Sheffield

SOME ISSUES:

Do you think appearance matters?

Is the answer different depending on gender?

Why do you think people judged the performances differently based on the appearance of the player?

Do you ever judge people on their appearances?

Are you ever judged on your appearance?

Phi harmonic – to watch video clips with various different permutations of clothing, player and piece. All were invited to give each performance a score out of six for technical proficiency and musicality, and the results were inevitable.

For technical proficiency, performers in a concert dress were rated higher than if they were in jeans or a clubbing dress, even though the actual audio performance was exactly the same every time (and played by a separate musician who was never filmed). The results for musicality were similar: musicians in a clubbing dress were rated worst.

Experiments offer small constricted worlds, which we hope act as models for wider phenomena. How far can you apply this to wider society? Women are still discriminated against in the workplace, but each situation has so many variables it can be difficult to assess.

In the world of music, assessment of performance goals can be restricted to make individuals broadly comparable, and so there's a reasonably long tradition of the field being used as a test tube for bigotry. In the 1970s and 1980s, in an attempt to overcome biases in hiring, most orchestras changed their audition policy, and began using screens to conceal the identity of the candidate.

Female musicians in the top five US symphony orchestras rose from 5% in the 1970s to around 25%. This could have been due to wider societal shifts, so Goldin and Rouse conducted a very elegant study, Orchestrating Impartiality: they compared the number of women being hired at auditions with and without screens, and found women were several times more likely to be hired when nobody could see that they were a woman.

What's more, using data on the changing gender makeup of orchestras over time, they were able to estimate that from the 1970s to 2000 – the era which shifted from casual racism and sexism in popular culture, to more covert forms – the trend towards greater equality was driven simply by selectors being forced not to see who they were selecting. I don't know how you'd apply the same tools to every workplace. But I'd like to see someone try

Women were several times more likely to be hired when nobody could see that they were a woman

The Guardian, 3 September 2010
© Guardian News & Media Ltd 2010

Fear of racism should no longer be the veil covering up hard truths

Jack Straw is right to ask hard questions about Asian men says *Yasmin Alibhai Brown*

The unrepentant British Pakistani gang leaders who violated young girls in Derby have been rightly reviled and given indefinite sentences. Their victims were almost all white. There it might have ended but for Jack Straw, who rekindled passions on all sides when he said that such Pakistani men thought these females were easy meat who deserved no respect or consideration (I paraphrase). No solid evidence is provided by Straw to back these assertions. In fact, when he was Home Secretary he could have funded research on the matter, but failed to.

Still, even a man used to controversies must be nonplussed by the reaction to his comments. His words were thrown on to blazing pyres by fulminating leftie liberals, feminists, Muslims, Pakistanis, anti-racists and influential individuals who think of themselves as gravely responsible. It was unacceptable, they said, to racialise or ethnicise a particular crime; some even declared that any discussion of cultural factors was dangerous and racist.

Being avowedly a leftie liberal, anti-racist, feminist, Muslim, part-Pakistani, and yes, a very responsible person, I should be in the circle with these objectors – particularly as I can't stand the Rt Hon MP for Blackburn, his devious, shady politicking and moral expediency. However, just as when he criticised the full veil, I cannot condemn his views. How can I? Just before Christmas, I too wrote about these rapists and the anti-white cultural prejudices in some of their communities and families. It was a hard column to write, as is this one. Easier to pick your way barefoot through a dark park littered with broken glass. You need to think about every line, its effect, and know that you will step on the shard that will cut you, however carefully you tread.

I accept that on the basis of the evidence presented in court, this Derby gang was no different from that of the white grooming posse convicted in Cornwall in November. They too preyed on helpless, easily-pleased young white girls who were then used and destroyed. Most paedophiles in this country are white, and their victims too. Just because they harm their own doesn't make it less abominable or more acceptable. What does it matter to a young, white, rape victim whether her violator has pasty or dark skin? And it is gratifying that reputable figures like Barnado's Martin Narey and the judge in the Derby case have spoken out against wholesale racial scapegoating. We know extremists use race and crime statistics to stoke racial hatred against Britons of colour and from religious minorities. I have sometimes been a pin-up girl for the repellent BNP and English Defence League, whenever I criticise Muslims, or Asian values or black Britons who do wrong. You feel degraded and treacherous when this happens.

SOME ISSUES:

Do you think there is a difference between how men of different cultural backgrounds view women?

What do you think the general opinion is of young women in this country?

Is there a difference between how men view women of different cultures?

But I still say we need to expose and discuss more openly the underpinning values of the Asian criminal rings in many of our cities. If we don't, the evil will grow. Fear of racism should no longer be the veil covering up hard truths. What the Derby gang did has planted and raised more

over the Sierra Leonean journalist Sorious Samura, who made a TV documentary on the gang rape of young girls in British cities. Censured by the usual slate of apologists, he accepted that the attacks were carried out by men of all backgrounds, but pointed out that a high

We need to expose and discuss more openly the underpinning values of the Asian criminal rings in many of our cities

racism – possibly even among good, benign people – than my words ever could. I am sure recruitment to extremist parties has gone up too. Prominent anti-racists know that, but will not openly say so.

The criminals feel they did no wrong. These girls to them are trash, asking to be wasted – unlike their own women, who must be kept from the disorderly world out there. The whore and

proportion were black or mixed-race. "As a black man as well as a journalist, I wanted to know what lay behind such attacks, the profoundly disturbing attitudes to females."

That is what I am seeking to do too, as a Muslim journalist who cares deeply about migrants and their progress. Let's ask questions we never ask, to find out more than we ever try to. Do these men have any idea of normal, pleasurable,

Ethnicity and sexual abuse cannot and should not ever be linked

the virgin are both feared and severely controlled and abused. A 2005 study in the Netherlands of Muslim males found the same bifurcation, and identified deep sexism as responsible for both.

The conversations can be heard every day around dining tables and on streets; they are embedded in thought and language. I once interviewed the mother of a man who had been convicted of repeatedly raping his young wife, who came from a rural village in Pakistan. The

healthy sex between a man and a woman? Are they maddened by their own frustration and fear of females? I am not impugning those Asian or Pakistani men who love women, but those who are too messed up to understand what that means; maybe those whose key choices, including their lifelong partners, have all been made by families operating as firms. And again, is this the most appalling pay-back for white racism? Black writers in the US, including Eldridge Cleaver, have

Let's ask questions we never ask, to find out more than we ever try to

head of the nursery school the couple's child attended had helped the victim report what was happening. In Urdu, the mother hissed: "How lucky was she to get my son? The dirty, ungrateful bitch – went to a white woman to complain. They sleep with everybody. She just didn't know how to make him happy. We have thrown her out. She can go on the streets like those whites now."

I have been writing about these culturally-sanctioned injustices for two decades, and have interviewed countless people. I will not melt the misdemeanours into generalities, and do not accept that ethnicity and sexual abuse cannot and should not ever be linked.

Some years back, a similar furore was raised

written movingly about some of the unconscious, vengeful urges that impel black men to take up with white partners to assert power, sometimes to annihilate the person who trusts them.

Shouting down Jack Straw, busying ourselves with warnings about feeding the BNP, are displacement activities that will do nothing to stop Asian groomers, who, from childhood have developed distorted ideas about themselves, society, females, vice and virtue. Like Samura said, it is up to insiders to examine and reveal what lies beneath these crimes. We owe that to ourselves, to our future generations, and to the country we have made ours.

The Independent, 10 January 2011

Too many of us treat young white women as trash

The case in Derby has revealed some truly unpleasant attitudes to the status of young women
Barbara Ellen

Is Jack Straw right: are white girls viewed by some Pakistani men as "easy meat"? He spoke after the sentencing of Abid Mohammed Saddique and Mohammed Romaan Liaqat, ringleaders of a group that targeted girls between 12 and 18 in the Derby area, grooming them for sex.

Straw said that this was noticeable in his constituency, Blackburn: "There is a specific problem which involves Pakistani heritage men… who target vulnerable young white girls." Mohammed Shafiq, of Muslim youth group, the Ramadhan Foundation, called it racism. "These young men do not see white girls as equal, as valuable, of high moral standing as their own daughters, and their own sisters, which is wrong."

Elsewhere, there was talk of a "conspiracy of silence", a politically correct muzzling of this issue. What no one is saying is that if Asian boys view white girls as drunken, worthless, sub-human trash, then, frankly, so does much of non-Asian Britain. In recent years, haven't we all become rather too comfortable with seeing girls portrayed like this?

Of course such victims are targeted. However, far more significant than colour is the fact that many of them are in care and, therefore, more vulnerable generally. Elsewhere, the supposedly all-important "Asian" element doesn't bear much scrutiny.

What no one is saying is that if Asian boys view white girls as drunken, worthless, sub-human trash, then, frankly, so does much of non-Asian Britain.

SOME ISSUES:

Do you think media coverage of young white women is realistic?

Is it mainly negative?

Do you think people of different cultures think different things about women and girls?

Who is to blame – the media, the family, the girls themselves?

See also:
Gender section,
p100-104, *Essential Articles 13*

A photograph issued by Derbyshire Constabulary of Abid Mohammed Saddique (left) and Mohammed Romaan Liaqat, ringleaders of a gang that committed a catalogue of offences against vulnerable young girls

The authors of the widely quoted "on-street grooming" research have already expressed concern that their limited case samples have led to racial generalisations. Straw talks of young Asian men being like any others, "fizzing and popping with testosterone, but Pakistani girls are off limits", as if this weren't true of all young males, fizzing, popping, exploding, whatever, who find that some girls are sexually available, others not, for myriad reasons.

Likewise Mohammed Shafiq's comment about Asian men not viewing white women as equal or valuable as "their own daughters, their own sisters". Well, join the chauvinist club, Asian guys. It seems to me that many men don't view females outside their immediate family circle or acquaintance as "equal, valuable or of high moral standing".

Whenever sex workers are murdered there is an effort to frame them as daughters, sisters and mothers, precisely because this is the easiest way to humanise them.

Even if Asian men tend to view white girls as easier meat, then where have they learned all this? Not only on the streets where they live, but also in the images surrounding them. There's endless coverage of drunken "ladettes" out on the lash, young girls being sick into gutters, lying in streets, smoking, getting pregnant, looking gormless, telling people with research clipboards that "all they wanna be is famous, innit".

In the vast majority of cases, the girls featured are white. Not because only white girls spend a period of their youth

Even if Asian men tend to view white girls as easier meat, then where have they learned all this? Not only on the streets where they live, but also in the images surrounding them.

making mistakes, living and learning, but presumably because it is less tricky to use pictures of white girls. Images of young black girls making mistakes, living and learning, could so easily look a bit racist. Therefore, any coverage of them must be framed in more sombre reportage, which to me seems racist in itself.

Likewise, Asian girls mainly crop up when there are arranged marriages to fret over. All of this when figures show that all girls, regardless of race, tend to do better than boys at school and presumably, therefore, are pretty similar in other ways too.

Are all non-white girls so much better behaved or is this inverted racial stereotyping, evocative of a society that's become far too comfortable with images of young, female, white trash, to the extent that many white and black boys probably also think they're "easier"? As the abuse in Derby involved children as young as 12, something even darker was going on. However, in the main, if young Asian guys have concluded that white girls are "easy meat", then there could be a lot more to this than good old handy "cultural differences".

*The Observer,
9 January 2011
© Guardian News &
Media Ltd 2011*

In the vast majority of cases, the girls featured are white. Not because only white girls spend a period of their youth making mistakes, living and learning, but presumably because it is less tricky to use pictures of white girls.

Health

Stroke
Locked In Syndrome
Family Hospital
Science Donation
Diagnosis TB
NHS Artificial limbs
Relationships

BIONIC IMPLANTS:

'WE HAVE THE TECHNOLOGY'

As scientists restore sight to a blind man, *Richard Gray* explains how human beings can now be rebuilt from top to toe with artificial parts

SOME ISSUES:

What do you think are the pros and cons of such medical advances?

Is the idea of 'bionic' replacement parts disturbing?

Is there a limit to how much humans can or should be improved by scientific developments?

For the first time in more than a decade, Miikka Terho was able to glance at a clock and read the time. It was a simple task, but one he had been unable to do since he was robbed of his sight by disease. Mr Terho, 46, a financial consultant from Finland, was one of three patients who had their sight temporarily restored using artificial light sensors and microchips placed on the retina at the back of their eyes by doctors in Germany.

This extraordinary melding of man and machine proves that we finally have the technology to create real-life bionic humans. In the 1970s TV series, The Six Million Dollar Man, Lee Major's character had his body rebuilt using bionic technology, leaving him "better, stronger, faster". Now, cutting-edge research is producing synthetic body parts to replace damaged tissues, limbs, organs and senses. In most cases it is used to improve a patient's quality of life, but in others it is saving lives.

Here we examine how science can potentially kit out a human being from head to toe to create a real bionic man.

BRAIN

By far the most important, and also the most complex, organ in the body is the brain. It controls our movements and our breathing, makes sense of the world and stores the memories that help form our personalities. Damage to the brain from accidents or illnesses such as strokes can be catastrophic, ranging from paralysis to memory loss. But some scientists believe they may have found a way to repair this damage – a prosthetic brain.

Dr Theodore Berger, from the University of Southern California, has been developing a device that can be implanted into the brain to restore memory functions, modelling the complex neural activity that takes place in the hippocampus, which is responsible for forming new memories.

The device – a microchip that encodes memories for storing elsewhere in the brain – has been tested using tissue from rats' brains, and researchers are planning trials on live animals. They hope it will provide a way of restoring memory function in patients who have suffered damage to their hippocampus from a stroke, an accident or from Alzheimer's disease.

EYES

Around one million people in Britain suffer from two of the most common forms of blindness: macular degeneration and retinitis pigmentosa. But doctors in Germany last week restored sight to three blind patients by implanting chips lined with electronic sensors – similar to those found in digital cameras – into the back of their eyes. When light hits these sensors, they produce electrical impulses that pass into the optical nerve behind the eye and into the brain. The patients reported being able to distinguish objects such as fruit and cutlery, and even read their own name.

Miikka Terho was one of the first to have the implant and saw his life transformed over the three-month trial, before the implant was removed. He went from being completely blind to being able to make out fuzzy black-and-white shapes that allowed him to read the time.

"When I first got the implant I could tell I was seeing something, but I couldn't really make out what it was – it was like my sight was a muscle that I hadn't used in a long time and it needed training to get used to recognising things again," he says.

"Later I was able to see people and tell if someone lifted their arm or if someone was taller than someone else. They were too fuzzy to distinguish faces, but being able to see like that would help me to be more independent and walk in unfamiliar surroundings – to live a more normal life."

Professor Eberhart Zrenner, who led the research at the University of Tuebingen, has already begun work on improving the detail that the patients can see by changing the power supply – currently the chip has an external supply that must be transmitted through the skin via a magnetic link.

"We also want to have the implant do some intelligent processing that can help to enhance the contrast and the graininess of the image," he says.

A larger trial of the device is now being planned and will include patients from the UK – but it is by no means the only approach being taken. While most research is aimed at helping patients who have lost their sight, some scientists hope they may be able to enhance the vision of healthy people, too. Artificial lenses that have microscopic circuits fixed to them could be used to produce wearable displays that beam maps, computer displays and even zoom functions to the wearer.

EARS

The bionic ear has been around for more than 40 years, and many thousands of patients are already wearing them. Cochlear implants turn sound into electronic pulses that are transmitted to the brain, allowing the wearer to "hear". Unfortunately, the devices are unable to tune in to specific sounds, so in noisy environments patients can struggle to hear speech and find music hard to enjoy.

However, scientists at La Trobe University, Australia, have, by studying the way in which the ear transmits information to the brain, produced a device that behaves far more like a human ear.

HEART

Artificial hearts, essentially miniaturised pumps, are often implanted into patients to help their damaged organs pump blood around their bodies while they are waiting for transplants. And last month doctors in Italy gave a 15-year-old boy the first permanent artificial heart implant. One company in France, Carmat, has developed a prototype for a fully artificial heart that would replace the organ altogether. Heart specialist Alain Carpentier, the doctor behind the device, uses hydraulic pumps to push blood around the body. It works like a natural heart, where blood is drawn into cavities inside the organ before being pushed out to the arteries. Surgeons plan to perform the first implant in humans in late 2011.

ARMS

In July, Patrick Kane, a 13-year-old schoolboy from London, was transformed into a bionic boy when he was fitted with a prosthetic arm by the Livingston-based firm Touch Bionics. Their revolutionary iLimb Pulse hand means Patrick, who lost his left hand after falling victim to meningitis when he was nine months old, can even squash grapes between his fingers. "It's the little things that the hand allows me to do that have really made the difference," says Patrick. "I can open bottles with both hands now, hold my fork and tie my shoelaces."

His prosthesis works by using two electrodes that make contact with the skin on his upper arm. When he tenses a muscle, tiny pulses of electricity from the nerves beneath the electrodes cause the hand to close; when he tenses another, the hand opens.

Researchers are working on prosthetic limbs that will allow wearers even more control. By mapping how the neural networks are used to control limb movements, they can learn how robotic arms can be controlled in the same way as a real, natural arm. Some approaches use electrodes implanted beneath the skin; others use ones on top of the skin. By picking up tiny signals from the brain when someone thinks about moving their arm, the robotic prosthesis can be made to replicate the movement.

Hugh Gill, chief technical officer at Touch Bionics, says: "What we're looking at is how you can map the signals from the brain so that you can have discrete control of individual digits on a prosthetic hand and rotate the wrist. The ideal situation is that when you go to reach for an object, the hand responds in the way you would expect a real hand to.

"One of the other things a number of people are looking at, and again we are interested in, is adaptive devices that fit around existing limbs like an arm or a leg and provide additional power."

MUSCLES

Some researchers are attempting to find ways of replacing individual muscles rather than whole limbs to provide bionic treatments for people who have suffered serious sporting injuries or lost muscles in accidents. They are using synthetic polymer gels that expand and contract in response to small electrical currents to create synthetic muscles for replacing heart valves, sphincter muscles and, eventually, larger muscles.

Scientists at Nasa's Jet Propulsion Laboratory in Pasadena are aiming to develop an arm powered by bionic muscles made from these "electroactive polymers" that would be capable of winning an arm-wrestling contest. Dr Richard Baker, from the University of St Andrews, is also working with polymer gels, but hopes to produce material that will contract and expand in response to the kind of chemical signals that are found in the body.

Scientists at the University of Texas have produced artificial muscles that are more than 100 times more powerful than natural muscle, using an elastic metal wire that bends when it is heated and returns to normal when cooled down.

TENDONS

Researchers at Manchester University are developing artificial tendons to help patients who have severed or injured their own. Using finely spun fibres of plastic material, the synthetic tendons behave just like the natural tissue and can be implanted into a patient to restore movement.

Professor Sandra Downes, from the school of materials at Manchester University, says the implants would encourage the body to heal itself and would gradually break down.

The team is about to start pre-clinical trials and hopes to have bionic tendons on the market within five years.

TOUCH

Even with the most advanced prosthetics available, patients with robotic arms still suffer from being unable to feel what they are touching. This important sense allows us to enjoy sensuality, control how hard we grip objects and even helps us form opinions about people we meet, for instance from their handshake.

Scientists in Italy have been working on a synthetic skin that gives robots a sense of touch. Although this was initially developed for robots, some researchers at the Italian Institute of Technology are developing ways of feeding information back from the synthetic skin to patients' nerve cells.

The Sunday Telegraph, 7 November 2010
© *Telegraph Media Group Ltd 2010*

A letter to my silent mother

Emmeline Hundleby

SOME ISSUES:

Do we take our loved ones for granted?

How would your life change if you could no longer speak?

How do disabilities affect family life?

The writer says "Had I known what was to come..." What would be different?

It's been years now since your first stroke. I didn't even know you had had one; you rushed off to the States to care for my father, who had had a heart attack, instead of seeking help yourself. That pretty much sums you up. A victim of your huge heart, caring so much for everyone, at the cost of your own health.

I can't remember the last "normal" conversation we had. I really hate that. Even though it was most likely something mundane, like what veg to

Had I known what was to come I would have treasured it more, every word, whatever was said

plant, or what mushrooms you had found on one of your crazy forest rambles. Knowing me I most likely cut you off to get on with the housework or rush off out. What an idiot. Had I known what was to come I would have treasured it more, every word, whatever was said. I would have come over and we could have sat in the garden with a cup of tea and chatted until your words ran out. Your aphasia happened slowly at first, then your voice was suddenly gone for ever. It is a shock that I don't think any of us will ever really accept.

There is no point getting angry any more, but I still do get very upset. There is no justification for what has happened. Nobody deserves to lose their voice or freedom of movement, but for it to happen to such an extraordinarily expressive and creative woman, well, it just seems somehow worse. It's cruel and unfair, to you and to us. It bothers me that people who meet you now for the first time don't know who you really are inside. They are missing out on something really special.

I love dreaming about you – you can always talk in my dreams. It's the most comforting sound, like a warm, comfy blanket to my soul. Waking up can be quite painful.

There are so many questions I still had to ask you. It took a long time to learn to stop myself from grabbing the phone mid-recipe to ask you what I was doing wrong or what I needed to make something. Oh God, I miss your cooking too. Your food was as important as your words – hearty, tasty and just bloody yum! The centre of family life, just like you.

Our food was as important as your words – hearty, tasty and just bloody yum! The centre of family life, just like you

I don't want to reminisce just about what has been lost; you are still very much needed in my life. Just in a new way, a way that we have to still figure out fully. We will get there with a little more patience and a few hiccups I'm sure. When

It's important that you really believe me when I say your eyes still sparkle, and hearing you laugh when you can is reassuring and a testament to your spirit and strength

my baby is older I promise to tell her all about how you were, and pass on your stories and funny tales and all the adventures we would get up to. Your legacy will be handed down and she will know who you are, past and present. I promise your old self will never be forgotten.

It's important that you really believe me when I say your eyes still sparkle, and hearing you laugh when you can is reassuring and a testament to your spirit and strength. Your spirit is still in there, even if you feel it has faded. That can never be taken away by any illness. I can still hear your voice inside my heart, please don't forget that. My mum, the mad mushroom picker is immortal!

The Guardian, 9 October 2010
© Guardian News & Media 2010

TB 'I was a medical mystery'

For months, fitness trainer Imla Hazaiah struggled with a crippling illness. Doctors diagnosed flu – then terminal cancer. But the reality was something much rarer

No one knows how I caught it. I could have walked by somebody while they were coughing. I could have got it from damp in the walls. It's impossible to tell.

For eight months, they kept testing me. My motor skills went, my memory became patchy. I'm still getting flashbacks, five years later. My face was gaunt and my skin had gone grey. I was using a walking stick to get around.

There were moments when I felt that I was looking down on my body from the ceiling. Just looking, convincing myself to choose life.

Tuberculosis – TB – isn't something you associate with life in England. It's not like getting the flu. When you hear of it you think of Victorian times, of the Black Death. Before I had it, I couldn't really have told you anything about it.

The first sign of trouble came at work. I'm a fitness trainer and complementary therapist, and I noticed how exhausted I felt. Initially I assumed my fitness wasn't up to scratch and simply pushed myself harder. Then one day, when I was cycling, I realised I didn't have the strength to continue. I decided to go to the doctor.

Maybe I was burned out, I thought – in need of a holiday, or anaemic. My GP told me I had the flu – though it didn't feel like it. A week or so later I returned, feeling no better. Again, he said it was the flu.

On my third visit, he was away and I was given a different doctor. From his surgery, I was sent straight to hospital. They took some X-rays before referring me to another hospital – Guy's in Southwark. They were testing for

SOME ISSUES:

Was Imla Hazaiah failed by the health system or saved by it?

For more information about TB in the UK, visit www.thetruthabouttb.org

They were testing for everything: cancer, TB, AIDS. This was the first round of tests

The fact that doctors hadn't come back with a diagnosis made things more difficult

everything: cancer, TB, AIDS. This was the first round of tests.

When the tests came back, the doctors still didn't know what was wrong. It was at this stage that I started to wonder whether I was making it all up. Perhaps, I thought, there isn't anything wrong at all. I was getting weaker, but there was nothing to indicate what it could be. I went into denial and tried to carry on.

Increasingly, it became impossible to function. I wouldn't go to bed. I would get in from work and pass out in my armchair, waking in the morning with a drink poured down myself. In the night, it would feel like I had left my body. I cannot tell you if I ate dinner in those months; if I ever did, I don't remember it. I was very skinny; people began asking if I had AIDS. Still, the doctors couldn't find an answer. I was passing blood and my stools were black from internal bleeding.

I would try to go to work but it became more difficult. Several times I passed out and awoke not knowing where I was. I still find it fascinating that other people at work rarely mentioned it. I'm freelance and people in my class knew I was sick, but I felt like my employers never really took it seriously.

I had a nurse assigned to me; she came round twice a week. I always said I was fine but there were days when I couldn't remember how to walk. It took me an hour and a half to get to a friend's place, which was about 1 km from mine.

It became very isolating. The fact that the doctors hadn't come back with a diagnosis made things more difficult. People would ask what was wrong. What could I say? I'm not close to my family, and so

there wasn't a network of people who could offer advice. I did have some people: friends who were willing to do my shopping, people to voice concern. They would tell me everything was going to be all right, that it would all work out. But that's not practical. It doesn't put your mind at rest. It doesn't help you look in the mirror when you can't face yourself, it doesn't help you get back your motor skills and it doesn't make you stop wondering whether, if you died that day, you had lived your life properly.

Then, eight months in, there was a breakthrough. The doctors had concluded that I must have lymphatic cancer and I was admitted to hospital. My first reaction was a strange one. I thought: "I'm not having chemotherapy or anything like that." I felt that I had lived my life and perhaps it was my time to go. They were going to cut open my chest and take out one of my lymph nodes so they could see how far it had spread. Of course, after they had operated they realised it wasn't cancer after all. I had TB within my lymph nodes – a new strain of TB. The doctor told me that I'd made history, and then – out of the blue – began to celebrate. "I knew you were too young to die," he said. It was the first time I realised how close I was to the end.

On the one hand, I felt very confident. On the other, there was no cure. That was an eye-opener because TB is supposed to be treatable. The doctors' solution was to give me 22 antibiotics a day. In other words, to throw everything plus the kitchen sink at it. They had me on a five-year plan where we started off with 22 per day and then, after a year or so, cut down to 11.

But within eight months, I was off the antibiotics altogether. I went back into the gym. I started meditation. I ate healthily.

The doctors said they couldn't believe it: I was well again. It was

THE TRUTH ABOUT TB

* Tuberculosis, known as TB, is commonly known as a lung disease, but it can affect any part of the body. Bacteria are inhaled and can travel in the blood to other organs.

* So long as it is diagnosed quickly, TB – in any form – should be curable.

* Common symptoms include: a cough lasting for more than three weeks, unexplained weight loss, fever, night sweats, fatigue and a loss of appetite.

* Tuberculosis is less infectious than a cold but people who are in close and frequent contact with a patient are vulnerable. Infection happens when airborne droplets – usually emitted by coughing – are inhaled.

* It is extremely rare for children with TB to be infectious.

* There is a vaccine against TB called the BCG, but it does not prevent all forms of the disease and – in the UK – is offered only to those at particular risk of the illness.

a huge relief. I started to relax in my mind, and allowed myself to remember what I'd been through.

A lot has changed since then. I have changed. Just before my illness, I had joined a meditation group and, as part of that, a discussion group. We would speak about problems and how we could turn them around. Throughout my illness, I never missed a session. If I hadn't been doing that, I probably would have gone back to that illness. The counselling has kept me in balance.

I'm still teaching and training. I'm still doing the things that I was doing before. And I've been doing a lot more for TB Alert, too. Going to work has become more important – but at the same time, it's not about the money. Everything in my life has become about the amount of joy that I feel each day, about trying to have as much fun as I can. Unhappiness is like bondage.

One of the biggest emotions for me now is relief that my TB was in my lymph nodes. That is what made it non-contagious, and that's a saving grace for anyone who was around me for those eight months.

Sometimes I think to myself: "Did it really happen?" Nobody can tell me how I got it, nobody can tell me how it went and nobody can tell me if it'll come back again. Subconsciously, it sits in my mind but I don't know what to do with it. I don't know what to do with the little information I have. I certainly can't spend every day wondering if it will return. I just need to focus on living.

Interview by Alice-Azania Jarvis

The Independent, 5 April 2011

The biggest gift

A lot of us get satisfaction from passing our old clothes, books and toys on to charity shops, knowing someone else, someone who will enjoy them for years to come, will treasure them. We may pass on items that were once special – a deceased loved ones' clothing, or a trinket once treasured, now unused – knowing that they will find new life with someone else. But when it comes to the most precious thing of all, human life and the body parts we no longer need, we are far more reserved.

When a person offers their organs for transplant they could vastly improve someone's health and quality of life – or even save a life. A single donor can help several people with their various organs such as kidneys, liver, heart, lungs, small bowel and pancreas. Tissues that can be donated include the cornea (the transparent layer at the front of the eye), bone, skin, heart valves, tendons and cartilage. Like charity shop trinkets, redundant body parts can be a precious gift to someone else. And most of us actually want to help – 90% of people say they support organ donation – yet just 28% are on the NHS Organ Donor Register.

But the need is urgent – more than 10,000 people in the UK are currently waiting for a transplant. Of these, 1,000 each year – that's three a day – will die on that waiting list, as there are just not enough organs available. And the list is growing. The number of people with severe kidney disease, for example, is increasing in all western societies leading to an increase in the demand for kidney transplants. The number of deceased donor kidneys available in the UK has not really changed in the last 10 years and so the gap between patients and donors has grown.

If we needed it, we would most certainly be grateful for a donated organ – so why aren't we prepared to support this system and act on our good intentions? For many of us it may just be that we intend to join the donor register but never get round to it. For some there may be some squeamishness around the thought of our bodies being 'messed about with' – although it is often the relatives of the deceased who are more upset by this idea.

This hesitation is the reason why some organisations would like the UK to move from our system of registering – opting in – to one where we are all automatically donors unless we opt out.

The British Heart Foundation says, "Heart transplants offer the best chance of long term survival for critically ill heart failure patients. We want the organ donation system to be changed to ensure that there are more organ donors available and help save lives.

Unfortunately there is a shortage of donor hearts for use in transplants across the UK. We want to see a change in the law to an opt out system, meaning that everyone would automatically be an organ donor unless they chose not to be. This change would encourage people to talk to their families about their wishes and increase public support for organ donation".

Others, however, would argue that an opt out system gives too much control to medical institutions and worry that the rights of individuals might be ignored.

For those on the waiting lists however, any measure that increases their chance of a successful transplant would be welcome. Some even argue for payments for organs donated from living donors – though this raises another set of ethical issues.

Sources: NHS, British Heart Foundation and others

SOME ISSUES:

Do you think we should have an opt out system for organ donation?

Would you donate your organs after death?

How would you suggest we reduce the waiting list for organ donations?

See also:
Organ donation,
p98, *Fact File 2011*

Internet & media

Abuse

Protest

Images Watershed

Big Brother

Tabloids X Factor

Newspapers

Propaganda   TV

Bullying

How the internet has turned old-school bullying into a virtual hell

EVA WISEMAN

Teenage bullying is at an all-time high. Much of it, though, is not the sly pinches and whispers that were so common in my teens, the cold giggles or occasional screamy slaps; much of today's is done online. In this week's survey of American teenage boys, one in 20 admits to uploading a "humiliating" photo of their ex-girlfriend, and 10% of boys and girls have received threatening mobile messages from a romantic partner.

In the UK, the Sun reports that cyberbullying is responsible for a 50% rise in teenagers self-harming. The problem has become so rife, so huge, blanketing schools like the smoke from a factory fire, that in the US they've just coined a new phrase for it: "electronic dating violence".

Whereas bullied teens could once find refuge at home from tormenting classmates, mobile phones mean that today they're never quite alone. Instead of scrawling someone's sexual history on a bathroom wall, today fake Facebook accounts lure broadcastable confessions. Girls' webcam stripteases are uploaded to YouTube, their intimate camera phone shots emailed from school to school, engraving themselves on the internet like initials in a tree trunk, fading but never quite disappearing, lingering, herpes-like, long after the relationships that spawned them have ended in tears and scratches. The thought of all those private pictures hovering bruisily above their original owners, just out of

Whereas bullied teens could once find refuge at home from tormenting classmates, mobile phones mean that today they're never quite alone.

reach (I always think of the internet as existing a metre over our heads, like a pixellated, static-y limbo), is depressing enough – these girls' small reservoirs of trust emptying in seconds – but this week's study also suggests that electronic violence and "traditional" offline dating violence are often related.

Is it wrong to be nostalgic for the bullying of the 90s, when things were bloodier but less virtual? When bullying faded in time, rather than remaining online forever, lingering on Google like a taste, colouring a girl's life like an unbleachable stain?

The Observer, 7 November 2010
© Guardian News & Media Ltd 2010

SOME ISSUES:

Bullying is never right, but has it become worse through the internet?

Is it just girls who are victims?

How much personal information do you think you should reveal online?

Would you trust your friends or partner with pictures of you?

See also:
Click Clever, Click Safe,
p124, *Fact File 2011*

Face up to Facts,
p126, *Essential Articles 11*

Videos on this issue at:
thinkuknow.co.uk
www.ceop.police.uk
www.bullying.co.uk

There is nothing petty about abuse and threats

Paul Taylor discusses online abuse – starting with the vicious responses to beauty contestant Shanna Bukhari

I am no great fan of beauty contests. It seems a strange thing to elect any kind of 'ambassador' based chiefly upon how well the candidate fills a swimsuit.

But I don't fume at what the hard-core feminists would call the objectification of women. This is a world in which Katie Price can make an entire career out of an artificially inflated chest. In today's more complicated landscape of sexual politics, there are thousands of intelligent women just begging to be objectified.

One of them is Shanna Bukhari from Rochdale, who hopes to become the first Muslim to represent Great Britain at the Miss Universe contest later this year. When this newspaper reported Shanna's ambition a couple of weeks ago, it was as a gentle talking point – an intriguing slant on a number of cultural questions.

The spelling and syntax of many is so poor that it is obvious the writer has not even read his own words before pressing 'submit'

Shanna's family has backed her ambition, and she expressed the hope that other Muslim girls would follow her lead. This seemed the opposite of the familiar debate about whether Muslim women should preserve their modesty behind the veil.

"It is not all about appearance," Shanna said of the beauty contest. Well, actually, Shanna it IS all about appearance. But as activities involving consenting adults go, a beauty contest is, though a little cheesy, fairly innocuous.

But then the beauty debate turned ugly. Days later, Shanna was fielding 300 messages a day on her Facebook page, several of them abusive. There were fellow Muslims accusing her of denigrating the name of Islam, white supremacists denying the right of someone of Asian heritage to represent the UK and women condemning beauty pageants and accusing Shanna of betraying her gender.

Then came a veiled death threat. After Shanna closed down her Facebook page, a friend was sent internet links to images of people

SOME ISSUES:

Why are people more confident about saying things online than in real life?

Is it your right to post offensive things online?

Then came a veiled death threat... Shanna closed down her Facebook page

murdered for standing up for their principles.

Shanna likens her tormentors to those who support 'honour' killings, and believes all this says something about multiculturalism in Britain.

All of which may be true. But this welter of invective is also a good illustration of the kind of sadistic and spiteful dialogue that many now believe the internet entitles them to indulge in.

The sinister side of trolling' – posting inflammatory comments – has extended even to people mocking the recently-deceased.

A Facebook memorial page to 15-year-old Natasha MacBryde, from Bromsgrove, who died beneath a train last month after allegedly being bullied, attracted sick comments such as this one: "I caught the train to heaven LOL".

In the USA, the grieving family of an 18-year-old who had died in a car crash were emailed leaked pictures of her corpse.

These are extreme examples, but the instant nature of online conversation, and the anonymity it affords have caused a huge shift in the way we express ourselves. Many of the comments beneath stories on newspaper websites

now drip with a bile and bitterness rarely seen in the days when you had to take the time to put those thoughts on paper, stick a stamp on the envelope and walk to the postbox.

The spelling and syntax of many postings is so poor that it's obvious the writer has not even read his own words before pressing 'submit', let alone given a moment's thought as to whether he is advancing the debate, making a nuisance of himself or perhaps even worse.

Jeff Pearlman, a writer for Sports Illustrated in the USA, decided to track down some of the people who sent him sick and poisonous online comments. These people melted apologetically when challenged face to face. "The internet got the best of me," said one.

Perhaps these idiots regarded online debate like a shoot-'em-up video game – a virtual reality in which no one's feelings could actually be hurt.

But Shanna Bukhari is now left wondering whether one of those poisonous cowards will come out from behind their cloak of anonymity and make good on a threat... all because she wanted to stand before some judges looking pretty and hoping for world peace.

Manchester Evening News, 23 March 2011

Photo courtesy of MEN syndication

WHAT DO WE WANT?
DIGITAL DISRUPTION

Photo BEEE/Shutterstock.com

Digital activists now have the tools to change the world.

Expect disruption – Adrian Hon

How many people does it take to topple VISA's website – a company that can process 10,000 transactions per second? A million? Surely hundreds of thousands, at least?

Just 2,000. That's how many were needed to overwhelm VISA.com. The actual damage was relatively minimal since credit card transactions take place on a separate system, but for "Anonymous", the online collective that co-ordinated the attack, and those on PayPal and Mastercard, it was an unparalleled propaganda coup – and as word spread, with curious internet users trying to visit VISA.com, the company's servers were only strained further.

While Anonymous has been breathlessly described as a group of expert hackers, this kind of "distributed denial of service attack" (DDoS), in which thousands of computers repeatedly visit the target website is a relatively simple operation – it just requires volunteers to download and run a piece of software that does all the work. Other activists are using Twitter, Facebook, Google Maps, and weblogs – similarly simple technologies – to organise protests and flashmobs in the real world, whether they're against tuition fees, government spending cuts, Philip Green's Topshop, or The X-Factor's hegemony over the music charts.

With more and more of our lives spent online, virtual protests like those by Anonymous – who were carrying out "revenge" attacks on companies that had withdrawn support for WikiLeaks – make a correspondingly bigger impact. In the past, even a large protest by tens of thousands might struggle to make a few headlines for a single day, but now a small number of online activists can block websites and organisations used by hundreds of millions of people globally. The activists' anonymity certainly helps, given that DDoS attacks are illegal in many countries including the UK, and that targets like the Church of Scientology are well known for their swift litigation.

But would people still protest if they weren't anonymous? Perhaps not quite with the same confidence or disregard for the law, but the recent protests against tax avoidance and tuition fees were all organised out in the open using Facebook and Twitter, with activists using their real names and profiles. Even members of Anonymous were willing to put themselves on the line when they organised protests in the real world against Scientology, with most not wearing masks.

Anonymity isn't necessary or even desirable when it comes to the new wave of direct-action protests. What distinguishes them from the past is their speed and decentralisation, made possible by the widespread uptake of social networking tools like Facebook and Twitter. It's almost as if millions of people were holding their breath, waiting for the opportunity to pursue their pet cause, when the tax avoidance protests and WikiLeaks showed that you don't need to set up an office or appoint directors to create a movement – you just need a Facebook page, a Twitter hashtag, and a free blog.

SOME ISSUES:

Do you think that the internet has improved awareness of political issues?

Do you think that online protest is a good way of demonstrating?

Have you ever signed a petition online?

Are cyber attacks on businesses justified?

Anonymity isn't necessary or even desirable when it comes to the new wave of direct-action protests. What distinguishes them from the past is their speed and decentralisation, made possible by the widespread uptake of social networking tools like Facebook and Twitter.

These new online tools have traditionally served two purposes; first, to make money for their Silicon Valley creators, and second, to disintermediate a wide range of otherwise time-consuming and tricky processes, from setting up social groups (Facebook) to publishing (Twitter and blogs) and receiving payments (PayPal). That they are being used to organise highly effective direct-action protests and movements is not particularly surprising to anyone who's read a William Gibson novel, but their sheer speed and effectiveness has shocked even the most die-hard futurists.

The importance of these tools, not just to online activists but to everyone, explains why people get so upset when they don't work in the supposedly neutral way expected of them. The anger of The X-Factor audience, who suspected that their votes were being tampered with, might strike most people as being unbelievably trivial, but it speaks to the betrayal of the trust we place in organisations and institutions that purport to represent our interests.

So imagine the fury when Facebook and Twitter – darlings of the internet, both of them – removed Anonymous' profiles, and Amazon and PayPal ditched WikiLeaks. People had thought that these companies shared their ideal of the internet as being a place for unfettered free speech and commerce, whereas in fact these internet giants were only interested in free speech insofar as it didn't interfere with commerce (of course, Anonymous created replacement profiles only a few minutes later). Yesterday, we had the bizarre spectacle of Anonymous debating whether or not to attack Twitter hardly a company associated with evil; eventually, Anonymous decided that Twitter was too important as a medium of mass communication to disrupt.

Many citizens stopped believing long ago that their elected representatives actually represented them, but they expected better from their new internet leaders. Now it appears that there is no one they can trust, and so disparate groups of activists are learning from each other about how to use social networks and DDoS tools to pool their individual resources, and taking matters into their own hands. You can only imagine the bind that Twitter and Facebook are in – they need the goodwill of their users, but they don't want to upset governments, or even worse, advertisers.

Is this development good or bad? Are we about to see a revitalised citizenry exposing corruption and improving the world, or will bands of anonymous activists start shutting down critical parts of the web? It's worth noting how internet users see it themselves. A popular notion amongst them, taken from role-playing games, is that the world can be classified into moral and ethical "alignments". This system combines a moral continuum (from good to neutral to bad) with an ethical continuum (from lawful to neutral to chaotic) to create nine alignments, such as 'Lawful Good' and 'Neutral Evil'.

Whether or not they, or others, see themselves as forces for good in the world, activists act in a rapid, decentralised, and unpredictable way – in other words, they're Chaotic, not Neutral, and certainly not Lawful. That's not to say that they go around breaking laws all the time, it's more that they don't adhere to any explicit structures or rules of behaviour. Within the student protest movement, nimble grassroots organisations taking direct action, such as the UCL Occupation, have arguably made more of an impact than lumbering entities like the NUS, even as the traditional media erroneously insists on identifying movements with single figureheads.

It's even more difficult for governments to respond to this level of chaos. The short-term effect of WikiLeaks is that US diplomats will circulate markedly less candid cables to fewer people, and use the phone more often; but by doing so, they deny themselves the very technologies that allow online activists to move so quickly.

Nor can Western governments step up monitoring or begin restricting the use of social networking tools without appearing hypocritical (see the West's criticism of censorship in Iran and China) and generating a massive backlash from internet users, who might even resort to routinely encrypting private communication – a development that security services truly dread. In a way, David Cameron has got the Big Society he wants, a nation of volunteers self-organising for the pursuit of shared interests – it's just that they aren't the same as his.

By itself, technology can't do anything; its creators can't even predict the full range of uses to which it might be put to. It takes real people to demonstrate applications, and over the past few months, WikiLeaks, Anonymous, student protesters, and X-Factor activists have all shown the rest of the world exactly how to use Twitter and Facebook – familiar tools to millions – in a new way. They've shown that self-organisation is possible, it's easy, and for the most part, it goes unpunished.

Expect disruption.

The Daily Telegraph, 9 December, 2010
© Telegraph Media Group Ltd 2010

Q: When does a tabloid become crude propaganda?

A: When it starts printing it

Star Photos by secretlondon123

Photo by Gene Hunt

Charlie Brooker

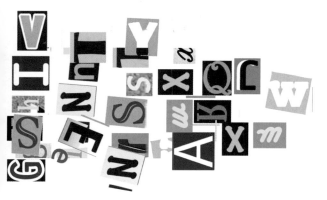

Tory chairman Baroness Warsi recently complained that Islamophobic chatter had become acceptable at dinner parties. I hate to break it to you, Baroness, but if they're saying anti-Islamic stuff while you're sitting at the table, imagine what they come out with when you nip off to the loo.

A few weeks later, David Cameron delivered his speech on multiculturalism, and Warsi's notional dinner-mates doubtless nodded in agreement, even though the very word "multiculturalism" has so many definitions it almost requires translation. It's not black and white. Which is ironic.

As a result it was possible to draw almost any conclusion from Cameron's speech, from "segregation is unhelpful" to "send 'em back". Cameron is many things – including an android, probably – but a racist he is not.

So he was doubtless dismayed that his speech went down well with the BNP's Nick Griffin, who interpreted it as a "huge leap for our ideas into the political mainstream". When I read that, my sense of hope took a huge leap into a s***-filled dustbin.

The speech was also welcomed by Tommy Robinson of the English Defence League (EDL) – and Stephen Lennon of the English Defence League. Who are both the same person, Robinson being Lennon's pseudonym. Mr Robinson-Lennon claims he's opposed only to extremist Muslims, not moderate ones, although how he hopes to tell them apart when he seems unsure of his own name is anyone's guess.

But then certain elements of the EDL seem confused by names in general. Several of them have been heard chanting "Allah, Allah, who the f*** is Allah?" If they don't know who he is, perhaps they ought to read that book they want to ban.

SOME ISSUES:

If something is printed in the newspapers, do you presume it is true?

What do you think about the headlines mentioned from newspapers like the Daily Star?

Is it right that they should print things like this?

What problems might it cause?

Does of freedom of speech, mean that anyone has the right to print anything?

The Daily Star is either grossly irresponsible in its sloppy representation of the facts, or engaging in overt anti-Muslim propaganda.

Robinson-Lennon recently appeared on Newsnight, up against Paxman. Not a classic battle of wits, but nonetheless the EDL's man came out on top: while middle-class viewers may have chortled at Robinson-Lennon's relative inarticulacy, others may have seen a member of the establishment sneering at a working-class white guy. Admittedly, Paxman sneers at everybody; he can't catch sight of his own reflection in the back of a spoon without asking who the f*** he thinks he is. But it reinforces the view that the white working classes are marginalised and looked down on by the media.

Not the entire media, mind. Some tabloids do little more but speak up for the white working classes – the Daily Star in particular. Which would be great, if the Daily Star didn't patronise its readers by repeatedly publishing lies.

Sometimes they're daft ies. Take the lie about the company behind Grand Theft Auto planning a game called Grand Theft Rothbury, inspired by the Raoul Moat saga. "We made no attempt to check the accuracy of the story before publication... We apologise for publishing a mock-up of the game cover, our own comments on the matter and soliciting critical comments from a grieving family member," read part of the paper's subsequent grovelling apology.

Sometimes they're visual lies. Take the time it Photoshopped a bald scalp and headscarf on to an image of Jade Goody in a wedding dress, to make it look as though she'd posed for the picture during chemotherapy.

Sometimes the lies appear on its front page, in a way that might alter a reader's view of Muslims. When not furiously recounting whichever grotesquely offensive stunt professional button-pushing irritant Anjem Choudary's* come up with this week – stories which are not lies – it gets worked up over other "Muslim outrages" with little or no basis in fact. Take the story "MUSLIM-ONLY PUBLIC LOOS: Council wastes YOUR money on hole-in-the-ground toilets". Weeks after that appeared, the Star admitted that "the loos may be used by non-Muslims and were paid for by the developer".

And sometimes it doesn't quite lie, but misrepresents by omission. Take the story on 8 February "WE'LL STAND UP AND FIGHT FOR BRITAIN'S BRAVE WAR HEROES", in which it is reported that "The English Defence League is planning a huge march after two Muslim councillors snubbed a British war hero given the George Cross".

It refers to an incident in Birmingham where two Respect party councillors remained seated while more than 100 other politicians gave a soldier a standing ovation. Nowhere in the article does the Star mention that there were many other Muslim councillors (Tory, LibDem and Labour) present at the same event – all of whom did stand and applaud.

In other words, the Daily Star is either grossly irresponsible in its sloppy representation of the facts, or engaging in overt anti-Muslim propaganda. Who can blame a reader who, after reading such a skewed version of events, is gripped with anti- Muslim fervour?

On the same page was a phone poll: DO YOU AGREE WITH THE EDL POLICIES? 98% of the respondents did. If I read the Star every day, and believed it, I'd join the EDL too.

Not that you have to be a dedicated reader to be exposed to its influence. Just pop into WH Smith's. There they are, those headlines, the steady drip-drip-drip: MUSLIM-ONLY LOOS and BBC PUTS MUSLIMS BEFORE YOU and MUSLIM SICKOS' MADDIE KIDNAP SHOCK (No, I haven't made that one up). Drip drip drip. Bullshit or exaggeration masquerading as fact. And to what aim?

On 9 February the Star ran a front-page headline claiming ENGLISH DEFENCE LEAGUE TO BECOME POLITICAL PARTY. Even that turned out to be dubious – their leader had merely said "we aren't ruling it out". Inside, another phone poll asked whether readers would vote for the EDL. 99% said yes.

Do they believe what they read in the Daily Star?

I believe this is a wonderful country. All of it. The people are inherently decent and fair-minded. All of them. We should resist crude attempts at division, wherever they come from. Because we deserve better. All of us.

If I read the Star every day, and believed it, I'd join the EDL too.

The Guardian, 14 February 2011
© Guardian News & Media Ltd 2011

* Anjem Choudary was the spokesman for extremist group Islam4uk before it was banned. He has praised the terrorists involved in the September 11th events and mounted demonstrations when soldiers' coffins were returned from Iraq & Afghanistan

X FACTOR SHOULD BE X-RATED...

Adrian Goldberg

After recently slating the Saturday night parade of talentless TV talent shows, I decided to give the box one more chance last weekend by tuning into the X Factor final.

I seriously wish I hadn't bothered. Here was living proof that 20 million people really can be wrong.

Three supremely average karaoke singers were battling for the right to become Simon Cowell's puppet – and it wasn't even a fair competition.

The figures show that checkout attendant Mary Byrne polled more public votes in the semi final than crybaby Cher, but was still booted out in a sing-off – making a mockery of all those who'd spent their hard earned cash phoning in.

Still, it's a free country, and if watching a bunch of mediocrities slug it out for the right to have the Christmas Number One turns you on, who am I to quibble?

What should concern all of us, I hope, is the opportunity the programme gave for the top shelf exhibitionism of Rihanna and Christina Aguilera.

Sorry to come over all Mary Whitehouse, but for a pre-watershed programme

Rihanna's gyrations wouldn't have been out of place at the Rocket Club, while Aguilera's basque and suspenders get up were straight out of the Ann Summers' catalogue.

SOME ISSUES:

Do you think performers such as Rihanna are not suitable for younger children?

Do they influence how teenagers dress and behave?

See also:
I'd Hate to be a Teenage Girl Today,
p101, *Essential Articles 13*

were straight out of the Ann Summers' catalogue.

How ironic that just a few days earlier, the government had announced plans to crack down on the sale of titillating clothing for pre-teen girls.

It's these vulnerable youngsters who provide the bedrock of the show's audience.

I'm no prude, and generally take the view that adults should be allowed to do whatever they wish as long as no one is harmed.

But kids are different.

The span of childhood is all too brief, and Cowell and Co have no right to corrupt the innocent in the chase for ratings.

Birmingham Mail, 15 December 2010

How ironic that just a few days earlier, the government had announced plans to crack down on the sale of titillating clothing for pre-teen girls

supposedly suitable for family viewing, it veered dangerously close to porno – more Sex Factor than X Factor.

Rihanna's gyrations wouldn't have been out of place at the Rocket Club, while Aguilera's basque and suspenders get up

Rihanna performing at the Brit Awards 2011

BIG BROTHER
IS WATCHING US

Adrian Goldberg

GEORGE Orwell's classic novel 1984 wasn't just a work of fiction – it was also a stark warning about the emergence of a surveillance society where civil liberties could be plundered from the people in the name of ensuring their safety.

What's remarkable is how much of the dark fantasy he created has become a daily reality in modern Britain – and with scarcely a whisper of protest.

People are locked up for weeks without trial, super injunctions ban the reporting of sensitive court cases, CCTV cameras monitor our every movement and strict rules give the police power to ban protests outside parliament.

Against this background, Birmingham City Council obviously thought there was nothing odd in encouraging schools to distribute a free software programme called Cyber Sentinel that allows parents to spy on their children's internet viewing habits.

We've all heard stories about paedophiles using social networking sites to groom youngsters. Online bullying is another baleful phenomenon of the modern age, not to mention the ease with which porn can be downloaded. Given that little lot, you could argue that only an irresponsible parent would refuse this spyware when offered the chance. Yet at least one mother makes an eloquent case against it.

ARM YOUR KIDS WITH KNOWLEDGE OF THE DANGERS SO THAT THEY CAN PROTECT THEMSELVES

Sibyl Ruth, from Kings Heath, contacted my BBC West Midlands show to argue that she would rather develop a relationship with her daughter based on trust – and that to snoop on the teenager denies her basic human right to privacy.

Sure, there are risks involved in surfing the net – but isn't it better, she says, to arm your kids with knowledge of the dangers so that they can protect themselves when you aren't around.

Like all good stories, this one clearly has two sides, but what frustrates me is the council's unwillingness to even debate the matter. They received more than £200,000 to fund the software programme from the technology quango BECTA, but won't answer questions about it in a live radio interview. Why? Surely someone at the local authority is willing to justify spending that much taxpayers' cash?

Apparently not. Big Brother may be watching you – but it seems the cat has got his tongue.

Birmingham Mail, 19 January 2011

SOME ISSUES:

Do you think this type of software is intrusive?

How do you think parents should help young people to be safe on the internet?

Do you think the council should be made to answer public questions about this?

For more information visit:
www.ceop.police.uk

Law & order

Riots
Protection
Gender Police
Forgiveness
Family Courage
Media Fear Rape
Restorative Justice
Protest

Restorative justice:

Why I forgave the man who raped me

Jo Nodding © Restorative Justice

Joanne Nodding was raped by a boy she knew...

In 2004 Jo Nodding was raped by a boy she knew. At first he didn't plead guilty to the rape, so Jo was faced with the extra stress of the trial. That changed, however, once Darren was presented with the DNA evidence and admitted his guilt. The first time Jo faced Darren was in Court when he received a life sentence.

For weeks after the rape I was in a daze trying to cope with what had happened not only to me, but also to my family. Almost a year later I had a visit from the probation Victim Liaison Officer and she mentioned the possibility of restorative justice (RJ) – of a meeting with Darren. From that time on it was always at the back of my mind. I knew as soon as she said it that I wanted to meet him because this was about me taking control of the situation, re-balancing what he had taken away from me that day. The judge had said to Darren in Court 'you have destroyed this woman's life' – but that wasn't what I wanted, and that wasn't how I saw it.

Nearly four years later, in 2009 I heard that Darren had agreed to meet me. There were lots of preparation meetings with the RJ workers over the next nine months, and some of it was emotionally exhausting, but

SOME ISSUES:

Do you think Joanne Nodding was right to see her rapist?
Do you think criminals should *have* to see their victims if the victim requests it?

Could this help the victims of different types of crimes or are some crimes unforgivable?

See also:
Police Record,
p131, *Fact File 2011* &
Crime Survey,
p140, *Fact File 2011*

I knew it was something I had to do. The meeting took place at the end of January 2010. I wasn't nervous beforehand as I had waited so long, and I'd made sure I didn't have any expectations, so I couldn't be disappointed.

When I walked in our eyes met straight away. He looked a lot older, but still looked like a child as well. I started by thanking him for agreeing to meet me as I knew it must have been a difficult thing to do. I asked why he had agreed to meet me and he said "I did something really bad and now I can do something good."

Then I went straight into telling him what it had been like for me on the day of the rape, how scared I had been and that I thought he was going to kill me. I went through every detail of the attack from start to finish. I could see the impact that I was having on him. As I told him the impact of the offence, the terror and confusion I felt that day, he actually cried. And I could see it was genuine. I could see for myself he found it really hard, but he listened to everything I had to say, and didn't try to make any excuses. He heard it from me that day, what he'd done to me, not from someone else saying how I might feel. I think if they hear it from the victim themselves they get a much better understanding.

I knew it was hard for him to listen to, so a couple of times I changed the conversation to what he was doing now and what he was hoping to do once he was released. We even had a laugh together, something which a few people have found difficult to understand.

I hadn't gone to the meeting expecting him to apologise, but towards the end he said "I'm sorry, and that's a proper sorry" – and I could see for myself he really meant it. He told me would never do anything like it again.

As the meeting was finishing I was asked if there was anything else I wanted to say, and I gave him what I've later come to think of as 'a gift'. I said to him "What I am about to say to you a lot of people would find hard to understand, but I forgive you for what you did to me Hatred just eats you up and I want you to go on and have a successful life. If you haven't already forgiven yourself, then I hope in the future you will." I didn't say it to excuse what he did, or to minimize it, but

> 66 I went through every detail of the attack from start to finish. I could see the impact that I was having on him. As I told him the impact of the offence, the terror and confusion I felt that day, he actually cried 99

> 66 I'm not a victim any more, I'm a survivor. I've been able to make sure something good has come out of something bad 99

because I wanted myself to be free of that burden of grievance, and as importantly for me, I hoped Darren could learn, move on, and forgive himself.

This had a massive impact on Darren – I could see he was shaken by the parting 'gift' I had given him. As I was leaving I wished him good luck for the future. His step mum who was there with him looked at me and just said "Thank you".

As I left that room I felt on top of the world. Meeting him gave me closure, because I had said everything I had wanted to say and I had taken back some kind of control over my life. I know it had an impact on him. I'm not a victim any more, I'm a survivor. I've been able to make sure something good has come out of something bad.

The Forgiveness Project

For further information visit:
www.restorativejustice.org.uk
theforgivenessproject.com/

JOAN SMITH: HOW ABOUT TELLING MEN, NOT WOMEN, TO STAY INDOORS?

In the wake of Joanna Yeates' murder, why is the onus placed on only one half of the population to make radical changes in their daily routine?

SOME ISSUES:

Do you feel safe being out alone after dark?

Does police advice like this keep people safe or just increase fear?

Are women more likely to be victims than men?

Should men be told to stay indoors to reduce crime?

See also:
Police Records,
p131, *Fact File 2011* &
Crime Survey,
p140, *Fact File 2011*
Fear Factor,
p131, *Fact File 2010*

Imagine the scene: thousands of students are about to return to a university city where a young woman has been brutally murdered. The police do not know where or when she died but they announce that her killer "remains at large". They call on men not to go out after dark until the killer is caught. "We ask men to go out in the evening only if their journey is really necessary, and to make sure they're accompanied by a woman," says the senior investigating officer.

Well, that's my fantasy. What the police have actually done in Bristol, where they're under huge pressure to identify the killer (or killers) of a young landscape architect, is issue an appeal to women not to walk home alone after dark. They've issued this alarming edict even though there's a glaring hole in their logic: detectives say they're "satisfied" that 25-year-old Joanna Yeates arrived at her flat in Clifton on 17 December, the night she disappeared, which suggests that home isn't a particularly safe option for local women either.

That message has been reinforced by police advice to "householders" to make sure that their premises are secure and take care when answering the door to strangers. But the specific advice to women to avoid walking home alone after dark means that the onus is once again on one half of the population to make radical changes in their daily routine. How on earth are women and girls in Bristol supposed to avoid going home alone in the dark when the sun sets at around 4.15 in the afternoon? Do Avon and Somerset police seriously expect the city's female population to observe an unofficial 16-hour curfew?

Just think of the chaos on public transport if women teachers, supermarket cashiers, office workers and indeed female police officers – there must be one or two, even if the top brass haven't noticed – rush home before it gets dark. Then there are the cleaners and bar staff whose jobs require them to work unsocial hours; some of them are bound to be students or single mothers, and unable to afford taxis home at the end of a shift.

I was going to write that it's incredible, in the 21st century, that the police are still issuing this thoughtless and insulting advice to women. Sadly, it isn't: it's easier to impose an unofficial curfew than to think about how the streets can be made safer, even if that means accepting the astonishing proposition that our cities and towns are no-go areas for women during the hours of darkness. Could there be a more damning indictment of the police in this country?

I WONDER HOW MEN WOULD FEEL IF THE ENTIRE MALE POPULATION WAS PERIODICALLY ADVISED TO STAY HOME BETWEEN DUSK AND DAWN IF THEY WANT TO AVOID BEING MURDERED?

Everyone wants more officers on the streets but they're especially needed at night when women are leaving restaurants, waiting for buses and walking home from bus stops. Last year, when I reported a spate of car crime in my street, a PC let slip that there are no routine patrols after 6pm, even though it's a popular late-night cut-through for pedestrians from one main road to another.

It isn't just girls and women who should be angry about this cavalier attitude to public safety. I wonder how men would feel if the entire male population was periodically advised to stay home between dusk and dawn if they want to avoid being murdered? Such advice is more than an imposition; it's an outrage.

It isn't a big step from telling women to stay indoors at night to questioning why we have to go out at all during the hours of darkness when a murderer is "at large". I mean, are we stupid? Guilty of "contributory

Joanna Yeates

Joanna Yeates was a 25-year-old landscape architect from Hampshire, who went missing on 17 December 2010 in Bristol after an evening out with work colleagues.

Her boyfriend Greg reported her missing when he returned to Bristol on December 19 following a weekend away visiting family in Sheffield.

Her frozen body was found on Christmas Day dumped on a verge, three miles from her home in Clifton, Bristol. She had been strangled.

Vincent Tabak, a 32-year-old Dutch engineer and neighbour of Yeates, was arrested on 20 January 2011. After two days of questioning, he was charged on 22 January 2011 with Yeates' murder.

negligence"? In Bristol, women are already telling reporters how frightened they are in their own homes, let alone on the streets; they don't know what to do and the situation has been exacerbated by confusing and contradictory messages from senior officers on the Yeates investigation. A "suspect" has been released on bail and suddenly there is talk of more than one killer; it still isn't clear whether Ms Yeates was followed home by a stranger, let someone known to her into the building where she lived, or confronted the killer inside her flat.

What's particularly distressing about this case is that the victim was a modern young woman, doing a job she loved in a vibrant city. On the night she disappeared, she did perfectly ordinary things like stopping on the way home for a pizza; if this could happen to her, it could happen to anybody.

Against this background, making local women feel even more vulnerable isn't helpful, especially when the advice they're being offered is next to useless. What's needed is the reassurance of extra patrols, police travelling on buses at night, and a much greater readiness on the part of officers to look out for and challenge men on dark streets. And if you think that's a breach of civil liberties, it's no more so than expecting half the population to stay at home after dark.

A similar edict was given in the 1970s, as the number of women murdered by the Yorkshire Ripper continued to climb. Ripper squad detectives warned women not to go out alone after dark – a fat lot of good to me, since I often had to work night shifts on a radio station in Manchester, a city where the Ripper had already killed two women. Long before Peter Sutcliffe was caught, I realised that the police were making a terrible mess of the investigation, largely because of their outdated and misogynist attitudes to women's lives.

Now senior officers in Bristol appear to be treating local women like Victorian ladies who are accustomed to needing chaperones. In 1977, women students in Leeds responded by organising the first Reclaim the Night march in this country, and similar demonstrations were soon taking place in other towns and cities. The message – that women would not be terrorised off the streets either by the Ripper or the police failing to do their job properly – was unambiguous.

I understand why the murder of Joanna Yeates has gripped the nation, and I want her killer or killers to be caught. In the meantime, local women are right to be anxious – and entitled to advice that recognises how they live and work. If Avon and Somerset police can't provide that, I hope women in Bristol will come on to the streets and once again Reclaim the Night.

The Independent, 5 January 2011

WHAT'S NEEDED IS... OFFICERS TO LOOK OUT FOR AND CHALLENGE MEN ON DARK STREETS. AND IF YOU THINK THAT'S A BREACH OF CIVIL LIBERTIES, IT'S NO MORE SO THAN EXPECTING HALF THE POPULATION TO STAY AT HOME AFTER DARK.

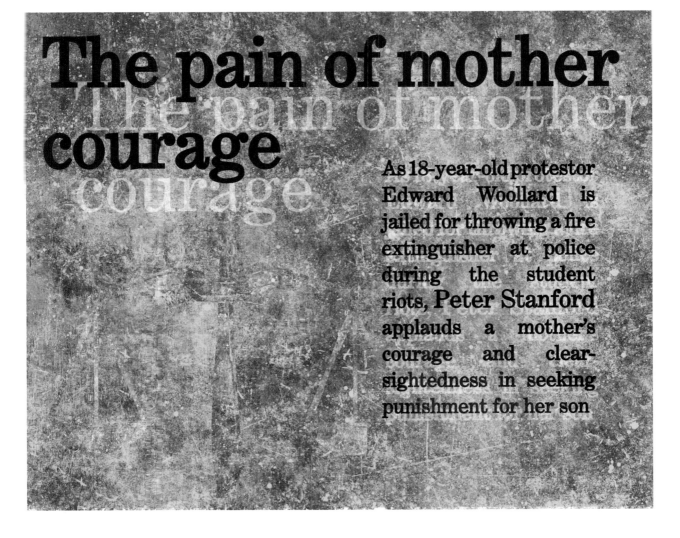

The pain of mother courage

As 18-year-old protestor Edward Woollard is jailed for throwing a fire extinguisher at police during the student riots, **Peter Stanford** applauds a mother's courage and clear-sightedness in seeking punishment for her son

SOME ISSUES:

If a member of your family broke the law, would you protect them, or seek justice?

Is there a typical law breaker?

Will this boy suffer more from his prison sentence than most offenders?

See also:
When is it right to take the law into your own hands?
p 43, *Essential Articles 13*

www.crimeandjustice.org.uk/

A parent's first instinct is to protect their child. So when there's an incident in the playground, we all pretend to be objective, give both sides a fair hearing, but nature has predisposed us to side with our offspring. Even if we think they're at least part way culpable, we seek to take the edge off any outside punishment they may face in the belief that we can put them back on the straight and narrow when we get them home.

Then children grow up and, as the adults our teenagers are constantly telling us they have become, there comes a point when they have to bear the adult consequences of their actions. But when is your boy or girl old enough to face the music?

This is the dilemma Tania Garwood has faced, albeit in a pretty extreme form. Her 18-year-old son, Edward Woollard, was

"I believe," she said before sentencing, "he deserves to be punished." And the judge applauded her for her actions

yesterday jailed for two years and eight months for violent disorder after he threw a fire extinguisher from the roof of the Conservative Party headquarters, narrowly missing a policeman during November's student protests in London. Should the mother of this apparently well-brought-up, well-spoken sixth former at the high-achieving Brockenhurst College in the New Forest – the principal has just been awarded the CBE – plead in mitigation that her boy is not your stereotypical criminal in the making, that he was really little more than a naughty boy who got carried away on what was his first demonstration, and now has more than learnt his lesson by having to attend court?

It is easy to see why she would have been tempted. By her own account, Edward is gentle, kind, caring and walks the family Labrador on the beach near their Hampshire home.

Or should Mrs Garwood accept that her son is old enough, and well-educated enough, to know that dropping a large metal object down seven floors could kill someone, that even if on this occasion it

Edward Woollard and his mother Mrs Garwood arriving at court

Picture by: Jeff Moore/Jeff Moore/Empics Entertainment

hadn't, his misdemeanour was extremely serious, and that he must therefore suffer the consequences laid out by the law for such actions? Tania Garwood chose the latter: "I believe," she said before sentencing, "he deserves to be punished." And the judge applauded her for her actions, the implication being that without them her son may have faced even longer in jail.

The current government, as well as previous administrations,

Too often mums and dads choose to believe ministers are talking about someone else's kids, not ours

have all talked at length about parental responsibility for the anti-social behaviour of their teenagers, but too often mums and dads choose to believe ministers are talking about someone else's kids, not ours. After all, we've made sacrifices to send them to good schools. We pay our taxes, keep the front garden tidy and have never claimed benefits in our life. Even if our son does suddenly choose to sport a hoodie, we refuse to imagine any circumstances in which he might end up in the criminal justice system. That is for other people's children.

To all who recognise the sentiments, Edward Woollard's case should act as a wake-up call. Like the judge, I admire his mother's clear-sightedness and courage. Moreover I hope I would follow her example if my son ended up in the same circumstances. But a part of me can still see, when challenged to reconcile my own picture of my boy — and who knows him better than me? — with evidence of involvement in a potentially fatal attack on police officers, how easy it would be to shy away and sweep it under the carpet.

Save for one thing. In the community where I grew up, there was a mother who years ago faced a similar choice. Her privileged, privately-educated 18-year-old son had become involved in a financial scam that included her among its victims.

Had she pressed charges, as the police wanted her to do, he would have faced a prison sentence, but she demurred. It was sufficient lesson to face her wrath, not the courts, she said. He wouldn't do it again.

He did, and the next time she couldn't save him from jail. He has been in and out ever since. It might have happened anyway, but he was allowed to carry on believing for longer than he should have that criminal actions were just an extension of childhood games and had no real consequences.

There are, of course, plenty of excuses for turning a blind eye to a child's law-breaking. Tania Garwood has spoken of her fears that her son's education will be damaged in prison — he was about to begin his 'A'-Level examinations when he was sentenced — and his life "ruined".

There are examples for and against that proposition. And while waiting to see how this toughest of all ways to learn a lesson will affect your child would be heart-wrenching for any parent, is the alternative any more palatable — risking raising a young adult whose bad behaviour is excused, covered up, blamed on others, until one inevitable day they do something so terrible that no amount of parental pleading can make it right?

The Daily Telegraph, 12 January 2011
© Telegraph Media Group Ltd 2011

> **There are, of course, plenty of excuses for turning a blind eye to a child's law-breaking. Tania Garwood has spoken of her fears that her son's education will be damaged in prison**

Restrain, contain –

Victoria Moore at the
Metropolitan Police
Training School

Photo: Alison Baskerville

What is it like to police a riot? Victoria Moore spent a day at the Met's training centre – and then watched officers in action during Saturday's violent protests

SOME ISSUES:

How do you think police should be trained for violent situations?

Is it fair that the police face violence at protests?

Do you think the protective clothing they wear is a help or a hindrance?

How do you think the police should behave in a protest situation if it turns violent?

The first missile thrown is obviously aimed directly at my head. I raise my arm to deflect it and it clatters hard against the shield I'm carrying, sending a jolt through my shoulder.

Looking up, I can see there are plenty more where that came from. The air is filled with flying wooden bricks – two more smash into me as I try to take in the scene – and a hundred yards ahead, I notice that a bunch of scruffy-looking blokes have supermarket trolleys filled with what look like petrol bombs.

"Dress right!" shouts the police officer standing beside me, waving to indicate to his colleagues and me that under the onslaught of bricks and jeers we've let our line of riot shields falter and need to get back into position.

I'm surprised by the violence of our aggressors – all the more so because this is an exercise at the Metropolitan Police's Public Order

Essential Articles 14 • www.carelpress.com

and duck

The reality is that all that clobber is disabling, uncomfortable and very hot

More than 250,000 people attended a march in London against public spending cuts

Photo: Lewis Whyld/PA Archive/Press Association Images

Trying to introduce a non-confrontational approach; not easy when people tend to respond to a police officer wearing a helmet and carrying a shield as if he is in full battle-dress.

Training Centre at Gravesend in Kent. A few weeks ago, I spent a day there to experience the way officers are trained to respond to situations such as Saturday's protests in central London. While praised for its broadly restrained approach, in the face of intense provocation, the Met has been criticised for failing to do more to prevent the trouble starting. But the line between controlled, effective policing and actions that can lead to accusations of heavy-handedness – or negligence – is difficult to tread.

The Met has come in for a lot of flak over its handling of protesters, and those caught up in protests, in the past few years. The inquest into the death of newspaper vendor Ian Tomlinson, who collapsed at the G20 riots in 2009 after being pushed to the ground by a policeman, began this week. And the Joint Committee on Human Rights has expressed concern over the containment – or "kettling" – of peaceful demonstrators that became a controversial feature of the student riots before Christmas.

Strategies have adapted accordingly; anyone caught in a kettle will now have a "containment officer", whose responsibility is to check that the right people are contained. Much of the new thinking is about crowd psychology: using Twitter to dispel false rumours that horses are being brought in to make a charge; and taking care not to run unless necessary, because the sight of a police officer legging it can incite enough panic to turn the mood of a crowd.

The focus is on smoothing edges and trying to introduce a non-confrontational approach; not easy when people tend to respond to a police officer wearing a helmet and carrying a shield as if he is in full battle-dress.

The reality is that all that clobber is disabling, uncomfortable and very hot. It takes three policemen 15 minutes to strap me into the leg pads, arm pads, groin guard, Kevlar-plated stab vest, heavy boots (with steel toe cap and sole, so they

instructor as we kettle some of the brick throwers towards the end of my training day, "lift up your visors and pull down your balaclavas so they can see your faces and try to

I consider myself to be reasonably fit – I ran a marathon last week – but I flunk the "shield run" fitness test that requires officers to jog 500 metres in 2m 45s while wearing this gear and carrying an unwieldy 17lb shield

can't be penetrated by broken glass), thick leather gloves, flame retardant trousers and jacket that zip together at the waist, flame retardant balaclava (added after someone ended up with what is wryly described to me as "a very cheap face peel") and helmet.

I consider myself to be reasonably fit – I ran a marathon last week – but I flunk the "shield run" fitness test that requires officers to jog 500 metres in 2m 45s while wearing this gear and carrying an unwieldy 17lb shield. I feel more clanking medieval knight than crack fighter.

Do people forget it's actually protective clothing, I ask Commander Bob Broadhurst, head of Scotland Yard's public order branch when I catch up with him in the Met's Special Operations Room in Lambeth on the morning of the TUC march. "They do. The dilemma for the commander is if they put the kit on too early it can exacerbate the situation. Too late and officers get hurt." A recent innovation is to supply officers with a baseball cap to put on as things calm down. "It's more relaxed, you can hear better, you can see better – it does seem to work," Commander Broadhurst says.

There is no dedicated force of "riot police"; just officers who all have another job but are trained to level 3 (the most basic, so they know how to set up a cordon or block off a road), 2 (they must pass the shield run test and renew their training with two days every 12 months) or 1 (these will be fitter, have more expertise and are deployed to more contentious areas).

In a fake town at Gravesend they're taught how to co-ordinate a safe advance through streets in which there's plenty of trouble, including petrol bombs exploding at our feet. "Now," shouts an

talk to them calmly and clearly, to explain what's going on."

More than the drills it's the temperamental grounding that is so important. "How to carry the shield is the smallest part of the job. We try to expose people to hostile situations so they can remain calm and controlled and rely on their knowledge and experience when they're out at work," says Sergeant Adam Nash from CO11 public order branch. "It's all about being part of the unit and taking pride in your job."

In Trafalgar Square on Saturday there was a chance to see how well these exercises would help officers to maintain composure. While paint was thrown and windows smashed on Oxford Street, the day passed fairly quietly here. But at 9.45pm, with only around 300 people left in the square, trouble suddenly flared up around the Olympic clock. "There was a pre-emptive strike from a large section of the crowd who had physically grabbed and tried to drag an officer away from his colleagues," said Chief Inspector Ian Hackett, who was in charge of the area. "There was a lot of glass thrown in Duncannon Street where they'd gone round the back of one of the restaurants and got bag-loads of recycling to use as ammunition. We had to use batons to drive the crowds back."

One activist blamed the police for starting the trouble, saying that it was caused by the attempted snatch arrest of a man suspected of damaging a shop front earlier in

We try to expose people to hostile situations so they can remain calm and controlled

Most people would be on their chin straps if they had to handle what the officers in Trafalgar Square handled at the end of an 18-hour shift

the day. Either way, scores of reinforcements in protective clothing were brought in, and ugly scenes followed, with bonfires lit and missiles thrown, before the melee eventually subsided with the activists kettled at the foot of Nelson's Column.

By this time, four or five police officers (who hadn't been wearing helmets) were in hospital with head injuries and another had a broken collar-bone. Activists in the kettle were protesting at being held and resisting arrest – which created more physical scuffles.

It was after 1am when I talked to Ciara Squires, 18, a student at Queen Mary, University of London, whose friend had just been arrested. "Look at this," she said, indicating police forming a barrier with their shields, "It's Orwellian. It's unacceptable." Others approached stoic, silent officers, thrusting their faces forward to scream, "We're doing this to protect YOUR pensions, to protect YOUR children's education."

It's true that the officers peeling protesters off Nelson's Column, either to arrest them or send them home, were having to be physical, but neither I nor the photographer saw anyone using unnecessary force, despite the frequent screeches of protest from a raggle-taggle bunch of observers. "Most people would be on their chin straps if they had to handle what the officers in Trafalgar Square handled at the end of an 18-hour shift," says Adam Nash when I discuss it with him later.

"The challenge for us is about finding the balance," Commander Bob Broadhurst had told me that morning. Back then he had been defending charges of the heavy-handed use of containment to maintain order. But at the end of a long day, as criticism began that the police had not been proactive enough, he must have been reflecting that you're damned if you do and damned if you don't.

The Daily Telegraph, 28 March 2011
© Telegraph Media Group Ltd 2011

Religion

Conversion
Acceptance
Homophobia Media
Christianity
Britain Islam
Persecution
Ground Zero
Superstition

'Ground Zero mosque'? The reality is less provocative

Millions of Americans are furious about the 'Ground Zero mosque'. But it doesn't exist – Charlie Brooker

Things seem awfully heated in America right now; so heated you could probably toast a marshmallow by jabbing it on a stick and holding it toward the Atlantic. Millions are hopping mad over the news that a bunch of triumphalist Muslim extremists are about to build a "victory mosque" slap bang in the middle of Ground Zero.

The planned "ultra-mosque" will be a staggering 5,600ft tall – more than five times higher than the tallest building on Earth – and will be capped with an immense dome of highly-polished solid gold, carefully positioned to bounce sunlight directly toward the pavement, where it will blind pedestrians and fry small dogs. The main structure will be delimited by 600 minarets, each shaped like an upraised middle finger, and housing a powerful amplifier: when synchronised, their combined sonic might will be capable of relaying the muezzin's call to prayer at such deafening volume, it will be clearly audible in the Afghan mountains, where thousands of terrorists are poised to celebrate by running around with scarves over their faces, firing AK-47s into the sky and yelling whatever the foreign word for "victory" is.

I'm exaggerating. But I'm only exaggerating a tad more than some of the professional exaggerators who initially raised objections to the "Ground Zero mosque". They keep calling it the "Ground Zero mosque", incidentally, because it's a catchy title that paints a powerful image – specifically, the image of a mosque at Ground Zero.

When I heard about it – in passing, in a soundbite – I figured it was a US example of the sort of inanely confrontational fantasy scheme Anjem Choudary* might issue a press release

SOME ISSUES:

Why do you think people were outraged by the proposal?

Are the media responsible for people's responses?

Photo: Swoan Parker/AP/Press Association Images

For one thing, it's not at Ground Zero. Also, it isn't a mosque.

about if he fancied winding up the tabloids for the 900th time this year. I was wrong. The "Ground Zero mosque" is a genuine proposal, but it's slightly less provocative than its critics' nickname makes it sound. For one thing, it's not at Ground Zero. Also, it isn't a mosque.

Wait, it gets duller. It's not being built by extremists either. Cordoba House, as it's known, is a proposed Islamic cultural centre, which, in addition to a prayer room, will include a basketball court, restaurant, and swimming pool. Its aim is to improve inter-faith relations. It'll probably also have comfy chairs and people who smile at you when you walk in, the monsters.

To get to the Cordoba Centre from Ground Zero, you'd have to walk in the opposite direction for two blocks, before turning a corner and walking a bit more. The journey should take roughly two minutes, or possibly slightly longer if you're heading an angry mob who can't hear your directions over the sound of their own enraged bellowing.

Perhaps spatial reality functions differently on the other side of the Atlantic, but here in London, something that is "two minutes' walk and round a corner" from something else isn't actually "in" the

same place at all. I once had a poo in a pub about two minutes' walk from Buckingham Palace. I was not subsequently arrested and charged with crapping directly onto the Queen's pillow. That's how "distance" works in Britain. It's also how distance works in America, of course, but some people are currently pretending it doesn't, for daft political ends.

New York being a densely populated city, there are lots of other buildings and businesses within two blocks of Ground Zero, including a McDonald's and a Burger King, neither of which has yet been accused of serving milkshakes and fries on hallowed ground. Regardless, for the opponents of Cordoba House, two blocks is too close, period. Frustratingly, they haven't produced a map pinpointing precisely how close is OK.

That's literally all I'd ask them in an interview. I'd stand there pointing at a map of the city. Would it be offensive here? What about here? Or how about way over there? And when they finally picked a suitable spot, I'd ask them to draw it on the map, sketching out roughly how big it should be, and how many windows it's allowed to have. Then I'd hand them a colour swatch and ask them to decide on a colour for the lobby carpet. And the conversation would continue in this vein

New York City firefighters and journalists stand near the area known as Ground Zero after the collapse of the Twin Towers September 11, 2001 in New York City *Photo: Anthony Correia / Shutterstock.com*

According to a recent poll, one in five Americans believe

Barack Obama is a Muslim, even though he isn't

until everyone in the room was in tears. Myself included.

That hasn't happened. Instead, 70% of Americans are opposed to the "Ground Zero mosque", doubtless in many cases because they've been led to believe it literally is a mosque at Ground Zero. And if not . . . well, it must be something significant. Otherwise why would all these pundits be so angry about it? And why would anyone in the media listen to them with a straight face?

According to a recent poll, one in five Americans believes Barack Obama is a Muslim, even though he isn't. A quarter of those who believe he's a Muslim also claimed he talks about his faith too much. Americans aren't dumb. Clearly these particular Americans have either gone insane or been seriously misled. Where are they getting their information?

Sixty per cent said they learned it from the media. Which means it's time for the media to give up.

Seriously, broadcasters, journalists: just give up now. Because either you're making things worse, or no one's paying attention anyway. May as well knock back a few Jagermeisters, unplug the autocue, and just sit there dumbly repeating whichever reality-warping meme the far right wants to go viral this week. What's that? Obama is Gargamel and he's killing all the Smurfs? Sod it. Whatever. Roll titles.

The Guardian, 23 August 2010
© Guardian News & Media Ltd 2010

* Anjem Choudary was the spokesman for extremist group Islam4uk before it was banned.
He has praised the terrorists involved in the September 11th events and mounted demonstrations when soldiers' coffins were returned from Iraq & Afghanistan.

THESE B&B OWNERS HAVE BEEN PUNISHED FOR BEING FAITHFUL TO CHRISTIAN TEACHING

Christian hotelier Hazelmary Bull, whose husband Peter could not appear due to ill health, reads a statement to the media outside Bristol County Court after a judge ruled that she and her husband acted unlawfully when they refused a gay couple a double room at their hotel.
Photo: Ben Birchall/PA Wire/Press Association Images

Where is the tolerance for which our country was once celebrated?

FRANCIS PHILLIPS

SOME ISSUES:

What do you think should happen when religious beliefs are in conflict with the law?

Should religious beliefs be tolerated when they are not tolerant beliefs?

What do you think about the way the hoteliers have been treated?

What do you think about the way they treated the gay couple?

See also:

Fostering Prejudice, p82
Gay UK?,
p30, *Fact File 2011* &
Religious matters,
p34, *Fact File 2011*

Everyone now knows about the case of Peter and Hazelmary Bull, the Christian couple whose home in the Cornish village of Marazion is also run as a B&B. Refusing to give a double bedroom to civil partners Steven Preddy and Martin Hall, they fell foul of the Sexual Equality Act, were ordered to pay £3,600 compensation by the judge and now risk losing their business (and their home).

Coincidentally, the Gospel text for yesterday's Mass was the Sermon on the Mount: "Blessed are you when people abuse and persecute you…" Just now the Bulls are probably not feeling very "blessed"; they have been punished, purely and simply, for being faithful to Christian teaching. They are not "homophobic" (whatever that means); they are not child abusers. They simply adhere to ancient Christian belief that sex is meant for marriage. Indeed, they treat unmarried heterosexuals wanting a bed for the night in the same way as they treated Preddy and Hall.

Some would argue that what goes on in the bedroom is nobody's business but its occupants and that 'we mustn't judge'

The judge told them that times had changed and that the law had moved on. An article in Saturday's Telegraph by Judith Woods went further: she referred to their "hardline stance", 'their bizarre 1950s house rules" and described them as "narrow-minded, eccentric, singularly lacking in business nous in their batty rejection of modern mores, gay and straight". All this gratuitously unpleasant mockery is directed at an unassuming, courageous couple who want to stick with beliefs that were held as right by common consensus for many centuries in this country – until very recently.

Some would argue that what goes on in the bedroom is nobody's business but its occupants and that "we mustn't judge". But for Christians marriage is a solemn sacrament and has public repercussions; the double bed symbolises the lifelong union of the man and woman and their openness to the children that might come from the consummation in that bed. So if you are Christians running a B&B there will be an important symbolic as well as practical distinction between twin beds and double beds. Others, probably those who have directed hate mail at

them, would argue that the Bulls should shut up shop and good riddance to their "hardline", "narrow-minded", "batty" values. But where is the true tolerance here for which this country was once celebrated? When you read of cases like the Bulls, or that of the Christian registrar who lost her job, or the Christian foster parents rejected by their local social services, you might reasonably think that an anti-Christian ideology is at work.

It so happens that I know a Catholic couple who run a B&B from their own home, like the Bulls. Like the Bulls they offer double bedrooms to married couples only; others are offered twin or single rooms. Like the Bulls they have reminders of their faith on the walls of their house: in their case it is crucifixes and pictures

The judge told them that times had changed and that the law had moved on

of Our Lady and the Sacred Heart. Judith Woods, although a "church-goer" (whatever that means), wrote in her article that the Christian reminders at Chymorvah, the Bull's B&B, made her "want to run a mile". But for the Bulls and this Catholic couple you don't separate your faith from your life. It isn't something you display on Sunday mornings for an hour of "church-going"; it informs your thinking and your actions every day of the week.

The difference between the Bulls and the Catholic couple is that the latter stopped advertising their B&B several years ago, fearing the very scenario that has now overwhelmed the Bulls. They simply rely on word of mouth recommendations from guests who have stayed with them and enjoyed the experience. Will this discreet filter system also come up against the Sexual Equality Act?

Why cannot this same law recognise the rights of conscience, similar to that in the Abortion Act, which allows an opt-out clause for doctors and nurses who will not take part in abortions?

Catholic Herald, 31 January 2011

Persecution? These Christian hoteliers have no idea

By Ben Summerskill, Chief Executive of the Lesbian, Gay and Bi-sexual charity Stonewall

The ruling against Christian hoteliers who turned away a gay couple sends an important message on equality

Within the past three weeks, dozens of Christians have been murdered in acts of organised violence in Iraq, Egypt and Nigeria. In Pakistan, Sudan and Indonesia hundreds of thousands more live in fear.

They might all have something to say about the fatuous suggestion that two British hotel owners, Peter and Hazelmary Bull, are also being "persecuted" for their faith. Last month, the Bulls' right to turn gay people away from their hotel was challenged. Thankfully, Bristol county court has found that the couple acted unlawfully.

If the Bulls had a sense of humour, something they don't seem God-blessed with, they might have spotted the irony of spending the Christmas season fighting for the entitlement to turn guests away from their inn.

During passage of the 2006 Equality Act, Stonewall fought hard to secure pioneering "goods and services" protections for lesbian and gay people, protecting them for the first time against discrimination in the delivery of public and commercial services. The preceding legal entitlement to deny gay people a service was every bit as offensive as the notorious signs outside guesthouses that once said: "No blacks. No Irish." And people certainly took advantage of it, as lesbians denied smear tests and gay men refused holiday bookings were well aware.

The Bulls suggest that it's their freedom, and not that of a gay couple, that is compromised by the existing law. But no part of the current and carefully calibrated compact in Britain's equality

SOME ISSUES:

Is it right or wrong to follow your religion even if it discriminates against others?

Why is it wrong to discriminate against people because of their sexuality?

See also:
Fostering Prejudice, p82
Gay UK, p30 &
Religious Matters, p34,
Fact File 2011

www.stonewall.org.uk

Civil partners, Steven Preddy and Martin Hall, were refused a double bed at a Bed & Breakfast belonging to a Christian couple

Steven Preddy (left) and Martin Hall Photo: Ben Birchall/PA Wire/Press Association Images

To deny gay people a service was every bit as offensive as the notorious signs outside guesthouses that once said: "No blacks. No Irish"

legislation forces anyone to do anything. However, if a couple choose to turn their home into a commercial enterprise, why should they be any more entitled to exempt themselves from equality legislation than from health and safety laws?

No one should take progress towards a more equal Britain for granted. (It was the leading Lib Dem peer Shirley Williams, after all, who moved a Lords amendment last spring that would have entitled adoption agencies to refuse to place gay teenagers.) But the coalition

government has, happily, thus far suggested that it's alive to the danger of compromising when it comes to intolerance.

If you allow businesses or public services to turn away gay people at will on trumped-up grounds of principle, as the Bulls would wish, then our public services will soon have to deal with the Jewish registrar with an ethical objection to marrying out, or a Muslim nurse who doesn't wish to care for an unmarried mother. So the really important message from Bristol county court is simply that the appropriate "balance of rights" for modern Britain is one that keeps private prejudice out of the public space.

The Bulls' shadowy supporter, the Christian Legal Centre, suggests it may turn to the law again. If so, it might reflect that, for the estimated £30,000 this court

case has cost it, Oxfam or Save the Children could have vaccinated 100,000 people against meningitis in sub-Saharan Africa. Now that would have been a genuinely Christian way to spend its money.

The Guardian, 18 January 2011
© Guardian News & Media Ltd 2011

For the estimated £30,000 this court case has cost it, Oxfam or Save the Children could have vaccinated 100,000 people against meningitis in sub-Saharan Africa. Now that would have been a genuinely Christian way to spend its money

Photo: Jon smith 'una nos lucror'

The Islamification of Britain: record numbers embrace Muslim faith

The number of Britons converting to Islam has doubled in 10 years. Why? *Jerome Taylor* and *Sarah Morrison* investigate

SOME ISSUES:

Why do you think people change religions?

What do you think the appeal of Islam is to people?

See also:
Muslim population,
p180, Fact File 2011
Why the burka is part of Britain,
p26, *Essential Articles 13*
They are right to ban the burka, even if it is for the wrong reasons,
p29, *Essential Articles 13*

The number of Britons choosing to become Muslims has nearly doubled in the past decade, according to one of the most comprehensive attempts to estimate how many people have embraced Islam.

Following the global spread of violent Islamism, British Muslims have faced more scrutiny, criticism and analysis than any other religious community. Yet, despite the often negative portrayal of Islam, thousands of Britons are adopting the religion every year.

Estimating the number of converts living in Britain has always been difficult because census data does not differentiate between whether a religious person has adopted a new faith or was born into it. Previous estimates have placed the number of Muslim converts in the UK at between 14,000 and 25,000.

But a new study by the inter-faith think-tank Faith Matters suggests the real figure could be as high as 100,000, with as many as 5,000 new conversions nationwide each year.

By using data from the Scottish 2001 census – the only survey to ask respondents what their religion was at birth as well as at the time of the survey – researchers broke down what proportion of Muslim converts there were by ethnicity and then extrapolated the figures for Britain as a whole.

In all they estimated that there were 50,699 converts living in Britain in 2001. With no new census planned until next year, researchers polled mosques in London to try to calculate how many conversions take place a year. The results gave a figure of 1,400 conversions in the capital in the past 12 months which, when extrapolated nationwide, would mean approximately 5,200 people adopting Islam every year. The figures are comparable with studies in Germany and France which found that there were around 4,000 conversions a year.

Fiyaz Mughal, director of Faith Matters, admitted that coming up with a reliable estimate of the number of converts to Islam was notoriously difficult. "This report is the best intellectual 'guestimate' using census numbers, local authority data and polling from mosques," he said. "Either way few people doubt that the number adopting Islam in the UK has risen dramatically in the past 10 years."

Asked why people were converting in such large numbers he replied: "I think there is definitely a relationship between conversions being on the increase and the prominence of Islam in the public domain. People are interested in finding out what Islam is all about and when they do that they go in different directions. Most shrug their shoulders and return to their lives but some will inevitably end up liking what they discover and will convert."

Batool al-Toma, an Irish born convert to Islam of 25 years who works at the Islamic Foundation and runs the New Muslims Project, one of the earliest groups set up specifically to help converts, said she believed the new figures were "a little on the high side".

"My guess would be the real figure is somewhere in between previous estimates, which were too low, and this latest one," she said. "I definitely think there has been a noticeable increase in the number of converts in recent years. The media often tries to pinpoint specifics but the reasons are as varied as the converts themselves."

Inayat Bunglawala, founder of Muslims4UK, which promotes active Muslim engagement in British society, said the figures were "not implausible".

"It would mean that around one in 600 Britons is a convert to the faith," he said. "Islam is a missionary religion and many Muslim organisations and particularly university students' Islamic societies have active outreach programmes designed to remove popular misconceptions about the faith."

The report by Faith Matters also studied the way converts were portrayed by the media and found that while 32 per cent of articles on Islam published since 2001 were linked to terrorism or extremism, the figure jumped to 62 per cent with converts.

Earlier this month, for example, it was reported that two converts to Islam who used the noms de guerre Abu Bakr and Mansoor Ahmed were killed in a CIA drone strike in an area of Pakistan with a strong al-Qa'ida presence.

"Converts who become extremists or terrorists are, of course, a legitimate story," said Mr Mughal. "But my worry is that the saturation of such stories risks equating all Muslim converts with being some sort of problem when the vast majority are not". Catherine Heseltine, a 31-year-old convert to Islam, made history earlier this year when she became the first female convert to be elected the head of a British Muslim organisation – the Muslim Public Affairs Committee. "Among certain sections of society, there is a deep mistrust of converts," she said. "There's a feeling that the one thing worse than a Muslim is a convert because they're perceived as going over the other side. Overall, though, I think conversions arouse more curiosity than hostility."

Photo: Funkdooby

How to become a Muslim

Islam is one of the easiest religions to convert to. Technically, all a person needs to do is recite the Shahada, the formal declaration of faith, which states: "There is no God but Allah and Mohamed is his Prophet." A single honest recitation is all that is needed to become a Muslim, but most converts choose to do so in front of at least two witnesses, one being an imam.

Converts to Islam:

Hana Tajima, 23, fashion designer. Hana Tajima converted to Islam when she was 17. Frustrated by the lack of variety in Islamic clothing for converts she founded Maysaa, a fashion house that designs western-inspired clothing that conforms to hijab.

"It's true that I never decided to convert to Islam, nor was there a defining moment where I realised I wanted to be Muslim. My family aren't particularly religious. I was interested in religion, but very uninterested in how it related to my life. I grew up in rural Devon where my Japanese father was the ethnic diversity of the village. It wasn't until I studied at college that I met people

> **I was pretty popular, had good friends, boyfriends, I had everything I was supposed to have, but still I felt like 'is that it?'**

who weren't of the exact same background, into Jeff Buckley, underground hip-hop, drinking, and getting high. I met and became friends with a few Muslims in college, and was slightly affronted and curious at their lack of wanting to go out to clubs or socialise in that sense. I think it was just the shock of it, like, how can you not want to go out, in this day and age.

"It was at about that time that I started to study philosophy, and without sounding too much like I dyed my hair black and wore my fringe in front of my face, I began to get confused about my life. I was pretty popular, had good friends, boyfriends, I had everything I was supposed to have, but still I felt like 'is that it?' So these things all happened simultaneously, I read more about religion, learned more about friends of other backgrounds, had a quarter life crisis. There were things that drew me to Islam in particular, it wasn't like I was reaching for whatever was there. The fact that the Qur'an is the same now as it ever was means there's always a reference point. The issues of women's rights were shockingly contemporary. The more I read, the more I found myself agreeing with the ideas behind it and I could see why Islam coloured the lives of my Muslim friends. It made sense, really, I didn't and still don't want to be Muslim, but there came a point where I couldn't say that I wasn't Muslim.

"Telling my family was the easy part. I knew they'd be happy as long as I was happy, and they could see that it was an incredibly positive thing. My friends went one of two ways, met with a lack of any reaction and lost to the social scene, or interested and supportive. More the former, less the latter."

Paul Martin, 27. Paul Martin was just a student when he decided to convert to Islam in an ice-cream shop in Manchester four years ago. Bored of what he saw as the hedonistic lifestyle of many of his friends at university and attracted to what he calls "Islam's emphasis on seeking knowledge," he says a one-off meeting with an older Muslim changed his life.

"I liked the way the Muslims students I knew conducted themselves. It's nice to think about people having one partner for life and not doing anything harmful to their body. I just preferred the Islamic lifestyle and from there I looked into the Qur'an. I was amazed to see Islam's big emphasis on science.

"Then I was introduced by a Muslim friend to a doctor who was a few years older than me. We went for a coffee and then a few weeks later for an ice cream. It was there that I said I would like to be a Muslim. I made my shahada right there, in the ice cream shop. I know some people like to be all formal and do it in a mosque, but for me religion is not a physical thing, it is what is in your heart.

"I hadn't been to a mosque before I became a Muslim. Sometimes it can be bit daunting, I mean I don't really fit into this criteria of a Muslim person. But there is nothing to say you can't be a British Muslim who wears jeans and a shirt and a jacket. Now in my mosque in Leeds, many different languages are spoken and there are lots of converts.

"With my family, it was gradual. I didn't just come home and say

... was a Muslim. There was a long process before I converted where I wouldn't eat pork and I wouldn't drink. Now, we still have Sunday dinner together, we just buy a joint of lamb that is halal.

"If someone at college had said to me 'You are going to be a Muslim', I would not in a million years have believed it. It would have been too far-fetched. But now I have just come back from Hajj - the pilgrimage Muslims make to Mecca."

> Islam has bought peace, stability, and comfort to my life. It has helped me identify just what is important to me.

Stuart Mee, 46. Stuart Mee is a divorced civil servant who describes himself as a "middle-of-the-road Muslim." Having converted to Islam last year after talking with Muslim colleagues at work, he says Islam offers him a sense of community he feels is missing in much of Britain today.

"Everything is so consumer-driven here, there are always adverts pushing you to buy the next thing. I knew there must be something longer term and always admired the sense of contentment within my colleagues' lives, their sense of peace and calmness. It was just one of those things that happened - we talked, I read books and I related to it.

"I emailed the Imam at London Central Mosque and effectively had a 15 minute interview with him. It was about making sure that this was the right thing for me, that I was doing it at the right time. He wanted to make sure I was committed. It is a life changing decision.

"It is surprisingly easy, the process of converting. You do your shahada, which is the declaration of your faith. You say that in front of two witnesses and then you think, 'What do I do next?' I went to an Islamic bookstore and bought a child's book on how to pray. I followed that because, in Islamic terms, I was basically one month old.

"I went to a local mosque in Reading and expected someone to stop me say, 'Are you a Muslim?' but it didn't happen. It was just automatic acceptance. You can have all the trappings of being a Muslim - the beard and the bits and pieces that go with it, but Islam spreads over such a wide area and people have different styles, clothes and approaches to life.

"Provided I am working within Islamic values, I see no need in changing my name and I don't have any intention of doing it. Islam has bought peace, stability, and comfort to my life. It has helped me identify just what is important to me. That can only be a good thing."

The Independent, 4 January 2011

SUPERSTITION: MY COMFORT IN CREDULITY

Whether it's magpies or horoscopes, of my many bad habits this is the hardest to shake

Morven Crumlish

SOME ISSUES:

Do you have any superstitions?

Do you believe them?

Are they similar to religious beliefs?

What is the difference between religion and superstition?

See also:
Touch wood,
p30, *Fact File 2009*

When I moved into this house in spring, the tree outside the kitchen window was heavy with blossom. During the summer, the leaves shivered with shrieking birds every time my cat stalked through the garden, but now the summer has long gone and I can see two fat magpies sitting in the bare branches.

One for sorrow, two for joy: I am irrationally relieved that the magpies make a pair, and I see them as some attempt at comfort, though I know they are after my teaspoons,

perhaps my eyeballs. If there are two of them it is merely because there is not one, or three, or seven – they are not a sign, a gift, a premonition; they are simply sharply dressed birds of dubious character.

I know that a single magpie does not predict the future, that walking under a ladder will not send me on a path to ruin, that killing a spider won't leave me penniless, and that breaking a mirror has never resulted in seven years of luck noticeably worse than any other period;

yet all these superstitions rise as effortlessly to the surface of my consciousness as any dogma.

They say that if you don't believe in God you don't believe in nothing – you believe in everything I try not to conform to this stereotype of the gullible atheist and yet can't stop myself from turning to my horoscopes every time I pick up a magazine, or a free paper on the bus. Even as I read that Leo should attend to family matters, or her travel plans are well starred I know that it is nonsense – even if the stars aren't slapped together during a tea-break, but are compiled by a true believer, I know that they are designed for the weak-willed and unhappy. After all, if your choices were so easy you wouldn't be clutching at these semi-relevant straws of comfort; you'd be spending all the money or having all the sex (what horoscopes mainly deal in, after all); not reading the Metro on the top deck.

My rational brain never wins the argument. I look for signs, for patterns, for inanimate backup for decisions – I once got back together with a boyfriend because three sets of lights changed to green as I approached. It didn't end well. I should have learned, but I find superstitions harder to shake than any other bad habit; they lurk, unwanted, even untended, in the very back of my mind, dormant until a moment of weakness, when their tendrils of false certainty creep around my doubts and sorrows, imitating design and purpose.

A friend of mine died recently. There was no warning sign, no premonition. It was sudden, shocking, and inexplicable – though explained in the simplest of medical terms. There could be no reason for this death. It could not make anything better, it made no sense.

As we wondered where to put this new fact in our lives I envied those people who have God, who can believe that there is some kind of plan, or that there is something useful up ahead.

All that can be made sense of is what has already been. My memories of my friend are not monumental or filled with drama; but I don't have to try too hard to remember the stories that made me laugh, or hear him laughing along. There's no point at all to his being taken away so rudely – nobody benefits, we are all just left to make the most of the past, and to remember the empty place in the world where he should still be.

The pair of glossy magpies in their tuxedos still sit in the tree. The rhythm of the nursery rhyme is a repetitive comfort. One for sorrow, two for joy. I cling to my credulity, and I turn away from the window before one of them flies away.

The Guardian, 27 December 2010
© Guardian News & Media Ltd 2010

I KNOW THAT A SINGLE MAGPIE DOES NOT PREDICT THE FUTURE, THAT WALKING UNDER A LADDER WILL NOT SEND ME ON A PATH TO RUIN... YET ALL THESE SUPERSTITIONS RISE AS EFFORTLESSLY TO THE SURFACE OF MY CONSCIOUSNESS AS ANY DOGMA

Sport & leisure

Money Clubs
Participation Cricket
Football Teams
Spectators
Energy Olympics
Fun Sexuality

16

Stumble at the starting block

WORLD RECORD BREAKER RICHARD WHITEHEAD IS TOLD HE CANNOT COMPETE IN THE PARALYMPIC MARATHON, DESPITE BEING ONE OF THE WORLD'S BEST PARALYMPIC RUNNERS.

Is there any world-class athlete who is equally capable of competing in the Olympic sprints as in the marathon? Even record breaking Usain Bolt claims to have had enough after 400 metres. Yet Richard Whitehead can do just that.

The double leg amputee is already a 200m world champion in his category T42 – leg amputees. Whitehead's personal marathon best, of 2hrs 42min 52sec, has convinced most of the world that he is more than capable of competing in the Olympic marathon too but the International Paralympic Committee (IPC) disagree. Instead of being bowled over with Whitehead's wide-ranging running ability, the IPC have said he cannot compete in the 2012 Olympics.

The reason being that there is only one marathon event in the Paralympics and it is for category T46 – arm amputees – only. Whitehead – whose personal best time is inside the top 10 world rankings for T46 athletes – is desperate to have a chance to compete against T46 runners, even though there is a clear disadvantage in competing against athletes who have both lower limbs.

He said "My twin goals are to be able to compete in the race and inspire others by demonstrating that being a double leg amputee is no reason to be held back."

Despite his plea, however, the IPC, although sympathetic, have larger areas of concern as they suffer from the pressure to make the 2012 Paralympics as appealing as possible to sponsors and spectators. One thing they are doing to make the event more appealing, is trying to simplify the categories and people's understanding of them.

The way paralympians are divided into groups for the competition has long been a source of confusion and dispute. There are currently 200 different medal events in the track and field Paralympic world. The IPC argues that combining classifications would further complicate things for the public they are trying to attract to the games.

So, regardless of his skill, Whitehead cannot even get off the starting block. Expressing his disappointment, Whitehead said, "While I fully understand that logistically the IPC cannot run a separate event for every discipline, the simple fact that a race already exists, and I am being denied entry for no other reason than it has not happened before, is sickening."

The IPC has said it will consider the possibility of a leg amputee marathon category in 2016 – should there be enough world-class runners at that level – but for now the numbers do not add up. Whitehead has said "As the current World Record holder in my class for the full and half marathons, I am staggered that the opportunity to inspire leg amputees is looking increasingly unlikely due to the inflexibility of the IPC.

Sources: Various

SOME ISSUES:

Do you think Richard Whitehead should be able to compete against arm amputee runners?

Should they create an event just so that Richard can compete?

Do you think the IPC's decision is right or wrong?

Photo: Andrew Matthews/PA Archive/Press Association Images

The secret of sport comes in revealing the child within

By Simon Kuper

"Why do people love sport so much?" a woman I know burst out in exasperation recently. It is a question I have often asked myself in eight years of writing this column. Now – in my last sports column before I move on to write a general column – I can reveal the answer.

There is no mystery about why people play sport. It is fun. It releases endorphins that make you happy. It keeps you thin. It can even keep you alive. But why watch other people play sport – and worse, why argue afterwards about how they played? Why is the Super Bowl the most watched American television programme? Why was the recent, tedious World Cup final the most watched programme in history?

You could adduce many reasons. Arthur Hopcraft, in his 1968 classic, The Football Man, said that sporting genius was the one kind of genius the common man could comprehend. It takes a certain education to appreciate Joyce, but almost anyone can enjoy Lionel Messi. Supporting a team can also unite you with others. When the Red Sox win the World Series and half of Boston goes crazy, people are sharing something with their neighbours and passers-by.

That's a rare pleasure. But to say that some follow sport because others do is a circular argument. Why, this woman was asking, do we follow it in the first place?

What I have learnt these eight years – and it isn't much – is that being a sports fan allows you to return to childhood. Like most ideas, this is best summed up by a Peanuts cartoon. Charlie Brown and Peppermint Patty are lying under a tree

SOME ISSUES:

Why do you think sport is popular?

How does sport make you feel?

Do you prefer watching or taking part in sport?

Do you think sport is unimportant?

talking. He is telling her what security is: you're a kid, you've been somewhere with your parents. and now it's night and they're driving you home. "They're doing all the worrying," he tells her. "You can sleep in the backseat, and you don't have to worry about anything."

"That's real neat!" exclaims Patty. But there's a catch, warns Charlie Brown. "Suddenly, you're grown up and it can never be that way again. It's over – and you don't get to sleep in the backseat any more." "Hold my hand, Chuck!!" says Patty.

For many adults their one escape from worry is being a sports fan. Watching sport, you can become eight years old again. You have returned to the backseat. You cannot control who wins. And at bottom, you know it doesn't matter. The emotions are largely play. You curse the TV if your team loses. but then life resumes. When England fail in the World Cup people don't jump off tower blocks. They just go to work.

Watching sport connects you with your eight-year-old self in another way, too. When you grow up, almost everything around you changes. People age, move to different cities, divorce and die. Only sports teams barely change. The Red Sox and Liverpool were around when we were kids, and will be there when we are old. They give continuity.

It is no wonder fans often think like eight-year-olds. Many treat athletes as two-dimensional figures: "hero", "Judas", "cheat"

For many adults, their one escape from worry is being a sports fan. Watching sport, you can become eight years old again

It is no wonder fans often think like eight-year-olds. Many treat athletes as two-dimensional figures: "hero", "Judas", "cheat". Tiger Woods was a demigod. But I was in Toronto when he got into trouble and I remember opening a serious Canadian newspaper that spent pages trying to fathom the mystery: how was it possible that a handsome young billionaire had slept around?

Sports fans seldom get to peek behind the curtain to see the real people on stage. Over years of interviewing great athletes, I've made a discovery: they are just like us, only better at sport. They are good at their work, but they do see it as work rather than some magical mystery tour. That is why the word they use to describe themselves is "pro". And all they do is give us a brief release from care. I hope that is a good enough reason to have spent eight years writing about something that does not otherwise matter.

Financial Times
25 September 2010

Time to come out to play?

In 2011, for a sportsman to disclose his sexuality shouldn't be news - but cricketer Steven Davies made headlines when he revealed that he was gay. The England wicketkeeper, is only the third professional British sportsman to come out of the closet since the first, Justin Fashanu, in 1990. The second, Welsh rugby player Gareth Thomas, found his bravery in coming out was rewarded by a warm reception in that most macho of sports.

The reactions encountered by Davies and Thomas were almost entirely supportive but Fashanu's experience, back in 1990, was completely different. He was the UK's first £1m black player, but suffered abuse and rejection after he revealed that he was gay. His career and his life went downhill - not solely because of the pressures brought about by his revelation, but there is no doubt they added significantly to his decline. He committed suicide in 1998.

In contrast, Thomas received great support from his family, colleagues and coaches, as well as from fans. He spoke very movingly on the Ellen de Generes show in the US and elsewhere about the burden that had been lifted and about

SOME ISSUES:

Why do you think it is difficult for gay sports people to reveal their sexuality?

If most people are accepting of homosexuality in sport, what prevents footballers in particular from revealing their sexuality?

Do you think this will change over time?

See: http://youtube/X3OnU_hNVrA

Photo: Mike Egerton/EMPICS Sport

the warm glow of support. But he also admitted that he only found the courage to make his decision at the end of his career, saying he 'could never have come out without first establishing myself and earning respect as a player'. He had certainly done that - having played for his country more than 100 times. Yet this muscular 16 stone, 6ft 3in rugby hero still needed to muster all his courage to make his announcement

Steven Davies, however, is at the other end of his career. He is not an established member of the national side and potentially might have put his future at risk f reaction had been different. He says, 'I have to play my best for Surrey and get back in the England side. I want to be remembered as a good cricketer not a gay cricketer.' Despite that assertion he hopes his example will be of use to others: 'Gareth Thomas' story helped me. It showed me it can be done. He was brave enough to stand up and say who he was. If I can help anyone else like he helped me, that would be great.' The fact that he felt confident enough to make a statement at this early stage of his sporting life suggests that attitudes have changed significantly.

So.. if it is now possible in cricket and in rugby, why are there no openly gay players in the top ranks of our national game? Ellis Cashmore, Professor of Culture, Media and Sport, and Jamie Cleland, Senior Lecturer in Sociology at Staffordshire University conducted an online poll of fans' attitudes through the Topfan website. The conclusions of the first phase of their report are shown in the green box.

It would seem that the fans are not the problem but that there may be issues within the football hierarchy and the media.

When Fifa last year awarded the 2022 World Cup to Qatar, where homosexuality is illegal, president Sepp Blatter joked that gay fans 'should refrain from any sexual activities' if travelling there.

This brought a strong response from John Amaechi, the former NBA basketball star who revealed he was gay in 2007: 'It's not just his reaction but the fact that an entire room of sports reporters thought this something worth laughing about,' Amaechi said. 'He is football. This is football's

SUMMARY OF RESULTS FROM TOPFAN PHASE 1

- 93% of fans think there is no place for homophobia in football
- 7% think that football is no place for gays
- 60% want gay players to 'be brave' and come out, but ...
- 40% don't think gay players should be forced to come out, mainly because it's a private matter and straight players don't have to declare their sexual preferences
- More than 90% think the only thing that matters in football is how the player plays ... not his sexual preferences
- More than 80% think Max Clifford, who said football is stuck in the 'dark ages' is part of the problem not the solution
- More than 60% disagree with Gordon Taylor's 'cowardly' decision not to support an anti-homophobia campaign
- Fans believe gay players choose not to come out to protect their commercial value, not because they fear the reaction of fans or team mates
- Many fans see parallels between black players in the 1970s/80s and gay players today
- 3,500 fans, players, managers, coaches and referees have participated in the research, which continues at www.topfan.co.uk

'He is football. This is football's attitude. This man, who giggles like a six-year-old when asked a perfectly reasonable question'

attitude. This man, who giggles like a six-year-old when asked a perfectly reasonable question. This is yet another case where the epic, archaic, neanderthal ignorance of someone who wields the power to summon kings, princes, presidents and prime ministers uses that power not to foster positive change but to further entrench bigotry.'

In 2009, Max Clifford claimed he advised two gay Premiership players to stay in the closet because football was 'in the dark ages, steeped in homophobia'. Last year, Gordon Taylor, head of the Professional Footballers' Association, casually remarked that homophobia was not high on the Premiership's agenda after no footballers would front the FA's anti-homophobia video campaign. As can be seen from the survey results, fans very largely opposed these attitudes.

Max Clifford claimed he advised two gay Premiership players to stay in the closet because football was 'in the dark ages, steeped in homophobia'

As Professor Cashmore points out: 'There was a very strong argument from the fans about performance on the field of play. As far as they're concerned, this is the only thing that matters. If a footballer plays well, that's the only thing that counts. Fans blame the media for keeping gay players in the closet, so to speak. Many think the response of personnel at the club would probably be supportive, though by no means all fans thought other players would accept gay team mates. Some thought other players would turn sharply against them. Some thought managers would transfer them.'

Apart from the media response, the fear of ruining lucrative advertising deals might be another reason why footballers hesitate to reveal their homosexuality. Professor Cashmore again: 'One fan put it bluntly when he said players don't want to risk their 'brand' by declaring their sexual preferences. It's a powerful argument, but it opens up a question: would it actually hurt a professional footballer if it were known that he was gay?'

The question remains open. Recently one young footballer did come out as gay: Anton Hysén, the son of former Liverpool defender and Swedish international Glenn Hysén. Although he is part of a footballing dynasty, he is currently only playing in the fourth tier of Swedish football and working in the local Volvo factory to support himself. No more illustrious players have taken the opportunity to imitate him. As Hysén says, 'Where the hell are all the others? No one is coming out.'

Sources: Topfan and others
www.topfan.co.uk

War & conflict

Safety
Afghanistan
Objection
Awol Family
Child soldiers
Prison Support
Mental health
Danger Battles

Soldier Boys - and Girls

Child. Soldier. Two simple words that don't belong together yet describe the lives of a quarter of a million youngsters. Often hidden from the public eye, children are fighting in wars that are tearing their own lives and communities apart. Taken from their homes and communities, these children are victims but also commit appalling atrocities.

How do children become involved?

The Coalition to Stop the use of Child Soldiers has reported that whenever armed conflict breaks out children will almost inevitably become involved as soldiers. It is extremely difficult to obtain their release and the best hope for them is that peace can somehow be established.

These children are often kidnapped and forced to become soldiers - a tactic most notoriously used by the Lords Resistance Army, a rebel force, in Uganda. There have been raids on schools resulting in mass kidnappings. Sometimes a community might be forced to provide a certain number of children as soldiers in order to be safe from attack. For some children and their parents, who are living in extreme poverty, life in the army or rebel group might seem the only alternative to starvation.

Schools can also be used to brainwash youngsters or to identify likely recruits. The Coalition to Stop the use of Child Soldiers has reports of schools in Southern Thailand training children from age 6 so that later on there will be a supply of teenage soldiers.

In some rare cases children make an active decision to join armed groups either for reasons of political or religious belief or to avenge the death of family members.

SOME ISSUES:

What effects would being involved in combat have on children?

Why do you think this is happening in these countries?

What should be done to help the children?

How can we stop this happening?

For more information go to:
www.warchild.org.uk

This image is taken in Gbadolite, northern Democratic Republic of Congo. The rebel MLC forces kidnapped and conscripted many child soldiers. War Child responded to negotiate the release of these child combatants, actually dragging them off the aircraft that were bound for conflict. Working to support their demobilization and providing education and skills training, War Child has since been able to reintegrate hundreds of de-mobilised child soldiers with their families.
© War Child

Why children?

It seems strange to say that children make great soldiers but from the point of view of the adults using them they are ideal 'cannon fodder' An army of child soldiers is cheap to pay, costs less to feed, can be adaptable and is expendable!

It is much easier to brainwash a child than an adult into believing in a cause. In some cases the children were persuaded that they had nothing to fear because they were protected by magic. Since children have less understanding of the dangers of war it is easier to use them recklessly in dangerous circumstances - sending them directly into the line of fire, for instance. As they are small and quick they make good scouts and lookouts. And of course in developing countries a high proportion of the population is under eighteen - giving a ready supply of recruits, however unwilling

"Child soldiers are ideal because they don't complain, they don't expect to be paid, and if you tell them to kill, they kill."
Senior officer in the Chadian National Army

How are they used?

Because they are small and easily replaced children are often sent into battle first as scouts or as decoys or to draw the enemy's fire. But many children are also used as porters, cooks and spies. Girls are often forced to become 'wives' of the male commanders and often bear their children or are used for sex by other soldiers.

And there are reports across the world of children being used in other ways - as suicide bombers in Afghanistan, as human shields in Israel and the Occupied Palestinian Territories, to lay mines in Colombia and to transport weapons and fight police, and to fight alongside armed gangs against the police in Haiti.

And after the conflict?

It is very difficult to regain freedom once a child has become a soldier. Even those who can escape from the fighting groups are not free to return to their normal lives. They are often injured, some have become dependent on drugs (often a way of conditioning them as soldiers) almost all are mentally scarred. Because they have seen and taken part in extreme violence from an early age many of these child soldiers have become 'desensitised' - their reactions are not the same as ordinary people. They may also have forgotten or never learned about normal life. Often they cannot return to their families and communities. As part of their recruitment they may have been forced to kill a family member or neighbour to make sure that they could never go back.

For girls in particular the chances of returning to their former lives are very slim. Girls are included in fighting forces in combat and non-combat roles but are also victims of sexual slavery, rape and other forms of sexual violence. The programmes set up to bring the youngsters back into normal life tend to focus on the boys but girl soldiers have extra problems. When there are negotiations to rescue or exchange child soldiers the girls may not be included as they are still useful to the armed groups even in times of truce. Girls who are released may be suffering from physical and mental injuries, as a result of rape, for which there is no specialist care. Young mothers with babies from their time in the rebel groups may not be accepted by their families or communities. Because of the stigma attached to sexual activity (forced or not) many girls will try to avoid being identified as soldiers and therefore will not come forward for help.

While the international community and charities such as War Child try to intervene on behalf of child soldiers every situation is different and complex. After years of misuse and exploitation the children are often left with poor health, no education, no work and no hope. Some simply return to the rebel groups as they have no other way of feeding themselves.

Sources: Various

Voices of child soldiers

JOSEPH'S STORY – UGANDA

"I was forced to kill other children who tried to escape.

Most of us had nothing to escape to anyway – when the LRA rebels came to our village they killed my Mum and Dad right in front of me.

'We're your parents now' they told me.

They abducted virtually all the kids from my school and we spent the next 9 years in the rebel army.

The rebels took my family and my childhood. I'm determined that they won't take away my chance of an education.

Now I'm 19 and War Child are helping me go back to school. I won't ever forget what happened – but now I feel proud that I can help give something back to my community."

Photo credit: Pierre Holtz | UNICEF CAR | hdptcar.net

Name and image altered to protect identity

Uganda

"Sometimes in the bush, the rebels would beat us without mercy whether you made a mistake or not. We would also be made to carry heavy loads on our heads for long distances and made to assemble out in the cold each day as early as 5am."

Boy age 15, previously abducted by the Lord's Resistance Army (LRA)

Uganda

"I feel pain from the rape, as if I have wounds inside, and I am afraid to have a disease. I would like to get tested but there is nobody to help me. I was tested in the reception centre in Gulu, but I was never told the result. The doctor said that it is better not to know the result."

Girl age 17, previously abducted by the LRA

Myanmar (Burma)

"They filled the forms and asked my age, and when I said 16, I was slapped and he said, 'You are 18. Answer 18' He asked me again and I said, 'But that's my true age'. The sergeant asked, 'Then why did you enlist in the army?' I said, 'Against my will. I was captured.' He said, 'Okay, keep your mouth shut then,' and he filled in the form. I just wanted to go back home and I told them, but they refused. I said, 'Then please just let me make one phone call,' but they refused that too."

Maung Zaw Oo, describing the second time he was forced into the Tatmadaw Kyi (army)

Nepal

"They [the army] took us to the barracks. They beat us both with their guns and boots. After 15 days my friend died from the beatings. They beat me repeatedly. Once I was beaten unconscious and taken to the hospital. When I regained consciousness I was taken back to the barracks and beaten again. I nearly died. I don't know why they beat me."

Ram, recruited in 2004 by the Maoists when he was 14 years old describes his capture by the Royal Nepal Army one year later

Liberia

"I was living in Foya when government troops entered. I stayed with them from 1999-2003 when I was captured with other small girls. There were eight of us altogether. We were all used by this one commander who would rape all of the eight girls. Now I have stomach problems. I am told that I have an infection but when I take medicine I don't really feel better. I am still not all right fully."

Faith, now 18, was 13 when captured by government troops

I WENT TO PRISON FOR GOING AWOL

ABSENT **W**ITH **O**UT **L**EAVE

I was 22 when I joined the army.

It was always an ambition and I believed the army was a force for good, helping developing nations become more stable. I wanted to be involved in that.

My first operation was Afghanistan in 2006. I'd never even been on a plane before, so everything felt new and exciting. We all wanted to get out there and prove ourselves.

We were logistics specialists based in Kandahar, working with combat supplies. I remember one evening a rocket whistled overhead and hit. We came rushing out of our tent, and could see civilians lying on the ground. I was torn – I wanted to help, but we weren't allowed to leave our fortified camping area. Later, we dealt with the aftermath of the Nimrod air crash, where faulty equipment caused the deaths of 14 people. I remember seeing all those coffins laid out and thinking, what a pointless waste of life.

On tour, you try to shove feelings of doubt to one side. But one day a comrade said, "Why are we here?" and the question hung around. Nobody seemed to know. I suppose all young soldiers are naive. The culture of the army is obedience, and you believe your government has your best interests at heart. But when I returned home after seven months, I was determined not to be blind any more. I read about the

I RAISED MY OBJECTIONS WITH MY COMMANDER AND TOLD HIM I DIDN'T AGREE WITH THE WAR. HE CALLED ME A COWARD

history of the conflict and began to realise I had been duped. This wasn't a war about liberation, it was about strategic influence; about economics and mineral wealth.

At the same time I started experiencing nightmares and anxiety caused by PTSD (post-traumatic stress disorder). I started drinking to get to sleep. I told the army, but I didn't feel I was offered proper support. At least I knew I wouldn't be going back to Afghanistan. I was protected by "harmony" guidelines – the 18-month gap between tours. I decided to keep everything to myself and get on with my job, then sign off when I could.

But after seven months, I was told I had to go back. I raised my objections with my commander and told him I didn't agree with the war. He called me a coward and said, "You're a soldier, you go where you're told." By that time, we were on build-up

SOME ISSUES:

Should soldiers have an opinion, or just obey orders?

Once someone has joined the army, should they be forced to fight if she/he does not agree with a war?

'THIS WASN'T A WAR ABOUT LIBERATION, IT WAS ABOUT STRATEGIC INFLUENCE; ABOUT ECONOMICS AND MINERAL WEALTH'

training to go on tour, so I faced a stark choice. I booked a cheap flight to Bangkok and left.

My plan was to spend a month there, get some space and come home, but I fell apart. I started drinking and taking drugs, and drifted around As a before ending up in Australia. It was there I met my wife and began to get myself back together. Eventually I called the awol hotline in the UK. I'd been gone for a year and a half. It was such a relief to talk after being silent for so long. Six months later we flew home.

In the end, I spent nine months in Colchester Military Corrective Training Centre. I had massive support inside. I remember this big, scary commando coming over. I thought, uh-oh. He said, "You're that guy, aren't you? Good egg, good lad."

It was tense and strange going back to the army base The next day, I was charged with going awol and put back in my old job. I didn't want to tell my colleagues what had happened, but when the army raised the charge to desertion – which can carry a sentence of up to 10 years – I decided to make a stand. I spoke to the papers, and in front of 500 people at a Stop the War meeting. The army were shocked. They just kept promising me I'd go to prison.

The sentencing took nine months, and in the meantime I built up a case with my lawyers on the legality of the conflict. It was clear the army didn't want a public examination because, all of a sudden, the charges for desertion were dropped.

What happened to me isn't unusual: 11,000 have gone awol since 2003, but the army keep it quiet. The public needs to know because they're paying for courts martial and military prisons. They need to know why people are refusing to fight.

I've found a real passion for antagonising the state, and I'm going to keep at it. I'm off to university to study International Relations with Peace and Conflict studies. After everything that's happened, I still love the army. I'll miss the banter and the culture. And I'm proud of myself for joining up in the first place. I wanted to improve things, and went out to Afghanistan for all the right reasons. It's a shame these conflicts are being fought for all the wrong ones.

By Joe Glenton, as told to Becky Barnicoat

The Guardian, 14 August 2010
© Guardian News & Media Ltd 2010

Wider world

War
Pakistan Flood
Haiti Earthquake
Media China
Japan Work Marriage
South Africa

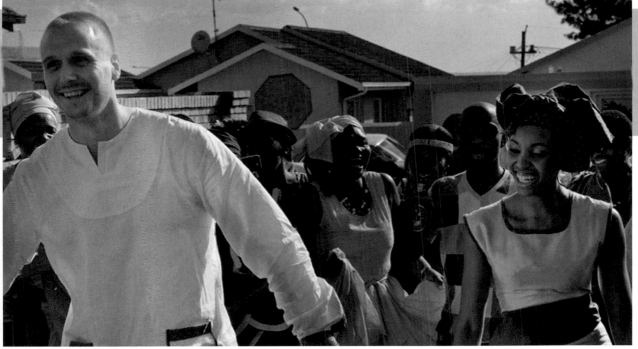

Photo courtesy of Stuart Phillips

GETTING MARRIED THE SOUTH AFRICAN WAY

Christian Parkinson, BBC News, Soweto

SOME ISSUES:

Are the customs discussed in this article charming or demeaning?

Would you follow customs out of respect, or challenge them if you didn't think they were respectful to women?

I'm sitting in my car, in a quiet side-street in Soweto, fidgeting. Beside me, my friend Mpho is telling lame jokes to try to ease the tension. Outside, I can see a long row of bungalows. Each with individually designed steel gates and brightly painted walls. There are BMWs and Mercedes parked on neat driveways.

These days most of Soweto feels like a cosy suburb. A far cry from the anti-apartheid street-battles of the 1970s and 80s. My mobile phone buzzes. It's a text from Bra Gugu. He's one of my key negotiators. "It's sorted," he says. I feel a surge of relief, and adrenalin.

Then Gugu and the team appear at the gate. And behind them, the tall, slim figure of Kutlwano – the woman I've just paid for. According to local custom, we are now man and wife.

AFRICAN WAY

Here in South Africa they call it lobola or bohali. But the tradition of paying a dowry of cattle for your wife is practised across Africa. When I first met Kutlwano, two years ago, the tradition

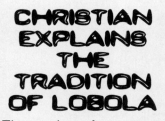

CHRISTIAN EXPLAINS THE TRADITION OF LOBOLA

The paying of money or cattle to the family of the bride is a common cultural practice across Africa and some parts of Asia. The tradition varies between different ethnic groups and the rules and subtleties can be bewildering to an outsider. In South Africa it is often described by the Zulu word Lobola. Some people see it as a way to compensate the family of the bride for losing their daughter to another family, while others regard it as a way to thank the bride's parents for raising her so well and allowing the groom to take her hand in marriage. All though agree that it is an honourable custom that unites and binds two families together.

struck me as archaic and somehow demeaning to women. But I've seen how important it is here and how seriously it's taken.

When I realised that I'd finally met the woman I wanted to marry, I knew I had to do things the African way - and hopefully earn the respect of Kutlwano's family. Bohali isn't a simple procedure. It is a long, elaborate process with many rules - each depending on the tribe and inclinations of the families involved.

My first duty was to write a letter to Kuts' father, informing him that my family intended to pay a visit. But the letter was supposed to be written in the Sesotho language - by my mother, who's English and doesn't speak a word of the language. Initially, Kuts' father wasn't inclined to compromise on this. But eventually he agreed that my mother could send him an e-mail, in English.

She let him know that she would appoint a team of South Africans to negotiate on her behalf. I turned to a friend, Bra Dan, who is from the same tribe as Kuts' family. He's a smart operator and good with people. I also asked a fellow cameraman, Gugu, and two other close colleagues, Ezra and Connie - all from different tribes.

PREMIUM PRICE

As for Kutlwano, she was excited but also worried that her family would expect too high a price for her. She is educated, beautiful and doesn't have any children. All of which puts her at a premium. And people here tend to assume that white foreigners are rich. (I'm certainly not.)

When I realised that I'd finally met the woman I wanted to marry, I knew I had to do things the African way - and hopefully earn the respect of Kutlwano's family

Kutlwano spoke in private to her mother. Word came back that we shouldn't worry. The price would be fair, and not based on my nationality. Back home in Leicester, mixed-race couples are not a big deal. Here in South Africa they are still very rare.

People often stare at us if we hold hands in public, though mostly they're just intrigued. When we're out shopping, young black women will approach Kutlwano and ask, in a whisper - how can they meet a white guy too? Apparently we have a reputation for being devoted and taking care of those we love. Race is still a complicated issue in South Africa. But I've found most people very open and welcoming.

Photo courtesy of Stuart Phillips

'WORTH EVERY COW'

Finally, a date was set for our negotiations. Outside Kutlwano's home, her family deliberately kept my team waiting for a good half hour. A traditional tactic. Eventually, they went inside without me. Bottles of whisky were exchanged, and the cash value of a cow agreed upon. Even in modern, urban South Africa, the cow remains the unit of negotiation. Then the bidding started.

It's considered bad form in South Africa to talk openly about how much you paid for a wife. Let's just say it cost me a herd. And it was worth every cow. But that's not the end of the wedding ceremony.

Twelve weeks later, I'm back on the same street in Soweto. This time I'm wearing a traditional lampshade-shaped Sotho hat, an off-white linen suit and brown sandals. Not my usual style. I'm dancing, clumsily, down the road - my entourage singing Sotho songs and laughing at my footwork. The whole neighbourhood is out in force, singing and shouting encouragement.

I reach Kutlwano's home, and push my way through the wall of people surrounding her, pulling her away from her family, and into mine, completing the ritual. The women ululate and the men grin and sip their potent home brew - Mqombothi.

It's a true township welcome. And suddenly I feel very at home.

BBC Radio 4, From Our Own Correspondent,
22 January 2011

Reporter's Dilemma:

'Elation and unease' at helping Pakistan flood child

When covering disasters, reporters can face the ethical question of whether they should help, or remain detached. When is it right for a journalist to help a weak and possibly dying baby? Jill McGivering was faced with this dilemma when reporting on the flooding in Pakistan which affected about 20 million people

Jill McGivering, BBC News, Sukkur, Pakistan

SOME ISSUES:

What do you think is a reporter's role in a crisis situation?

Is it right for someone to receive treatment just because a reporter has taken on their cause?

What effects might it have on events if a reporter gets personally involved?

See also:
Displaced by disaster,
p178, *Fact File 2011*

Sometimes the scale of a tragedy is so vast, it is hard to comprehend. Eight million people in Pakistan are homeless and hungry. Sometimes it takes just one to make it all seem real. That is how I felt in Sukkur 10 days ago. Overwhelmed.

People were flowing into the city at a ferocious pace, a ragged river of humanity, with shocked faces and frightened eyes.

They were fleeing on trucks, donkey carts, bicycles and on foot, clutching whatever was precious - electric fans, bedding, pots and pans, chickens and goats. Behind them, a great sinister mass of floodwater was pouring in.

Tiny scrap

Sukkur itself was overflowing with families, along the roadside, on river banks, on every patch of open ground. The heat was unbearable but they had no shelter.

When our car pulled up, they ran to it, flattened their faces against the windows, begged for food, for water, for help.

When I got out and started to record interviews, people pressed round. Then, in all the noise and heat and smell, someone told me about a baby, born by the roadside, and led me off to see.

She was a tiny scrap, silent and still amid the clamour.

She was lying motionless on her back, on a small mat under a tree. Flies were thick round her face. The passing traffic was just feet away. Her skin was almost translucent, her head smaller than my palm, balanced in a faded china saucer, propped up against a stone. Her eyes were closed and lifeless.

I thought at first that she was dead. Her young mother seemed vacant with shock. She had had a difficult birth, there on the road, with no-one to help. Now she sat beside her baby, looking dazed. The baby was not feeding, she said. She had not seen a doctor. She did not know where to find one.

I went down the road to a chaotic emergency clinic and interviewed a doctor there who promised to go and help. Then I went back to the hotel to work on a different report.

Metaphor for suffering

The following day, I was busy chasing more stories, but on the way back to the hotel in the early evening, I stopped off at the roadside, with some trepidation.

It seemed very likely that the baby would not have survived. But she had. She was weak, but whimpering now and trying to move. The doctor had visited and whatever he had done seemed to have made all the difference. Her mother had just named her Samina. Suddenly she had a name and a hold on life.

That evening I was elated. In all that misery and heat and exhaustion, I felt boosted by the thought I had helped someone, perhaps even played a part in saving a life. It eased my sense of guilt and helplessness.

The report I filed on baby Samina met with a tremendous response. Suddenly she seemed to be a metaphor for the general suffering. I was contacted by friends and colleagues and complete strangers.

An international agency got in touch, offering to help the family. Baby Samina was becoming, unwittingly, a poster girl for the floods.

In some ways, that is wonderful. But it also made me feel very uncomfortable. I see my job as to bear witness in a tragedy and to report - but not to interfere. I had urged that doctor to treat baby Samina.

He may have saved her, but was it at the expense of another patient? Is it unethical to attract resources to one family, when millions of others may be equally deserving?

Hope and disappointment

This week I went back to Sukkur to do a second report on Samina. Her family has a tent inside a camp now - tent number 59 - with a supply of food and clean water.

Samina seems stronger. She is lying on a pile of embroidered cushions, instead of the ground, wriggling and yawning. Her mother's health, too, seems much better. The family's future is still uncertain, but the immediate crisis is past.

Maybe I should stop there, with a happy ending that makes us all feel hopeful, but as I walked away from Samina's family, someone tugged at my sleeve. She led me to a tent nearby where another young woman had just given birth, a day or two earlier. Her relatives lifted a cover to show a tiny, wrinkled newborn.

The women turned to me, eager and expectant, as if they were thinking now this foreigner will help our child too. They looked disappointed when all I could do was to say thank you, congratulate them and then turn to leave.

BBC Radio 4, From Our Own Correspondent,
4 September 2010

Photo courtesy of Jill McGivering

Is it unethical to attract resources to one family, when millions of others may be equally deserving?

Jill McGivering is also the author of *The Last Kestrel* and *Far From My Father's House* published by Harper Collins

PRIDE AND PURPOSE

A massive 9.0 earthquake and tsunami hit Japan on 11 March 2011

The earthquake triggered a tsunami which washed away a warehouse and vehicles and left a road covered with a mountain of debris in Ishinomaki Fishing Port, March 31, 2011. The ferocious tsunami, spawned by one of the largest earthquakes ever recorded, slammed Japan's eastern coasts. The second photo shows the road of the Ishinomaki Fishing Port seen cleared and utility poles set up nearly three months after the 11 March earthquake and tsunami 5 June, 2011 (The Yomiuri Shimbun via AP Images)

A sea coast is filled with destroyed houses and debris at Ishinomaki, Miyagi prefecture, northeastern Japan, on 12 March, 2011, one day after the devastating earthquake and tsunami hit the area with the houses and debris. The second photograph shows the area cleared as photographed on 3 June, 2011 (AP/Press Association Images)

The latest calculation of the devastation suggests that there have been 15,372 deaths and there are 7,724 people still missing – a total loss of 23,096 inhabitants of the regions affected.

114,000 buildings were destroyed, 91,000 partially destroyed and 391,000 damaged, with still more to count. 80% of the 380 hospitals in Iwate, Miyagi and Fukushima prefectures were completely or partially destroyed.

Despite the size of the disaster, Japan has begun to rebuild and recover. The fact that it is a developed and relatively wealthy country has undoubtedly helped, but there is also something in Japanese attitudes and culture which makes the country very resilient. For example, a recent opinion poll showed that despite worries about the economy, most Japanese believe that their country will be left stronger, not weaker, after this disaster.

Sources: http://earthquake-report.com & Japan Times

SOME ISSUES:

Why do you think Japan was so well organised when it came to recovering from the devastation?

How does this compare to other disasters, in Haiti, for example?

Do you think Britain would recover as quickly?

See also:

Haiti: One year on... p184

Haiti then...

People, carrying scavenged goods, run away from the police in Port-au-Prince, Friday, 15 January 2010, just days after the earthquake.

(AP Photo/Ramon Espinosa)

Haiti: One year on, the scars of the earthquake have scarcely begun to heal

The fires are no longer burning, but precious little else has changed. These new pictures, and others from almost a year ago, lay bare just how slowly Haiti is recovering from the worst natural disaster in modern history

SOME ISSUES:

Why do you think Haiti is still so badly affected by the disaster?

Who do you think should take control of the situation?

Why do you think a lot of the aid has still not reached the country?

See also:

Pride & Purpose, p182
Displaced by disaster,
p178, *Fact File 2011*
Haiti: I want to go back,
p188, *Essential Articles 13*

By Guy Adams

At 4.53pm today, 12 January 2011, the Western world's poorest nation will pause to mark the anniversary of the moment when it was rocked by an earthquake measuring 7.0 on the Richter scale, which killed 200,000-300,000 people and made roughly one in four of its citizens homeless.

A minute's silence will be observed, across Port-au-Prince, the capital city, where 800,000 victims are still living in makeshift tents, and where 3,651 more people have died in recent months, after cholera hit their dangerously-crowded encampments. Thousands of white balloons will be released into the sky.

... and now

Marie La Jesula Joseph prays at a Cathedral destroyed by the earthquake in Port-au-Prince, Haiti, Sunday, 30 January, 2011, over a year since the earthquake struck.

(AP Photo/Rodrigo Abd)

In the city centre, large crowds are expected to celebrate Mass in the ruins of the Catholic cathedral

In the city centre, large crowds are expected to celebrate Mass in the ruins of the Catholic cathedral, which became a symbol of the destruction when it was photographed last January. Like most of Haiti's demolished buildings, it has yet to be rebuilt. On the outskirts of town, Haiti's political leaders gathered yesterday to pay their respects at one of the mass graves where bodies of victims were taken in bulldozers and dumped in the weeks that followed the disaster.

It marked a rare cessation of hostilities. The country, which has suffered generations of political instability, was recently forced to delay a presidential run-off election scheduled for 16 January after supporters of the eliminated candidate Michel Martelly, a popular singer, alleged widespread fraud in the first round of voting, which took place in November.

Until their complaints can be investigated, Haiti remains in a state of legislative limbo. Officially, the country is under the command of René Préval, the widely-criticised incumbent President. In practice, it is controlled by the United Nations, whose troops have lately been forced to quell occasional riots.

On almost every street, long lines of locals can still be found waiting for basic supplies. Although aid agencies have been able to provide food, medicine and other bare essentials, they have made little impact on unemployment. The economy remains almost totally reliant on overseas aid.

There are occasional signs of progress. Rubble has been cleared from Port-au-Prince's pot-holed major roads, and demolished buildings are slowly

Joel Met, 24, takes a shower using a public water tap in Port-au-Prince, Haiti, Monday, 24 January, 2011. A little more than a year since the devastating earthquake more than 800,000 Haitians still live in displaced camps, according to the United Nations.
(AP Photo/Rodrigo Abd)

Huge sums of money, in some cases more than half of all last year's donations, are still sitting in bank accounts. They claim, in their defence, to be reluctant to throw money at a dysfunctional economy, where fraud is rife and financial oversight non-existent

being loaded into dumper trucks and removed. The number of people in camps has fallen from a million and a half in the immediate aftermath of the disaster to roughly half that figure today.

But it will be some time before rebuilding can commence. Reconstruction efforts are complicated by the fact that many legal records, including most of the country's property deeds, were destroyed. One in five civil servants also perished.

Overseas governments and charities have meanwhile been criticised for spending only a small portion of the billions of dollars which were pledged to Haiti in the aftermath of the disaster. Huge sums of money, in some cases more than half of all last year's donations, are still sitting in bank accounts. They claim, in their defence, to be reluctant to throw money at a dysfunctional economy, where fraud is rife and financial oversight non-existent. But without bold action, many Haitians look at growing political turmoil and the threat of cholera, and fear that 2011 could be an even grimmer year than 2010.

The Independent, 12 January 2011

iSlave

Jenny Chan explores life and death at one of China's most successful companies.

While getting ready to start work on the production lines, management ask: 'How are you?' Workers must respond by shouting: 'Good! Very good! Very, very good!'

SOME ISSUES:

What do you think about the working conditions described here?

Should this be legal?

Do companies have a responsibility to make sure their goods are produced in a decent environment for workers?

What about consumers? Do they have a responsibility?

Would this affect what products you buy?

Last year a startling 18 Chinese migrant workers attempted suicide at Foxconn production facilities located in Guangdong, Jiangsu and Hebei Provinces. Fourteen died, while four survived with critical injuries. All were between 17 and 25 years old. Why did they, in the prime of youth, give up on their lives?

In 2010, Foxconn recorded all-time high annual revenues of $79.1 billion – even higher than some of its corporate customers such as Microsoft, Nokia or Dell. Consumers around the globe face a dizzying array of choice in the latest electronics gadgets such as the iPhone 4, the iPod, and, forthcoming, the slimmer tablet computer iPad 2. These are all produced by the million-plus Foxconn workers in China alone. The company is projected to capture 50 per cent of the world market share in electronics manufacturing and service by mid-2011.

Foxconn grew out of the Taipei-based parent company Hon Hai in 1988. Its strategy was to invest in the lower-cost Shenzhen Special Economic Zone bordering Hong Kong, where local government provided cheap industrial land and tax exemptions. And it had a ready labour force: the 230 million 'peasant-workers' of China – flexible, cheap, perfect for just-in-time production.

According to Foxconn CEO Terry Gou, a leader must be 'a dictator for the common good'. Under his leadership, one enormous factory has constructed its own 'city within a city' in Shenzhen, southern China, where company managers and security officers retain supra-governmental control over workers.

Every factory building and dormitory has security checkpoints with guards standing by 24 hours. Assembly workers wear uniforms colour-coded by their department. When they were interviewed, they constantly stressed how the multilayered electronic entry access system felt like a total loss of freedom.

While getting ready to start work or the production lines, management will ask the workers: 'How are you?' Workers must respond by shouting: 'Good! Very good! Very, very good!'

The management undertakes this drilling process to instil

forced to stand at attention to read aloud a statement of self-criticism. She must be loud enough to be heard. Our line leader would ask if the worker at the far end of the workshop could hear clearly the mistake she has made. Oftentimes girls feel like they are losing face. It's very embarrassing. Her tears drop. Her voice becomes very small.'

Anti-suicide nets are hung around outdoor stairways of dormitory buildings to prevent employees from jumping

Ma Zishan mourns his son Ma Xiangqian, the tenth protest suicide against draconian management at the South China firm. The suicides continue. Photo: Kin Cheung/AP/Press Association Images

discipline. Workers elaborated how they are scolded and punished when they talked on the line, failed to catch up with the high speed of work, or made mistakes in work procedures.

According to a woman working on the soldering line attaching speakers to MP3- and MP4-format digital audio players: 'After work, all of us – more than 100 persons – are made to stay behind. It happens whenever workers get punished. A girl is

Line leaders are also under pressure, and treat workers harshly to reach productivity targets. The bottom line for management is daily output, not workers' feelings. Branded electronic products are expensive and there is no margin for mistakes. A female worker interviewee was punished for forgetting to fix a screw in an iPhone. She was made to copy Terry Gou's quotes such as 'A harsh environment is a good thing' 300 times.

'I am just a speck of dust'

Workers told us that after a basic wage increase to 1,200 yuan per month (£113) in June 2010, an increase in production was scheduled. A member of a group of young workers responsible for processing cellphone casing testified: 'The production output was set at 5,120 pieces per day in the past but it had been raised by 20 per cent to 6,400 pieces per day. We were completely exhausted.'

'We cannot stop for a minute from work. We are even faster than the machines. During really busy times I don't even have time to eat or go to the bathroom'

Foxconn deploys time-and-motion studies, statistical control processes, and computerised engineering devices to test worker capacity. The target is to increase speed until worker capacity is maximised. According to one worker: 'We cannot stop for a minute from work. We are even faster than machines.' Another reported: 'During really busy times, I don't even have time to eat or go to the bathroom.'

Buyers of Foxconn products want their computers and iPhones fast. The company's moving towards 24-hour non-stop conveyor belts to meet global demand. This drive for productivity and quality means constant pressure on Foxconn workers. Posters on the workshop walls and between staircases read:

'Value efficiency every minute, every second;

Achieve goals unless the sun no longer rises;

The devil is in the details.'

Workers are organised into fixed seating or standing positions along production lines for a typical shift of 12 hours – of which four are overtime. The rotating day and night shift system takes away any feeling of freshness, accomplishment or initiative toward work. Typical worker comments to us were: 'The air-conditioners are only here for the sake of the machinery' and 'I am just a speck of dust in the workshop.'

Total management

Most migrant workers live in factory-provided dormitories because they are unable to afford even a small apartment. For companies like Foxconn the dormitory labour system is cost-efficient, ensuring workers spend their off-hours just preparing for another round of production. Workers are provided with 'conveniences' like dormitories and canteens to incorporate the entire living space in factory management. Food and drink, sleep, even washing are all scheduled tasks like those on production lines. Workers with different jobs and even different shifts are mixed in the same dormitory. They frequently disrupt each others' rest. Random dormitory reassignments break up friendship networks, increasing isolation and loneliness.

Workers live with strangers, are not allowed to cook, and cannot receive friends or families overnight. Whether you are single or married, private space is limited to one's own bed behind a self-made curtain.

Suicide as protest

In the wake of the suicides, Foxconn has installed three million square metres of safety nets – the so-called 'nets with a loving heart'. The anti-suicide nets are hung around outdoor stairways of dormitory buildings to prevent employees from jumping. This has not, however, stopped the suicides. On 7 January this year, a 25-year-old university graduate worker jumped to her death at Foxconn's flagship plant in Shenzhen.

In China, the new market economy – driven by the state, transnational capital and the people themselves – is based on a radical redefinition of needs and desires. Rural migrants long for a life attuned to the times, and the city is where everything is happening. Some young workers, who were born in the 1980s or 1990s, have been in the city since their childhood and do not possess farming skills. The higher the younger migrant workers' aspiration, the more obvious the contrast to harsh reality. Through various forms of protest, of which suicide is the most desperate expression, they are trying to reclaim their rights and dignity.

Suicide must not become the only desperate means to resist social injustice. Concrete improvements should start at Foxconn but not end there. Without stronger social and legal protection of workers' rights and support from the government, it seems certain we will witness a growing roll-call of deaths. Western consumers of electronic gadgets must become active advocates of humane production standards.

The New Internationalist, April 2011

Jenny Chan is an advisor at Hong Kong-based Students & Scholars Against Corporate Misbehavior (SACOM).
www.sacom.hk

Work

Aspiration

Responsibility Gender

A fair wage Qualifications

Benefits Ambition

Unemployment

Self-employment Money

Prospects

FAIR PLAY ON FAIR PAY

Why does pay matter? Well, apart from the obvious ability to feed and clothe yourself, pay is also often about status, about how much society values what you do. On a personal level it adds to your own feeling of worth if you are rewarded for your efforts – you feel recognised, valued and deserving.

What does it say then about our society when some people are paid 145 times the average wage? And when those people work almost exclusively in business and finance rather than in, for example, medicine, education or law and order, how does that reflect what we value as a society?

Boom at the top
The latest report from the High Pay Commission reveals that the Chief Executives of the 100 biggest companies in the UK earned an average of £4.2 million each in 2009/10 and if current trends continue will be looking at earnings of £8 million each by 2020. At the same time pay for most workers will remain at today's rate – meaning that top executives will then be earning 214 times the average.

The widening pay gap isn't confined to these few individuals. The top 0.1% of earners in the UK, that's 47,000 people, have seen their pay rise by 64% over eleven years (from 1996/7 to 2007/8). At the same time the bottom 50% of earners saw their income rise by about 7%. As an illustration – this year, the top paid banker at Barclays, Rich Ricci, will receive over £14 million – that's 1,128 times what Barclays' lowest paid employee receives. Or to put it another way, it's more than the average person earns in 11 lifetimes!

Despite the banking crisis, 2,800 staff in 27 banks received more than £1 million in 2009 and complex bonus arrangements in this and other sectors may mean that even bigger payments are being received but hidden.

But if you pay peanuts you get monkeys ...
The idea that very generous pay is needed to attract highly competent people no longer holds sway with the general public. Only 19% of us think that the banks, for example, are well run and 70% of us say executive pay makes the country 'grossly unequal'. With a tiny percentage of people earning so much while others are taking pay cuts or unpaid leave to preserve their jobs even the director of the employers' organisation, the CBI, has expressed doubts: 'If leaders of big companies seem to occupy

SOME ISSUES:

Do you think it is fair that some people get paid so much money when others are paid so little?

What kind of job do you think deserves a higher salary?

How can we stop the pay divide from increasing further?

See also

Let's take the housing fight to wealthy owners with empty spare rooms, p50 & Time to stop glossing over these artful tax dodgers, p52

a different galaxy from the rest of the community, they risk being treated as aliens,'

His image is a good one – the very rich are soaring away from the rest of society. Their incomes are increasing while many are facing reductions. This means that they do not share the lifestyle, the concerns or the experiences of the majority. They are an elite – the word 'private' comes in front of all their activities: healthcare, education, travel and even community. Yet they have a great deal of power, which influences the lives of the 'other' people who scarcely enter their world.

Wheels within wheels

The people within companies whose job it is to oversee pay at the top tend to come from the same background and culture as the executives whose pay they are monitoring. They have the same expectations. When executive pay is reviewed there is a subtle pressure to pay above the average since paying them below it might suggest that executive performance is below average too. And so, like a system of cogs, at each stage the pay level is ratcheted upwards – the average becomes higher and the pay increases continue to beat the average.

What's fair?

How should we pay a police officer? Or a firefighter? Or a nurse? What should we pay the teacher who gave them the education they needed for their jobs? Whenever pay is discussed we look at the idea of what someone is worth – in all the meanings of the word. Is someone who creates jobs in a business worth more than someone who saves lives in a hospital? Is a social worker a more valuable member of society than an estate agent? People like the idea of a fair day's work for a fair day's pay – but what's fair?

WHAT IS THE AVERAGE?

The Annual Survey of Hours and Earnings gives us some idea about the average wage earned by people in the UK. The figures are for full time jobs at adult rates and do not include the self-employed.

These are the amounts before any income tax or national insurance has been taken out, so they don't represent what people actually take home.

The amounts here are based on the median. The median is the value below which 50% of employees fall. It means that the 'average' is less affected by a small number of very high earners.

Sources: The High Pay Commission, ONS and others

2010 AVERAGE FULL TIME WAGES UK:

All employed people: £25,879
Men: £28,091 Women: £22,490

BY JOB CATEGORY

Managers and senior officials £37,837
Professional occupations £36,507
Associate professional and technical £29,338
Administrative and secretarial £19,761
Skilled trades £23,787
Personal service £16,984
Sales and customer service £15,598
Process, plant and machine operatives £21,708
Elementary occupations (manual/unskilled) £17,200

Averages, of course iron out the difference. For example within the Professional Occupations group Health professionals average £61,414 while teaching and research professionals £35,529

AGE...

The youngest workers earn least:

Those aged 16-17 average £9,042 and those aged 18-21 average £14,279.

THE MINIMUM HOURLY WAGE IS...

£5.93 – the main rate for workers aged 21 and over
£4.92 – the 18-20 rate
£3.64 – the 16-17 rate for workers above school leaving age but under 18
£2.50 – the apprentice rate, for apprentices under 19 or 19 or over and in the first year of their apprenticeship

WHAT ARE YOU WORTH?

Some bloggers try to answer

CHARITY WORKER

I am 30 years old and I work for a mental health charity. I get paid just under £21k. It's not a bad wage but it has taken me a long time to reach it.

I don't expect to earn a fortune as a charity worker but my job does require skill and it is a vital one. I've worked with people who are suicidal and people who are dangerous. We matter in people's lives. I'm not poor but I can't really afford any luxuries. My rate of pay does make me think about how much society values my work of caring for vulnerable people.

ADMINISTRATOR AT A COLLEGE

After I left university at age 21, my first job was in a bar on £4.50 an hour. I'm 26 now, I earn £17,000 a year as an administrator. This is the most money I've ever earned and it's too much for the work I do compared with the work I did then.

I used to work 12-hour shifts, on my feet all the time. I was constantly dealing with customers and changing situations. I was shouted at, insulted and assaulted. My current job means I have to use my brain but my first job was harder. In all fairness the pay levels should be the other way round.

I don't need to earn any more than I do and when I see bar staff and waiting staff working so hard for their minimum wage I feel ashamed of what I earn.

What does it say then about our society when some people are paid 145 times the average wage? And when those people work almost exclusively in business and finance rather than in, for example, medicine, education or law and order, how does that reflect what we value as a society?

REWARDS ANALYST

I earn £30k a year as a reward analyst. I'm 27. As well as my salary I have £3,000 a year which can either be spent on benefits or taken as cash. I can also earn bonuses.

My job is to work out pay and rewards for other people so I know a bit about how high salaries are. I know, for instance, that you can expect to sell your whole life to a company in return for high earnings.

I earn a lot more than most of my friends but because I have invested in a flat I don't have much money to spend.

LAWYER

I work as a specialist commercial solicitor in financial services. Last year I earned £512,000 before tax. How can I justify that salary? So far this year I've saved two companies from insolvency and as a result helped to save several thousand jobs. I don't get paid for saving jobs though – I get paid because I'm good at what I do. Basically I bring in much more money than I cost my firm and very few people could do my job.

I'm on duty whenever I'm awake – my main working day is about 9am to 8pm, I don't stop for lunch.

I know teachers, nurses, soldiers, policemen etc. are vital but it's not difficult to find people to do those jobs so you don't need to pay a big salary. In any case it's my huge tax bill that is paying their wages.

poor prospects for young people left trailing by a self-perpetuating elite

Jayne Dowle

SOME ISSUES:

Would you be willing and able to afford to work for free to gain experience?

Do internships seem fair?

See also:
For children today table manners still trump talent, p200, *Essential Articles 13* &

Future imperfect, p185, *Fact File 2011*

I KNOW a young woman who will graduate this summer. Her ambition is to work in events management and public relations. But – and this is a very big but – she is from an ordinary working class family in the north-east, and right now, she can see no way of getting a job in her chosen profession.

It is virtually impossible to enter this competitive industry without undertaking a period of work experience. And work experience, inevitably, involves living in another city, probably Manchester or London, and working for free for months. Unless she finds a fairy godmother – or moonlights as a pole dancer – she can't imagine how she will do it. Knowing this girl, she will.

Like a lad I know who grafted on a building site all winter so he could go to London, put himself up in cheap digs and work on Loaded magazine for three weeks. He lived on any free sandwiches that came into the office, but he got paid work in the end, and now runs his own business back in Barnsley. But I'm telling you about this girl in case you feel tempted to moan about over-qualified graduates who can't find a job, and how much it costs taxpayers to support them etc etc. For thousands, this is the reality:

A good degree, a winning personality, and the total frustration of being unable to get a foot in the door.

A recent survey found that 60 per cent of employers won't even consider employing a young person unless they have done work experience. In essence,

I agree with them. There is nothing more irritating than a graduate who enthuses about "wanting to be a journalist" but has never bothered to attempt to get a word in print. And I am glad that the Government is planning to extend the period of work experience for young people on benefits, hooking up with employers such as Punch Taverns, Homebase and McDonalds to provide up to eight weeks in the workplace to prepare them for securing a "proper" job.

I've been there and done it. The week after I graduated, went to London and slept on my university friend's floor for six weeks so I could work as a general gofer on women's magazines. That was more than two decades ago, and even though my parents sent money for my "keep", and in those days employers paid a nominal fee of "expenses", I was so skint I had to hide from the bus conductor.

Without it, I would never have got started. For years, I have drilled it into young people that the only way to get a job in the media is to get as much experience as possible. Over my time as an editor, I witnessed a procession of hopefuls. They would write in with their glowing CVs, turn up in the office terrified, and sink or swim. Some of them went on to become very successful. Some of them have even employed me.

But it is clear that the only young people who can afford to work for free these days are those whose families can afford to fully support them.

Well-off middle-class families, in other words. Grandly-named "internships" are often little more than slave labour. These kids don't even get travel expenses. Talking to friends on national newspapers, it is apparent that most interns are the sons and daughters, nieces, nephews and friends of established journalists, with somewhere free to stay in the capital. It's the same in the

law, the theatre and television. All this does is create a self-perpetuating elite, where the only kids who can get on the ladder are those with plenty of money. What hope for those like my young friend from the north-east?

It would be OK if she wanted to work for McDonalds. But like me at her age, she is more ambitious. And this is what angers me about her situation, and of those coming up behind her. No-one expects a job on a plate, but her life chances are being blighted because of her background.

At least she got to university, because she went to college to study for her A-levels supported by the Education Maintenance Allowance. Now I know there are students who abuse the EMA.

But I know too, that when it is scrapped, thousands of young people from modest backgrounds simply won't be able to afford to continue their studies. Ministers go on about offering higher education to all.

But there is a huge hole in their logic. If they don't support less

well-off kids doing their A-levels, how will these kids even get to university? I know they waffle on about special grants and so on, but these are no substitute for transparent, easily-accessible funding.

Call me a cynic, but could it be that this is all part of a grand plan to cut down on the further public funding such students would require if they actually made it on to a degree course? Talk about a self-perpetuating elite. It's bad enough now. What's it going to be like in 10 years' time?

*Yorkshire Post,
26 January 2011*

> A good degree, a winning personality, and the total frustration of being unable to get a foot in the door.

> Grandly-named "internships" are often little more than slave labour.

IS THE NEW WOMAN'S PLACE IN THE HOME?

Anne Johnstone

Glass ceiling. The phrase seems to have been invented by American feminist Nora Frenkiel when she wrote in 1984: "Women have reached a certain point – I call it the glass ceiling. They're in the top of middle management and they're stopping and getting stuck."

It's hard to believe that in Britain, four decades after the Equal Opportunities Act, I'm still writing about this subject. Today sees the publication of the report by Lord Davies about "diversity in the boardroom". What diversity? you may ask. In a recent interview he admitted that he was shocked and humbled by how difficult it is still for women to succeed in business. The figures are extraordinarily poor, especially at the executive level. It is bad enough that just 13% of directors on FTSE-100[1] boards are women. Worse is that nearly two-thirds of those are non-execs[2]. Female representation may be improving but at such a snail's pace that it will take 70 years to reach parity. (Equal pay for women managers will take even longer: 184 years, apparently.)

So a quarter of a century after Nora minted the term, women are still getting concussion from

SOME ISSUES:

Why do you think family commitments get in the way of women's careers?

Is this fair?

Do you think self-employment is the answer?

See also:

Work and play,
p190, *Fact File 2011*

Snail's pace,
p190, *Fact File 2009*

WOMEN IN FULL-TIME WORK SPEND 30% LONGER ON CHILDCARE THAN FULL-TIME MEN. AND THEY CONTINUE TO DO THE BULK OF UNPAID WORK IN THE HOME, EVEN IF THEY AREN'T MOTHERS

banging their heads on the glass ceiling. In fact, it's worse than that. They're still being asked to give it a quick squirt of Windowlene while they're up there. Even women at the top tend to have greater commitments at home than their male counterparts. Women in full-time work spend 30% longer on childcare than full-time men. And they continue to do the bulk of unpaid work in the home, even if they aren't mothers.

Flexible working remains the holy grail for women managers. Not the flexibility that is synonymous with unpaid overtime and the longest working hours in Europe, but the flexibility that lets you off for the school nativity play or to take your bleeding son to casualty.

The other half of this issue is about the Catch-22 situation, otherwise known as the Old Boys network, in which overwhelmingly middle-aged, white, male managers select their successors in their own image because they can't imagine the world being organised differently. The few women that make it through are either Nicola Horlick-style superwomen or those who behave like men. This is crazy because, as Davies will point out, diversity at board level increases a firm's competitive advantage in a world where women make a lot of purchasing decisions.

Some men blame this gender asymmetry on women themselves. Women are self-limiting and lack ambition, they argue. But this too is a circular argument when women look at the way power is exercised in their organisations and decide promotion would be unpleasant or unworkable. So all over Britain (and especially in Scotland) there are offices where a predominantly female workforce beavers away while ten men in shirt sleeves sit round a table in a glass box in the corner and take

the decisions. No wonder the few female success stories, like Michelle Mone[3], enjoy a high profile. Women need such role models. Some sectors have adapted better than others. It's a pleasure to see Theresa May and Yvette Cooper debating across the dispatch box, without Tory backbenchers making melon gestures. Women are also permeating the top tier in charities, where there is less outside recruitment and goals that are more worthwhile than hitting annual targets.

Are quotas the answer? Probably not. Token women on boards to make up a quota won't help and may be the focus of male resentment. Women promoted before they have the requisite experience merely exchange a glass ceiling for a glass precipice, over which they are likely to plunge amidst smug choruses of "Told you she wasn't up to it". Davies opts instead for a voluntary "comply or explain" strategy, with a target of 20% of FTSE 350 directors by 2013.

There is another answer. Work from the London School of Economics suggests that thousands of women under 30 are turning themselves into "kitchen table tycoons", creating businesses that they can run from home and run in a way that suits them. Self-limiting and unambitious? On the contrary. Women are doing it for themselves.

*Herald Scotland,
24 February 2011
Reproduced with
permission of Herald &
Times Group*

THE OLD BOYS NETWORK... WHICH IS MIDDLE-AGED, WHITE, MALE!

[1] FTSE 100 is a share index of the 100 top UK companies listed on the London Stock Exchange.

[2] Non-executive directors give advice on strategy and other issues but are not part of the day-to-day management team.

[3] Michelle Mone is the Creator of MJM International which includes the Ultimo Bra Company.

Maternity laws should consider employers too

Nick Freeman

The birth of a healthy child is priceless. Though in the case of little Matilda Scott, the stork also delivered a sack load of cash.

For her mum, Jacky, has just trousered a five figure payout after being sacked for getting pregnant with her baby daughter whilst on maternity leave with her older child, Jacob.

A tribunal found her company was guilty of sexual discrimination.

The gut reaction of the egalitarian masses is to praise this triumph for equality, but let's give the verdict a second glance. It's a fine result for the employee, but what about the employer?

Legislation concerning sexual discrimination is unfairly weighted in favour of the employee. It has no recourse to the collateral damage caused by female staff playing roulette with their family planning.

Employers of course have a duty to individual workers, but they also have a greater responsibility to ensure the overall health of their company. And if profitability is compromised by unpredictable absenteeism then everyone on the pay roll may ultimately suffer.

Employers are currently handcuffed by draconian laws surrounding maternity leave. They have no choice but to endure the prolonged absence of key members of staff – those whose work cannot simply be replaced by a jobbing temp.

Bosses should be allowed, when interviewing potential recruits, to ask whether they are planning to start a family – and if so when, and how many. This discussion should form part of a contractual obligation on both sides. And if breached, the employer should retain a discretion to sack and replace.

Why? Because someone struggling to steward their business in these economically choppy waters has as much right to plan their future as their employees do.

Evidently plenty of new mums rush back to work, either because they need the money or because they are sensitive to the demands of their role within a company. But there will always be those, like Jacky Scott, who place their boss in an impossible position. And thus do a huge disservice to the rest.

Look no further than Natasha Kaplinsky who spent much of her record-breaking £1m-a-year contract with Five on maternity leave after falling pregnant six weeks into the job. Two children later, it's interesting to note that the news reader said last week she is bored of motherhood and wants a job in TV again. I would not employ her as a tea maker.

The law needs to change so there is parity between a worker and their boss. Otherwise employing women, already an occupational hazard, could become a thing of the past. What would the cry babies say then?

*Manchester Evening News,
15 March 2011*

> **Employers are currently handcuffed... They have no choice but to endure the prolonged absence of key members of staff**

SOME ISSUES:

Is it fair to women to consider their family plans before employing them?

Is it fair to employers not to be allowed to ask women about their plans to have children?

See also:
Snail's pace,
p190, *Fact File 2009*

Rush-hour silence in a welfare ghetto

Two days ago, I stood in the middle of the Lower Falinge Estate in Rochdale, watching its version of the morning rush hour. There are more than two hundred flats here, and perhaps 500 residents.

In the hour and a half between 8 and 9.30am, only four of them emerged to go to work.

By Andrew Gilligan

The main roads that encircle Lower Falinge were crowded with cars and pedestrians on their way to town. But on the estate, spectral calm prevailed. Even by 9.30, a third of the flats still had their curtains drawn. There were, in fact, more people commuting into the estate – to work at the numerous official "outreach agencies" which have offices there, or doing council maintenance – than there were people commuting out.

Lower Falinge is the worst welfare ghetto in Britain. The Office for National Statistics (ONS) divides the country into 34,000 "lower layer super output areas," each making up about a quarter to a fifth of a council ward. The one which includes the estate and its surrounding streets, Rochdale 10C, contains 1,030 adults of working age. Eight hundred and sixty-five of them — 84 per cent — are unemployed.

The statisticians break down some of the figures even further, into "census output areas" of a few streets or council blocks. Census output area 00BQFD0025, as it's known to the ONS – or part

Stock photo

of the Lower Falinge Estate, as it's known to everyone else – appears to have more unemployment claimants (215) than working-age people (179). An unemployment rate of 120% is probably explained by a combination of benefit fiddling and outdated statistics. It also underlines the perils of focusing on very small areas: local politicians point out that most of Rochdale is more prosperous than Falinge, and resent the bad publicity it draws.

But there is no doubt that these grey low-rise blocks are places of almost total worklessness; no doubt, either, that some, perhaps much, of that worklessness is due to

the benefits system itself, a problem the Coalition promised last week to tackle.

Lower Falinge is a place where some of the usual excuses do not apply. It is across the road from the town centre, and 15 minutes' walk from a short train ride into the regional employment hub of Manchester. At Rochdale jobcentre last Friday, there were 903 vacancies on offer.

Many of the people we talked to on the estate were genuinely looking for work, or trying to better themselves. Before 9am, Mukuka Kalambayi was heading for the jobcentre. "I've been trying very hard for a long time to get a job," he

said. "I'm doing an accounting course to help."

Zahid Hussein was heading to college. A mother of two, Sabrina Cregan, said she was putting her children into nursery school so she could go back to work.

She gets about £260 a week on the dole, including housing and council tax benefits; many of the 903 jobs on offer pay little more than that. But others in Rochdale were living the stereotype. In the 20 minutes we spent at the

The Lower Falinge Estate appears to have more unemployment claimants (215) than working-age people (179). An unemployment rate of 120% is probably explained by a combination of benefit fiddling and outdated statistics

She gets about £260 a week on the dole, including housing and council tax benefits; many of the 903 jobs on offer pay little more than that

jobcentre, no fewer than three people arrived to sign on by taxi.

Back on Lower Falinge, two unemployed sisters came out of a ground-floor flat and into another waiting cab. Where were they going? Asda, their brother said. Asda is 10 minutes' walk away. Watching their departure with a kind of rueful anger was Granville, one of the housing department's maintenance men, doing a job on a flat.

"I can't afford to get around in taxis," he said. "We're working people. We struggle, but they get everything.

"There are jobs, but they won't take them. I've always been Labour, but if the Tories do what they say they'll do [on welfare] I might change to them."

The majority of the unemployed in Rochdale 10C – 440 people – are on incapacity-related benefits, far more than are on Jobseeker's Allowance.

Over the last 10 years, for all Labour's investments in the NHS, the number of incapacity benefit claimants in the area has risen by more than 25% (though it has dipped a little lately). Are people in this area really 25% more ill and disabled than they were 10 years ago? Or is the system being abused?

In a converted church building, Tracie Powers, an inspiring, dynamic woman with purple hair, runs the Spotlight on Falinge project. "People round here genuinely want to go back into work," she says. "One of the people who came here applied for 50 jobs. But a lot of it is lack of experience, and lack of confidence. The benefit system plays a part. If you haven't got confidence, it's security. The system for claiming is so long-winded that people are frightened to go off it."

The owner of the bed and breakfast I stayed in recalled advertising for a chambermaid and getting 50 calls, many of them from men and many of them desperate to work. But even that job demands high standards of spoken English and a good telephone manner — which many of the callers did not have.

Spotlight on Falinge has people in to calculate how much more they could be making from work than from benefit (contrary to popular belief, says Ms Powers, it usually is more: "They're often quite surprised to find they'd be better off.") Spotlight will literally walk with people down to the jobcentre.

Although it may not know it, the project is David Cameron's Big Society incarnate. "Every bit of this [the conversion] was done by volunteers," says Ms Powers. "We don't get any funding. There's no point asking for money that's not there."

She has mixed feelings about the new government. One of the key programmes Spotlight is involved with, the Future Jobs Fund, has taken three young people from her project into full-time work. It subsidises an employer to take them on for six months, helping build experience and confidence in the face of repeated rejection.

The fund is described by the Coalition's "poverty tsar," Frank Field, as "one of the most precious things the last government was involved in,

Over the last 10 years, the number of incapacity benefit claimants in the area has risen by more than 25%... Are people in this area really 25% more ill and disabled than they were 10 years ago? Or is the system being abused?

a lifeline that no amount of 'New Deal' or our rhetoric ever offered the unemployed."

The Future Jobs Fund was one of the first things the Coalition scrapped. "They've pulled the rug from under a lot of people," says the local Labour MP, Simon Danczuk.

Yet, like many people we spoke to, even the unemployed, Ms Powers likes the sound of some of the welfare reforms. "Reducing housing benefit to get people back to work is one of the best things they've done," she says.

Rochdale is about to announce a new project, bringing more than a thousand new jobs to the town. If some of them go to people from the Lower Falinge Estate, the new government will know its message is getting through.

The Sunday Telegraph, 10 October 2010
© Telegraph Media Group Ltd 2010

Young people

Ambition

Names Attitude

Employment School

Teachers Travel

Parents Money

Education

Friendships

I am an Actual Human Being

Hi, I'm a teenager. Excuse me while I verbally abuse my parents, smoke some marijuana, drink a load of vodka, get pregnant, breach my asbo, fail my incredibly easy GCSEs, mug a pensioner and destroy the English language with my dutty slang, terrible, like, grammar and mndlss abbrvtns lol. Simultaneously. Right, OK, I feel much better now.

I detest the word teenager and those inevitable prefixes "stroppy", "unreasonable" and "spotty". Lovely children do not turn into violent, smelly monsters on their 13th birthdays. If they do, there's something wrong with the cake.

Why is it OK to discriminate against teenagers? Human beings are allowed into shops in groups, can choose where they sit at the cinema, and can get on a bus without fear of being turfed out halfway home. Teenagers don't have these privileges. Can you imagine the outrage if an irate bus driver suddenly stopped and bellowed, "Right. All you over-60s, off the bus"?

A word describing an age group should not be synonymous with "irrational subhuman". It even encourages us to play to stereotype; when my parents say, "Chuh! Bloody teens", I'm likely to go off on one. It's a self-fulfilling prophecy.

So let's use something less specific. "Young people" is fine, or something cool like "transition tots". Or, hey, we could be put into the category of Actual Human Beings. That would be nice.

Rebecca Grant
Age 15

The Guardian, 16 July 2010
© Guardian News & Media Ltd 2010

Picture posed by model

SOME ISSUES:

Do you feel you are judged because of your age?

Do you think the teen stereotype is wrong?

See also:
Parents' perspective,
p74, *Fact File 2011*

I'd hate to be a teenage girl today,
p101, *Essentia Articles 13*

www.ikeitis.org

Name-calling ... if only I could

A teacher's view, by Ms Ann Thrope

SOME ISSUES:

Is it important for a headteacher to know every student's name?

When the writer talks about different tribes, do you recognise different 'tribes' in your school?

Do you think suicide has an appeal to teenagers?

I have a terrible memory. Three weeks in and I can still only remember the names of the pupils who occupy the four corner desks, the dyspraxic kids who are spattered in ink and the girl in Year 10 with irritable bowel syndrome and a note.

It doesn't help that all the girls in Year 9 are called Rebecca and half the boys in the school are Jack. In the naming ritual, whatever happened to individuality and derring do? It obviously gets sucked out of mothers in the delivery room along with the placenta and their desire for adventurous sex. You go into labour believing that you are giving birth to Thor and you come home and baptise him John. Then you pop into BHS for a winceyette nightie and a Teasmade. Is it any wonder that my husband left? At least we can rely on the hippies to liven up our registers: Sky, Scout, Freya and Kai were all conceived at Glastonbury by parents who can handle three Rizlas. As indeed can

At least we can rely on the hippies to liven up our registers: Sky, Scout, Freya and Kai were all conceived at Glastonbury by parents who can handle three Rizlas

their children, in the precinct, after dark.

In order to commit kids' names to memory, I often resort to visual aids. My planner is awash with letters and symbols that I will have to keep under wraps at parents' evenings. Three exclamation marks and an emoticon resembling Munch's The Scream is not how Mr and Mrs Baxter want their darling Bethany to be remembered, so if you are going to record unpleasant observations, remember to encrypt them using the Enigma code.

Tribal allegiances are another useful way of remembering who's who, as they give you a cultural hook to hang the kid's face on. In my school, we are down to four main tribes: the emos (who have just completed a management takeover of the goths to become the school's

Tribal allegiances are another useful way of remembering who's who, as they give you a cultural hook to hang the kid's face on

market leader in existential despair), the charvas (broadly anyone who eats haslet), the spice boys (snug-fitting v-neck tops and tight jeans, a look favoured by the young Joe Orton) and, of course, swots (anyone who has perfect attendance, full school uniform and a library card).

Of all of these tribes, the kids that I first commit to memory are the emos, the ones with pink eyeshadow, fingerless gloves and XXL black fringes and hearts. They have grown out of playing with dolls and are toying around with despair instead. It's a poignant rite of passage - they complete this virtual course in misery before leaving school, getting married and experiencing the real thing. And we help them along by giving them Sylvia Plath, Romeo and Juliet and Willy Loman to add to the chirpy company of Curtis and Cobain in their suicides' hall of fame.

It should probably worry us that suicide appears so attractive to young people. The writer Paul Morley described suicide in a recent RSC Romeo and Juliet

When I was a student I gained a lurid respect among my peers because my mother had attempted suicide. In terms of kudos it kicked divorce into touch. Years later when she did it for real, I only felt the terrible, senseless loss

programme as "(shimmering) in the distance as a kind of mischievous, tantalising friend", and you only have to think of Bridgend* to recognise its omnipotence. I understand its allure. When I was a student I gained a lurid respect among my peers because my mother had attempted suicide. In terms of kudos it kicked divorce into touch. Years later when she did it for real, I only felt the terrible, senseless loss. So study your emos, remember their names, and help them learn to love life.

Anne Thrope (Ms) is the pen name of a secondary teacher in the North of England

Times Educational Supplement Magazine, 24 September 2010

* Bridgend is a small town in South Wales which seemed to suffer a series of suicides of young people in 2007-08.

SARAH EVANS: ACTUALLY, KIDS ARE ALL RIGHT

On the dreadful morning last week when The Today Programme had been banished by striking journalists, I had to listen to a young woman on the radio telling us that her generation of 20-somethings had been cheated of their gilded heritage by the middle-aged. "I feel humiliated," she said, "that I can't live the lifestyle of my parents".

The theme is fashionable. Two ex-Birmingham heavyweights, MP David Willetts, in his recent book The Pinch: How The Baby Boomers Stole Their Children's Future, and Tim Brighouse, in a newspaper article last week arguing for a graduate tax for the 45-70 generation, have developed the same idea. It's a bad time to be young and it's the fault of the older generation.

Last weekend, I was organising a new passport for my 17-year-old son. The stamps in his passport brought forcibly to mind that he has travelled far more in his life than I have – not me at 17 (I had never been abroad) but me now.

His education in both the academic and broader sense has been stratospherically better than his parents. Then there is everything else. He has technology I never dreamed of. Eating out is part of normal life. Going to the cinema or theatre is not regarded as a special treat. And so it goes on. This is not because of some sudden upward social mobility in our family. It is because the affluence of his parents' generation has led to a much higher standard of living for their children.

Education and every other sort of opportunity for the young has changed out of all recognition. The percentage of those going into higher education continued to grow despite the introduction of tuition fees (which was greeted, as the news of the forthcoming rise has been, by predictions of huge decline in applications). Out of school, children have access to museums, art galleries, holiday courses, sports clubs and theatre.

Who knows what lies ahead? Society seems particularly bad at predicting it accurately. But a lot has been achieved for today's young people.

Their education should mean they are in a better position to solve problems. And as for not having the same lifestyle as your parents in your 20s – well, what generation ever has?

Sarah Evans is principal of King Edward VI High School for Girls, Birmingham

The Birmingham Post, 12 November 2010

SOME ISSUES:

What are the differences between your experience of being young and your parents?

Do young people now have more opportunities than their parents did?